THE FABLE OF THE BEES

BERNARD MANDEVILLE

THE FABLE OF THE BEES

And Other Writings

Abridged and Edited,
with an Introduction and Notes, by
E. J. HUNDERT

Hackett Publishing Company, Inc.
Indianapolis/Cambridge

CONTENTS

produced his last work, *A Letter to Dion*. This was a polemical reply to *Alciphron; or, The Minute Philosopher* (1732), in which the philosopher Bishop Berkeley attacked various freethinkers and cast Mandeville as Lysicles, a lawless libertine and atheist. Mandeville exposed in detail Berkeley's wholesale misrepresentation of the *Fable*. He also forcefully reasserted his thesis that a strict interpretation of Christian conduct, which requires self-denial and the sacrifice of impulse, fatally compromises Christians like Berkeley, who hypocritically pretend to charity and benevolence while reaping the benefits of modern forms of affluence and exchange.

Mandeville did his most creative work and produced a masterpiece during what until recently was considered the onset of old age, an accomplishment surpassed in the eighteenth century only by Immanuel Kant, one of the *Fable*'s great admirers. For his immediate audience, however, and then for succeeding generations of European intellectuals, "Mandeville" was less the person who wrote an infamous book than an ideologically charged symbol constituted by the eighteenth century's intense and prolonged dispute about how to understand and evaluate the liberation of acquisitive instincts engendered in modern polities by the infusion of commercial relations into the centers of public life.

Bernard de Mandeville was born in or near Rotterdam in 1670, the son of Judith (Verhaar) and Michael de Mandeville, who was a doctor, as was Michael's own grandfather. No portrait of Mandeville is known to exist, and little can be gleaned about the details of his life or character from the few surviving relevant documents. Indeed, more is known about the *Fable*'s critics than about its author. While his family name suggests French ancestry, the de Mandevilles were not recent immigrants to Holland but had lived in Leeuwarden in the Friesland region of the Netherlands from at least the late sixteenth century, later establishing themselves in the city of Nijmegen. After attending the Erasmian school in Rotterdam, Bernard followed his father and great-grandfather in the study of medicine, matriculating at the University of Leiden in 1685.

During his years of study at this major European medical faculty, Mandeville published a required dissertation, in which he argued the Cartesian case for animal automatism. After receiving his medical degree in 1691, he traveled in France, Italy and then to England to learn the language in which he would later excel, returning to Holland in 1694. A short time later Mandeville immigrated to England and settled in London, where he married Ruth Elizabeth Laurence in 1699, fathered at least two children, and remained until his death from influenza in 1733.

Until late in life, when fame assured him access to an audience, the ful-
fillment of Mandeville's literary ambitions depended upon the opportunities for writers provided by the dramatic enlargement of the English
reading public in the early eighteenth century. Most important, a writer's
success hinged upon the ability of the bookseller-publishers who organized the so-called London Grub Street presses to offer to a metropolitan
audience in search of diversion a continuing stream of inexpensively produced pamphlets, broadsides and, crucially for Mandeville, satirical verse.
Mandeville made his English debut with two anonymous works in 1703,
The Pamphleteers: A Satyr and *Some Fables after the Easie and Familiar
Method of Monsieur de la Fontaine*. In the first work, Mandeville defended
the Glorious Revolution of 1688–89 against the attacks of Tory and Jacobite "pamphleteers," as he was to do throughout his career, while the second work was the earliest English translation of twenty-seven of La
Fontaine's *Fables*, to which Mandeville added two of his own in the same
style. Probably in response to reasonable sales of *Some Fables*, an
expanded edition of these poems was printed under Mandeville's name as
Æsop Dress'd; or a Collection of Fables Writ in Familiar Verse in the next
year. In 1704 Mandeville again drew upon his familiarity with French
skeptical and libertine traditions, publishing *Typhon: Or the Wars Between
the Gods and Giants: A Burlesque Poem in Imitation of the Comical Mons.
Scarron*, a work whose dedication to the "Numerous Society of F[oo]ls"
was intended as an invocation of *The Praise of Folly* by Erasmus, one of
the very few Dutch writers whose work Mandeville ever praised. One
year later, Mandeville sought to advance his career as a fabulist in verse
with the publication of *The Grumbling Hive: Or, Knaves turn'd Honest*, a
433-line poem in octosyllabic verse. Pitched in the popular "low" style
which he had mastered, but attracting hardly any notice from the wider
reading public, *The Grumbling Hive* would later serve as the foundation of
The Fable of the Bees.

While Mandeville produced one final volume of poetry, some of it
erotic, in the 1712 collection *Wishes to a Godson, with Other Miscellany
Poems*, the remainder of his literary output was in prose, most often in the
then-popular dialogue form, in a conversational idiom which he
employed for the purposes of philosophical and social commentary. The
tone of Mandeville's mature writing is already evident in his first prose
volume, *The Virgin Unmask'd: or, Female Dialogues Betwixt an Elderly
Maiden Lady, and her Niece, On several Diverting Discourses on Love, Marriage, Memoirs, and Morals, &c. of the Times* (1709). Here, in ten sexually
charged dialogues on virginity, marriage and the designs of men, which

include many digressions on history and politics, the luscious and inexperienced Antonia is instructed in the ways of the world by her maiden aunt Lucinda. Mandeville again adopted a female persona in thirty-two numbers of *The Female Tatler* between 2 November 1709 and 29 March 1710. This journal employed the fiction of discussions of a "Society of Ladies," often joined by gentlemen, in order to ridicule the pretensions of Isaac Bickerstaff, the spokesman of Richard Steele in his popular *Tatler*, published between 1709 and 1711. Bickerstaff self-righteously proclaimed that the practice of moral virtue made society possible. In direct contrast, humility, temperance and frugality emerge in the discussions of Mandeville's personae as unpracticed, if much commended, virtues in opulent nations, virtues which flourish precisely because their wealthy members indulge the vices of self-aggrandizement, avarice and prodigality. As one of Mandeville's characters says, it is absurd because contradictory at once to desire a flourishing trade and the decrease of the vices of pride and luxury—a position Mandeville first enunciated in *The Grumbling Hive*.

By the beginning of the second decade of the eighteenth century, then, Mandeville had established a decidedly modest literary reputation. Few readers could have known the identity of "B.M.," the initials appearing on the title page of *The Virgin Unmask'd*, or the anonymous author of *The Female Tatler*. Nevertheless, he continued to claim the attention of publishers for the expression of his widening interests, particularly those in medicine and politics. In 1711 he published *A Treatise of the Hypochondriak and Hysterical Passions, Vulgarly call'd the Hypo in Men and Vapours in Women*, also in dialogue form, in which Mandeville's spokesman Philiporo (the lover of experience) expounds upon the mechanist theories of physiology then at the forefront of medical theory. Unlike his competitors, Philiporo treats few patients, because his scientifically grounded methods demand close and careful observation of patients over long periods of time, in contrast to conventional physicians, who engage in profitless speculations about symptoms whose meaning eludes them. Mandeville went on to publish an expanded edition of his medical treatise in 1730, adding to the speeches of its main participants, translating Latin passages for the general reader, and reflecting in some detail upon the scientific study of human behavior. The content of these reflections was an important feature of his wider arguments about the analysis of society.

Mandeville's political interests and commitments were not publicly apparent until 1714 (the year before he dropped the "de" from his name), when he made his debut as a Whig propagandist. In that year he published *The Mischiefs that ought to be Apprehended from a Whig-Government*,

a dialogue between Loveright, a Whig, and the Tory Tantivy, in which the
conventional Whig defense of the revolutionary settlement of 1689, the
Protestant succession, and the legitimacy of the Hanoverian line are primary elements of a dialogue which concludes with thanks to Providence
for sparing the British from the chains of popery and Stuart tyranny.
Many of these same themes reappear in Mandeville's final party political
tract, again published under his initials in 1720. As its title implies, *Free
Thoughts on Religion, the Church and National Happiness* discourses upon
the advantages of Whig governance, explaining that the apparent abuses
of politicians, so grumbled at by malcontents, are in fact trivial vices of
private persons who in their public roles efficiently administer a benign
constitution. In this work Mandeville also adopted an aggressively skeptical view of the religious establishment and of priestcraft generally, while
arguing for a rationally defensible religion. The humility of bishops, he
quipped, must be a very ponderous virtue, since it had to be drawn by a
coach and six. Such views evoked the specter of freethinking, as did the
book's title, and despite the patronage of Lord Macclesfield, the Lord
Chancellor from 1718 to 1724, Mandeville was never again employed by
the Whigs in the cause of political propaganda, something for which his
notorious reputation would have in any case permanently debarred him
once *The Fable of the Bees* became known as a scandalous book.

　　Mandeville's masterpiece first appeared under its full title in 1714,
when he transformed *The Grumbling Hive* into a small book by adding a
preface, "An Enquiry into the Origin of Moral Virtue," as well as twenty
prose Remarks ranging from single paragraphs to full essays which were
meant to elaborate the meaning of his original verses. In these essays,
Mandeville first achieved a register adequate for his larger philosophical
purposes, but the book in which they were contained seems to have made
only a small public impression. In the years immediately following, allu-
sions to it were quite rare, and since Mandeville's name was absent from
the book's title page, his small place in the public's imagination remained
confined to readers of his early verse and later political tracts. Only when
Mandeville published an enlarged edition of *The Fable of the Bees* in 1723
did he achieve the fame he sought. This edition included an amplified set
of Remarks and two new lengthy essays, "A Search into the Nature of
Society," in which Mandeville found it polemically useful to contrast *The
Fable* to the third Earl of Shaftesbury's *Characteristics* (1711 and 1714),
which famously argued that men were naturally sociable and beneficent,
and "An Essay on Charity and Charity-Schools," which ridiculed the
efforts of contemporary moral reformers. After the Middlesex Grand

Jury's presentment appeared in the press, Mandeville attacked his accusers in *The London Journal* of 27 July 1723, and shortly thereafter published the text of the presentment, together with his own defense, as "A Vindication of the Book, from the Aspersions contain'd in a Presentment of the Grand-Jury of Middlesex, and an abusive Letter to Lord C.," which he then appended to the 1724 editon of the *Fable*. A literary career was belatedly launched, as "Man-devil" became a synonym for immorality, while *The Fable of the Bees* quickly acquired an independent identity as an unsubdued mutiny in moral philosophy. As Dr. Johnson said, every young man had Mandeville's work on his shelf in the belief that it was a wicked book.

The immediate circumstances surrounding Mandeville's spectacular rise to fame were conditioned by the dominant civic humanist language of argument within which the emergence of modern forms of mobile property, public finance and enlarged government power were understood in early eighteenth-century Britain. *The Fable of the Bees* first came to prominence because it was implicated in an intense controversy about the nature of politics, modern commerce and their contemporary moral consequences. The presentment to the Middlesex Grand Jury claimed that the *Fable* was designed "to run down Religion and Virtue as prejudicial to Society, and detrimental to the State; and to recommend Luxury, Avarice, Pride, and all vices, as being necessary to Public Welfare, and not tending to the Destruction of the Constitution. . . ." This charge was couched in the language of traditional Christian moral perception, laced with Puritan idioms. In his "Vindication," Mandeville recognized it at once as the rhetoric of the Societies for the Reformation of Manners, whose campaigns for moral reform and whose program for the education of poor children he had savaged in the *Fable*'s "Essay on Charity and Charity-Schools."

The Grand Jurymen judging the case were opponents of the current Whig administration who shared Tory and possibly Jacobite sympathies. These men sought to assert their loyalty to the crown and their moral opposition to Robert Walpole, its chief minister, whose principles they now found politically opportune to claim were enunciated in Mandeville's book. In his *Free Thoughts* of 1720, Mandeville had argued that "dominion always follows property," and that the Glorious Revolution of 1688–1689 had brought the constitution into equilibrium with contemporary property relationships, a thesis which had become the official doctrine of the government party. Mandeville's argument was an elaboration of the government's well-known position, coupled with a satiric attack upon its opponents, who had denounced the government's financial manipulation of placemen in parliament, and came close to questioning its legitimacy as well. Government publicists like Mandeville not only sought to defend the Hanoverian succession against Jacobite claims of usurpation. In championing the new regime, Whigs were also obliged to claim that its institutions were not signs of what had, for nearly a half century, commonly been called "corruption": the ability of government through financial reward and the granting of office to manipulate parliamentary institutions. Mandeville's was a telling critique of the opposition's principles. He argued that what was formerly regarded as political unscrupulousness had become inevitable in modern conditions of affluence, and that it was now the function of a well-ordered state to govern men whose growing opportunities for private gain were at the same time prerequisites of contemporary prosperity. Mandeville infuriated his immediate enemies because he defended existing political practices by offering a compelling account of the social place of private impulse to explain their necessity.

In their assault on the *Fable* the Grand Jurors spoke as what was termed Old Whigs, in what has been variously called the language of the Commonwealth, of civic humanism or republicanism. They attacked Mandeville in the context of an intense and comprehensive critique of modernity, undertaken in the name of an ideal of virtue practiced in antique Mediterranean republics, particularly republican Rome and the quasi-mythical Sparta framed by Lycurgus's laws. In Augustan England, the primary language of political opposition engaged a vocabulary that opposed virtue to corruption, the dignity of landed to mobile property, and public service to self-interest. Behind this rhetoric stood a tradition of political analysis ultimately derived from Machiavelli's account of the Roman Republic in the *Discourses* (1518), which was translated into English by the republican Henry Neville in 1674, and then re-issued four times by the date of the *Fable*'s prosecution. This argument inveighed against tyrants, found the source of political corruption in self-interest, suspected material affluence as a sign of moral degeneration, and hailed a citizen militia as the necessary guardian of liberty. While the liberty of the people was a constant theme of this literature, general material betterment was viewed with suspicion since affluence, it was believed, would fan self-interest. Neither did those who spoke as Commonwealthmen encourage popular participation, since political judgment was seen to be embodied in hero-statesmen like Cincinnatus or Cleomenes (the name Mandeville ironically chose for his own spokesman in the *Fable*), whose virtue was thought to derive from their devotion to patriotic principles, and was sustained by an aristocratic, landed independence from material need.

Central to the civic humanist position was the assumption of a necessary connection between political liberty and landed property. Machiavelli and his Florentine contemporaries had insisted upon this connection, while advancing the complementary thesis that the pursuit of private gain threatened civil liberty. They held that the scramble for money was one of the major dangers to the maintenance of freedom and public virtue. Instead, land seen as a patrimony supporting men at arms and sustained political independence was understood as the necessary economic foundation of the virtuous citizen. The prospect of moveable wealth amongst the newly monied, and of land treated as capital in a volatile market of anonymous risk-takers, conjured up the specter of public opinion alone as the measure of one's standing, and of the self-interest and private pleasure through which luxurious nations declined, falling prey to their frugal, independent neighbors. In this way, so those who followed the civic tradition argued, Sparta triumphed over Athens and the Swiss preserved their freedom in the face of the huge, corrupt states on their borders. Mandeville's contemporaries John Trenchard and Thomas Gordon, whose publisher was charged along with the *Fable*'s, denounced in their influential tract of 1723, *Cato's Letters: or Essays on Liberty, Civil and Religious, and Other Important Subjects*, the public morality of affluence which they saw as engendering the panic and disaster of the South Sea Bubble (the collapse of the South Sea Company's shares on the London Exchange) less than three years before. Only a frugal population could maintain its freedom, and only a rigorously defended civil liberty stood between civilization and a luxurious decline into arbitrary government.

These were compelling and politically potent doctrines during the first half of the eighteenth century. They were modifications of an allied puritan outlook into less specifically Christian forms of rhetoric, and were put foward as a distillation of those principles which the Glorious Revolution supposedly confirmed. Moreover, these ideas helped to make coherent the position of what in the 1720's and after was called "the landed interest," families living on their incomes from rents and who derived few supplementary revenues from office holding, commerce or finance. In the thirty years following 1688 these persons found their political position eroding as rents, mortgages and sales of land rapidly became less profitable. The new machinery of public credit and government finance, epitomized by the Bank of England and the East India Trading Company, presented great opportunities for profit to individuals eager to invest their newly won surplus capital. This was particularly true of holders of Bank and East India Trading shares, and of those persons handling their affairs on the London Exchange. These jobbers, brokers and factors whom the traditional landed classes found so threatening to their status and power, so it was claimed, formed the nucleus of "the moneyed interest" on whose speculation, rather than parliament's grant, the government increasingly depended for its soaring revenues.

Great Britain had recently emerged from wars in Europe against France and her allies in 1689–1697 and 1702–1713 as a major power with Atlantic imperial ambitions, supported by an expanding professional army sustained by a system of public credit and a national debt. These phenomena were seen by the regime's opponents as vastly expanding the crown's already considerable capacities for patronage, thus threatening parliamentary supremacy and also making increasing numbers of individuals dependent upon the government for their social and economic fortunes. The "Country" party, as this group was called, opposed the new system, since it directly threatened its members' political power, social standing and self-esteem. It blended the themes of classical republicanism, civic humanism and puritan frugality into an ideological defense of English liberties and the constitution against the supposed intrusion into the public domain of both private wealth and arbitrary influence. It set "virtue" over and against "commerce" and "corruption," "frugality" against "luxury," and the independence of parliament against the desire of the crown for unbalanced dominion. It stressed the role of the independent proprietor against the rentier, speculator and placeman. It identified as threats to liberty and security the manipulators of moveable capital, "stockjobbers" and holders of government notes, self-made urban plutocrats, French Huguenots and (particularly Portuguese and Dutch) Jews, all of whom centered their activities in the City of London and lived with that amalgam of unrestrained passion and self-interest which supposedly eroded a devotion to the common good. Sections of the established ruling orders thus felt endangered by persons recently propelled into power by a mysterious finance capitalism whose imperatives seemed at once to subvert traditional morality and threaten their social standing. Most fervently expressed during the financial crises of 1696, 1710 and 1720, these ideas retained their force well into the 1760's and beyond as the vagaeries of fortune initiated by a revolution in public finance loomed as a threat to a landed, antique ideal of civic freedom and public personality.

Setting Mandeville's work within the framework of a multifaceted British debate about commerce and virtue helps to make historical sense of much of the remarkably hostile reception the *Fable* initially received. Mandeville's moral skepticism was carefully framed in a language suited to engender in a large segment of his immediate audience a threat to their own self-understanding. By adopting the Satyr's sneer and at the same time notionally affirming the most rigorous criteria of the inherited moral tradition, Mandeville successfully fashioned an intuitively compelling picture of a world dramatically transformed by new mechanisms of exchange, a world that frighteningly demanded from its members the relegation of their civic ideals to the realm of nostalgia, and the adoption of an intransigently egoistic morality.

The local circumstances surrounding Mandeville's rise to fame should not obscure the *Fable*'s central place in the moral imagination of Enlightenment Europe, however, where the greatest students of contemporary society felt obliged directly to engage with its arguments. Mandeville was a self-conscious member of the European Republic of Letters at the turn of the eighteenth century, and he drew upon a variety of resources at some remove from the native conceptual environment in which he first became known. He recast in an original form arguments from Continental traditions of political discourse, natural philosophy and Christian moral psychology with which most of his initial adversaries had only a casual acquaintance. Mandeville was a thinker for whom scraps of quotidian reality provided the most startling information about hitherto unexamined social processes. He introduced into the heart of European social understanding a series of arguments designed to sustain the radically unsettling conclusion that the moral identities of his contemporaries had been permanently altered by an unacknowledged historical tranformation. A rich understanding of Mandeville's achievement must include the sources and strategies of his project as he understood it, and should treat his work with the philosophical seriousness accorded to *The Fable of the Bees* during three generations, from Hume to Kant and Rousseau to Adam Smith. For Mandeville provided for eighteenth-century intellectuals a map, or rather a sketch from which various maps could then be drawn, of society itself, understood as a hitherto untheorized entity whose history and paradoxical structure were now for the first time amenable to systematic analysis. *The Fable of the Bees* decisively shaped the Enlightenment's encounter with what Mandeville insisted were the unique and uniquely disturbing paradoxes of modernity.

2. Mandeville's Project: A Science of Socialized Man

In the *Fable*'s Preface Mandeville declared himself to be a "naturalist" seeking to lay bare the mechanisms which conditioned human desires. He claimed that longings for power, esteem and sensual pleasure were innate and indelible, driving everyone to compete for scarce satisfactions. Contemporary moral standards could not coherently be accounted for in terms of the received platitudes of orthodox ethical reasoning, but rather by inspecting the social history of this necessitous being, one whose superabundant desires, he would show, paradoxically made him fit for society. The commonly held belief in personal rectitude as the source of public good, Mandeville claimed, derived from a long-standing and highly articulated ideological project in which elites laid claim to private virtue in order to disguise their own self-seeking, thereby ensuring the respect of subordinates. He sought to reduce to absurdity the idea that polities could have been established from any realistically conceivable process of communal deliberation. Instead, only the "dextrous management of skillful politicians" served to stabilize an anthropologically irreducible clash of escalating individual desires.

Mandeville also rejected as contrary to all experience the venerable notion of a moral hierarchy of goods naturally suited to human needs. There was no *summum bonum*. Men were, and would always be, driven by their commonly shared passions, whose individual intensities were shaped by their inborn temperaments, and whose communal expressions were simply the derivative functions of given social opportunities. The sociological importance of this psychological truth was thrown into bold relief in modern conditions of affluence, which Mandeville, virtually alone amongst his immediate contemporaries, viewed with unambiguous delight. Well-governed commercial states in modern Europe, he insisted, were required to confront recently altered economic conditions that encouraged and rewarded both aggressive individual enterprise and social mobility. Rather than striving to curb the supposed moral corruption encouraged by widening economic opportunities (which was in reality nothing more than the perfectly normal expression of universal human traits), politicians, so Mandeville argued, had now expressly to attend to the manipulation of egoism into communally useful purposes. Ruling orders were obliged to govern subjects whose massively enlarged opportunities for purely personal gain were at the same time prerequisites of national prosperity. Mandeville gleefully dismissed as romantic nostalgia the widely held opinion that the intense scrambles for wealth and power which characterized modern polities provided evidence of the growing corruption of public life. Instead, *The Fable of the Bees* offered a psychologically compelling account of the positive social function of greed.

Mandeville meant the *Fable* to have a broad conceptual purchase. His arguments concerning the sources of virtue and justice, rather than the criticism of any particular persons, groups or local institutions, inspired the intensely hostile reactions of so many of his critics. Mandeville's unvarying subject was the moral and intersubjective demands made upon individuals recently propelled into the novel political and social conditions of commercial societies. In his formulation, men had to become what he called "taught animals" in order to make life comfortable in civil society. Mandeville understood this demand not so much as a necessary condition of justice, or a local feature of contemporary political struggle, but as a requirement of the prosperity which commercial citizens were coming to expect. This essentially political project, he pointedly added, required the prosperous, and those who sought prosperity, falsely to proclaim their virtuous intentions, all the while encouraging docility and ignorance amongst the lower orders, whose hard, ill paid work and continued deference were required to sustain their opulent living.

It would be difficult to find an English contemporary with a similar intellectual profile during the first quarter of the eighteenth century, and more difficult still to locate a native English audience for whom these concerns collectively formed the basis of sustained social commentary. The *Fable*'s power to shock its readers, and much of its conceptual force too, was a function of Mandeville's ability to inject novel elements into an already established civic discourse on the volatile moral relations between public virtue and the demands of commerce. Many of these elements were distinctive features of a Dutch republican political theory founded on a science of harnessing the passions, a self-described "political science" which the brothers Johann and Pieter De la Court formulated in Holland in the 1660's, most notably in *The True Interest and Political Maxims of the People of Holland* (translated in 1702), where the crucial distinction between false and prudentially disciplined self-love was articulated in exemplary fables. The De la Courts grafted a reading of Descartes's *Passions of the Soul* (1649) onto the arguments of *Leviathan* (1651), in which Hobbes distinguished men from social animals like bees by virtue of their political ability to forge agreements and enter into contracts. They found in Descartes a psychological theory of the passions as naturally disposed to desire what is useful for the individual, but in principle subject to rational control. Such control was possible through a reorientation of individual self-seeking so as to direct it to the common good. This goal could only be realized, the De la Courts maintained, in a state founded upon contract, one in which individuals able and willing to calculate their future advantages agreed to form a community. The resulting state would prosper and its citizens remain free if and only if this polity preserved a republican political balance of individual passions and communal interests. While writing in a Hobbesian idiom of unavoidable prepolitical conflict, the De la Courts nevertheless argued that men in the natural state were fully capable of making political calculations about those institutions and societal arrangements which would best serve them collectively. This they expressly contrasted to a society in which men followed the example of the bee, which seeks its own pleasure without regard for others.

In the *Fable* Mandeville sought to render incoherent the De la Courts' argument about the beneficent control of impulse for the common good. His portrayal of the beehive, by contrast to theirs, cast a positive light on precisely those values of self-interest and the dominance of the passions which the De la Courts had condemned. The bee had long been a symbol of the orderliness of absolute monarchies, while in England economic writers commonly used the bee to represent Dutch frugality, discipline and commercial success. Mandeville refused these images and associations, concentrating instead on the beehive as a symbol of morally unbridled economic activity. In this he followed the poet La Fontaine, whose *Fables* he had previously translated, as well as the then contentious position of the French philosopher Pierre Gassendi on the absolute continuity of human and animal drives, famously articulated in Gassendi's *Objections* to Descartes's *Meditations,* published together in 1641. Mandeville aimed to demolish the De la Courts' assumption that the passions could only be harnessed in a republic, and to ridicule the claim that a genuinely civil life could only be led under a republican government—a type of regime he associated with the impoverished rudimentary societies of the antique Mediterranean. He challenged as absurd the supposition that ignorant savages living in the rude conditions preceding the imposition of laws would have been in any position to make the prepolitical calculations necessary for them to agree upon any sort of government for their common good. In Mandeville's view, the first unsocial and cognitively primitive "brutes" could never have entered into the morally informed agreements which characterized contemporary theories of contract. Instead, societies requiring even the most elementary forms of coordination and consent, he argued, had to have been formed by the artful manipulation of the passions of these unreflective primitives.

It was this thesis that connected Mandeville's enterprise to a subversive tradition of social theorizing associated with the revival in Europe during the sixteenth and seventeenth centuries of the materialist and morally skeptical doctrines of the ancient philosophers Epicurus, Sextus Empiricus and Pyrrho of Elis. These thinkers concentrated on what they termed *bios*, the common conduct of daily life, questioned the existence of any universal ethical principles across the spectrum of human communities, and sought to understand men as complex animals responding to their innate impulses. During the late seventeenth century, skepticism was strongly associated with the Protestant refugee philosopher Pierre Bayle (who taught in the Rotterdam school Mandeville attended), and with the French Catholic followers of the Augustinian theology of Cornelius Jansen (called Jansenists), notably Blaise Pascal and Pierre Nicole. Those influenced by skepticism sought to show that a person's apparent practice of Christian virtue in no way provided an observer of these acts with indubitable information about the underlying motives informing them. Since apparently virtuous acts were rewarded by public esteem, it was in the obvious interest of the vicious to mime the conventional signs of Christian piety in order to win the approval of their fellows. Forms of egoism, in other words, manifested themselves according to the socially prescribed conventions of propriety amongst skilled social actors. Moreover, if virtue could reasonably be understood as one of the masks available to fallen men in their pursuit of selfish interests, then the difference between virtue and vice would have nothing to do with behavior. Instead, the distinction between an act which stemmed from selfish desire and one whose source was Christian charity would, of necessity, depend entirely upon the judgment of God as He inspected each human heart.

Two unsettling consequences followed from these morally pessimistic arguments. First, it was assumed that the great majority of mankind merely feigned Christian commitments while being, in reality, driven by self-love. Yet the fact that their behavior was in principle indistinguishable from that of true Christians challenged the conventional assumption that believers who feared Hell and yearned for salvation were more powerfully motivated toward virtuous action than were pagans, Jews or atheists. Bayle drew the obvious conclusion in his *Thoughts on the Comet* (1680): any man, atheist or believer, could make a good subject, since civil conduct required only the outward conformity to standards of propriety produced by social pressure, underwritten by law. The rectitude of a citizen required no spiritually enriched conscience. Second, as was famously suggested by Pierre Nicole in his *Moral Essays* (1674), just as the selfish, and thus necessarily conflicting, wants of individuals could be harnessed to politically beneficial ends, so too could competing social and economic interests be made to obey similar constraints. Social utility and communal benefit could correctly be understood as unintended consequences of certain historically domesticated forms of self-aggrandizement. The seemingly anarchic tendencies of the scramble for wealth, for example, revealed themselves, at a deeper level, to be structured social regularities attending the common pursuit of material gratification. Gross cupidity and never-satisfied material interest created secret social bonds, while the intersubjective sources of commercial interchange in goods and money provided men, Nicole said, "as much peace, safety, and comfort, as if they lived in a Republic of Saints."

Mandeville remodeled this stark contrast between divine injunctions and everyday behavior. He set out to compare the fantasy of the otherworldly city of the true believer with the motivations of thoroughly egoistic actors. He stressed the role of the demands made by the social environment in shaping the emotions of all persons into expressive conjunctions of judgment and passion whose local embodiments could only be realized and understood within the established conventions and beliefs of a commercial public sphere. If the demands of pride and the need for esteem were constant and universal features of the human constitution, desires themselves were nevertheless realized or thwarted only in socially structured, rule-governed interactions with others. Mandeville could at once mock orthodox Christians, his republican opponents and the defenders of aristocratic ideals of human excellence, because of the truth he claimed to have discovered: that the conditions of commercial modernity had made the Christian saint, the classical citizen and the noble warrior anachronistic mental deposits of long vanished or quickly eroding social formations.

The *Fable* consolidated a revolution in the understanding of the relationship between motives and acts largely begun in France by setting this relationship in a new problem space, that of viewing commerce and sociability as reciprocal and historically decisive features of the modern dynamics of self-regard. Persons in the recently constituted commercial polities on which the *Fable* concentrated were obliged, Mandeville argued, to respond to a revised structure of priorities if they were to satisfy their impulses. They were not merely driven by the universal appetites for authority and esteem, as were all others. In the centers of

European commercial societies outward displays of wealth alone were now widely accepted as a direct index of social power, rendering absurd, he argued in Remark L, the conventional condemnation of luxury as immoral. As he put it in the *Fable*'s Remark M, in great commercial cities, where strangers are regularly encountered, people gain public esteem by their clothes and other accoutrements of wealth, "not as what they are, but what they appear to be." Mandeville showed that the aggressive pursuit of wealth had now to be understood not as an activity properly confined to marginalized minorities, but as central to the self-definition of urban and commercial populations. The enlarged mechanisms of and opportunities for consumption emerged in the *Fable* as the distinguishing mark of commercial sociability, and thus a necessarily central concern of public policy rather than the exclusive domain of moralists and divines. Most strikingly, Mandeville claimed that his work for the first time systematically comprehended from the perspective of society itself the consequences of the behavior of persons for whom monied wealth encouraged those forms of self-display that were in effect the vehicles through which they established their moral and social identities.

Mandeville did not simply enlarge and extend the practical reasoning of his French predecessors. His analysis of morals, by contrast to theirs, rested on what he insisted were scientific foundations, explicitly grounded in a thoroughgoing naturalistic anthropology. For Mandeville, the image of a virtuous but depopulated terrestrial Jerusalem was nothing more than an absurd figure of derision, as he made clear in Remark T, thus abandoning not only the assumptions of the Jansenists, but also the Calvinism of Bayle. Mandeville called his project an "anatomy" of "the invisible part of man" (Remark N) because he thought that persons living in modern conditions had lost touch with the "natural causes" of their actions. Highly polished civilized social actors had thoroughly internalized the codes of law and morality which systematically suppressed the instinctual and unsocial sources of communal life, thereby erasing them from consciousness, and permitting these rational egoists to pursue their desires with relatively little social regulation. When critics objected that Mandeville treated persons as if they were nothing more than animals, repeating a complaint put into the mouth of Horatio in the *Fable*'s Third Dialogue of its second volume, they captured a central feature of Mandeville's enterprise.

Mandeville's denial of any innate human propensity for sociability— seen by him as a political achievement—followed directly from his rejection of the Cartesian contrast between the springs of animal behavior and the workings of human passions. In human beings alone, Descartes argued, the passions were under the direction of the rational soul; all other animals behaved as strict automata. Mandeville took his medical degree at Leiden University during a period of intense controversy between Cartesians and their resolutely mechanist opponents on the question of animal automatism. By the time he began writing the *Fable*, he had thoroughly abandoned the pertinent Cartesian views that he had held as a student, and had adopted the position that there was no qualitative distinction between men and beasts. He claimed, against Descartes, that animals, just as men, do feel, that men and animals have nearly identical passions, even including envy, and that animals, like men, have calculating minds. This was the line of reasoning associated with modern Epicureanism and ancient skepticism, influentially revived by the philosopher and essayist Michel de Montaigne in his *Essays* (1580–1588) and, amongst natural philosophers (what we now call scientists), most importantly stressed by Gassendi, whose doctrines were made known to a wide European public in the *Abridgment* (1684) of his secretary, François Bernier. While beasts do not speak our language, so Gassendi argued against Descartes, they have their own forms of discourse. Animal intelligence does not differ from ours in kind; such differences as exist are a function of the varying degrees of physiological complexity in humans and other animals.

This materialist physiological premise became the scientific foundation of Mandeville's wider enterprise. His account of social formation in "An Inquiry into the Origins of Moral Virtue" began with an examination of the cognitively immature brutes who populated the "wild state of nature," and then sought to explain how "Savage Man," an "untaught," self-regarding animal, became the tame, sociable creature celebrated by philosophers. Mandeville argued that it was precisely the animal impulses naturally disposing men to seek their own satisfactions that made them fit subjects for manipulation by the "lawgivers" who civilized the race as they appealed to the universal appetite of pride. Flattery was the "bewitching Engine" of an ideological project through which individuals were disciplined by encouraging amongst them the belief that persons demonstrated their moral superiority through acts of self-denial. Following contemporary physiological materialists who argued that men were essentially distinguished from one another by their differing temperaments established at birth, Mandeville hypothesized that in the first ages of the race the strong and cunning induced the weak to believe "that it was more beneficial for everybody to conquer than indulge his appetites, and much better to mind the Public" than what seemed his private interests.

Mandeville argued that the origins of morality, and thus of the social discipline required by the rule of elites, followed from the discovery by these elites of what he called the "imaginary" rewards of praise to which complex animal organisms responded. Flattery was employed to tame men by generating within these prideful creatures a conception of self constituted in part by the opinions of others. Only creatures instructed in the rhetoric of honor and the theology of shame could then internalize politically fabricated ideals of virtuous conduct. The *Fable*, in other words, sought to explain the domestication of the savage mind. Mandeville accounted for the false but socially necessary belief that virtue was the distinguishing feature of the human race by subsuming socialized men under the larger category of domesticated animals.

Mandeville thus attempted to derive an explanation of moral motivation from the few psychological facts about human nature which were strongly supported, he argued, both by the claims of experience and scientific enquiry. His hypothetical history of social origins was a foundational hypothesis meant to sustain and further encourage a thoroughgoing empirical discussion of the microprocesses of social interaction. Moral behavior could suitably be understood to arise from the reactions of an egoistic and necessitous creature to the opinions of others because these opinions have important tangible consequences for one's well-being. Men come to have an interest in keeping their promises, for example, precisely because of their painful realization that others have an interest in their doing so. By virtue of their approval and disapproval of the actions of others, men mete out rewards and punishments. If human beings quite understandably seek the approval of their fellows, and thus unwittingly acquire an interest in the continuation of normal intercourse, "politicians" could then seek to promote this balance by playing the passions of individuals against one another once society becomes firmly established.

The Fable of the Bees, then, was part of an ongoing enterprise begun by Mandeville in 1705 with the publication of *The Grumbling Hive*, and first elaborated in 1714 as a satire of a Dutch and English moralized political idiom. Uniting the physiological presuppositions of his medical *Treatise* with a largely French discourse analyzing the passions, Mandeville in 1723 then produced a greatly enlarged version of what he had come to understand as a theory of sociability in commercial societies. This project only achieved what he regarded as a comprehensive and philosophically secure form, however, once Mandeville worked out the consequences of his skeptical and scientific commitments in the *Fable*'s second volume of 1728, which were then further elaborated in *An Enquiry into the Origin of Honor* (1732). Mandeville virtually abandoned his earlier satiric mode of writing by 1728. This shift in his work was accompanied by a changed mode of address. In the Preface to the *Fable*'s second volume, Cleomenes, Mandeville's principal spokesman, is introduced to the reader as a "student of anatomy and natural philosophy" who "had studied human nature," and whose stated intention is to explain and defend the *Fable*'s larger naturalistic objectives.

It was this explicitly naturalist attempt at constructing the foundations of a science of socialized man that became the specter haunting Enlightenment social understanding. Mandeville proposed that styles of individual behavior in any historical epoch, and the collective fashions in which they participated, should be regarded as biological phenomena or symptoms of hidden natural causes, those elemental drives men shared with the higher animals. All passions and instincts, he argued, tend to the preservation and happiness either of individuals or the species. Mandeville explicitly endorsed the foundational claim that men and animals shared similar cognitive capacities, and that their differences could only be discovered by abandoning the fanciful hypotheses of philosophers, relying instead upon strict empirical observation. The diverse functions of human cognitive capacities could sufficiently be explained only in biophysiological rather than moral or metaphysical terms. Men differ from bees not because the hive is composed of lower animals, but because the intellectual powers of men could be, and in fact were, "artfully managed" so as to suppress and redirect their primary drives, a civilizing project, he said in the Sixth Dialogue, and again in *Honor*, which is "the joint labor of several ages." Even the social function of wealth, Mandeville argued in the concluding discussion of the *Fable*'s second volume, had properly to be explained in terms of the way money "mechanically" works on the passions as an attractive force in polished conditions.

Mandeville's reconceptualization of egoism along these naturalist lines entailed a sketch of the workings of what he termed this "instinct" in order to comprehend the pervasive force of pride in the shaping of human affairs. "Self-liking," as he now termed it in the Third Dialogue, was the innate mechanism by virtue of which one could explain the decisive power of flattery in first domesticating the species, and then account for those alterations in the presentation of the self as an object of approbation which characterized successive historical epochs in the history of sociability. Mandeville distinguished three decisive causes in the long, slow progression to civility: the banding together of savages for their mutual defense against animals; the stimulation of man's innate pride and courage through threats and attacks of other men; and the invention of language and letters, by means of which laws would remain stable and trustworthy instead of being subject to the efforts and insecurities necessarily associated with societies governed by oral traditions. Each stage in the civilizing process was accompanied by an "invention" or further refinement of "morality," conceived by Mandeville as the norms of conduct formally enacted or tacitly designed by the ruling elites that governed every polity in order to stabilize forms of intercourse among beings whose radical egoism and constitutional unsociability remained an ever-present threat to social stability. Commercial societies, the most recent and, for Mandeville, the most pertinent of these social forms, were shaped, as were all others, by the domestication of violent passions. But commercial societies were historically unique in one crucial respect: material affluence and political security enable their members to satisfy self-regarding impulses in ways that largely transcend the conflict between the individual's pursuit of his own pleasure and the blatantly repressive demands of social discipline that previously characterized every social order. As never before, men could now indulge themselves in the world of commerce because in it they were free to compete in non-violent ways for the most valued "tokens" of public approbation. The civility and politeness which had come to characterize the social habits of modern elites were in fact regulatory devices governing an unprecedented, but in Mandeville's view, already dominant, process of conspicuous consumption of symbols for the promotion of self—a relentless accumulation of emblems that could be acquired by wealth in a commercial market of marks of esteem.

Modern manners thus comprised the last stage in the history of pride, and the most efficient way to manage it. The habituation to politeness had effectively, albeit unconsciously, domesticated the violence of an expanding elite within recent history, while redirecting its energies to the productively liberating (because economically expansive) end of luxury consumption. Once men were able to distinguish themselves by mannered social pretense underwritten by the marks of wealth, the stern and self-denying morality of virtue which first made communal life possible was effectively reduced to a nostalgic remnant of the politically defeated and downwardly mobile. The decorous intercourse of contemporary elites, then, was at once the initial target of Mandeville's satiric voice as he exposed the hypocrisy of its supposedly other-regarding pronouncements, and the terminus of his enquiry into the history of pride, which concluded with the achievement of polished sociability—commercial society's successful surrogate for self-denial.

Mandeville's physiological model of the passions licensed the foundational presumptions of this hypothetical history: men everywhere and at all times had identical psychological structures; these structures were expressed in basic impulses which predisposed individuals to be strictly self-seeking agents who desired only their own satisfactions. Consequently, the social development of the race must be understood to have resulted from the largely unplanned, though, because physically derived, not random consequences of persons pursuing the amoral and diverse ends which answered the pull of their passions at any given moment in their life histories. The narrative constructed from these premises described a history of the race's progress in stages, from instinct to morality and then to law. It charted the course of the most immediate needs of body and mind, needs which were at first both paramount and psychologically transparent, because unmediated by social symbolism. Beginning in conditions of bare subsistence and primitive survival, this story culminated in the commercial polities of contemporary Europe. While the fundamental passionate repertoire of the human frame remained undiminished, these passions were now effectively harnessed, redirected from violent ends to seek tokens of public esteem and then made largely unconscious to the social actors themselves during the long course of the civilizing process.

When Kant in *The Critique of Practical Reason* (1788), his treatise on the foundations of ethics, grouped Mandeville with Montaigne and Epicurus as the theorists who first discovered the principles governing the constitution of society, he grasped this crucial feature of *The Fable of the Bees*, whose importance for the Enlightenment understanding of sociability forcefully emerged in the generation after Mandeville's death. This is readily apparent in Hume's adoption of a Mandevillian perspective in Book III of the *Treatise of Human Nature* (1740), the same year in which the *Fable* was first translated into French, only to be ritually burned by the public executioner in Paris. Hume, who, like Mandeville, was accused of Epicureanism, famously characterized his own philosophical activity as akin to that of an anatomist, and served as a decisive figure in the European encounter with the *Fable*, most influentially among the French *philosophes* and Hume's Scottish colleagues and successors like Adam Smith. In his Introduction, Hume named Mandeville as one of the philosophers in England who had begun to put the science of man on a new footing.

Likewise, he fully exploited Mandeville's work for the purposes of his own science of morals, claiming that the passions have a strict correspondence in men and animals, and that identical qualities give rise to pride in each. For any comprehensive understanding of social progress to be philosophically defensible, Hume agreed with Mandeville, it would have to account for accepted conventions of politics and the emergence of rules of justice strictly in terms of the consequences produced by the passions of individuals. Moral rules, he argued, should be understood through a conjectural anthropology of morals which attempts to describe the necessary features from which our moral judgments, or those of any society, arise, explaining the way in which the actions of individuals unintentionally lead over time to uniform and orderly patterns of moral behavior.

After 1750, the date of its second French translation, and in part because of Hume's achievement, the *Fable* became a contemporary classic for the students of an emerging science of man. This can be seen, for example, in the Sorbonne's condemnation of Helvétius's *On the Mind* (1759) because its author's attempt to naturalize ethics in the service of political ends was seen directly to derive from Mandeville's. Most significantly perhaps, Adam Smith openly acknowledged the *Fable*'s importance in the constitution of Enlightenment social understanding. A vigorous critic of the *Fable*, Smith nevertheless recognized in the six editions of his *Theory of Moral Sentiments* (1759–90) that no matter how destructive of conventional moral reasoning Mandeville's arguments may appear, they could never have been so widely discussed, nor have occasioned so general an alarm, had they not bordered on the truth. When he reviewed Rousseau's immensely influential *Discourse on the Origins of Inequality* (1755) for *The Edinburgh Review*, Smith informed his audience that Rousseau could not properly be understood without reference to *The Fable of the Bees*. Indeed, Rousseau's conjectural history of humanity, while strenuously denying the *Fable*'s conclusions, was perhaps the most influential single text which openly injected Mandeville's naturalism into the wider Enlightenment debate on the human sciences. Rousseau modeled his theory of the emergence of culture on a Mandevillian account of social evolution, and he explicitly confronted Mandeville's arguments while attempting to provide a natural history of morals founded, as was Mandeville's, upon the modern physical sciences and medicine. In the process, Rousseau directed Kant's attention to the *Fable* and probably alerted the Sorbonne's censors when they condemned Helvétius two years after Rousseau's *Discourse* was published amidst considerable controversy. Within a generation, almost every significant Enlightenment intellectual had pronounced on the problem of the morally paradoxical nature of material progress. This problem, which was a staple of Enlightenment anthropology in France, formed a starting point during the Scottish Enlightenment for the project of constructing a natural history of humanity. Late in the century it became a central feature of German reflection on modernity, most notably in Kant's adoption of Mandeville's theory of "unsocial sociability" in his *Idea for a Universal History from a Cosmopolitan Point of View* (1784), and then in Friedrich Schiller's *Letters on the Aesthetic Education of Mankind* (1795).

It is important to note that none of these writers, Adam Smith included, saw Mandeville's primary importance as that of an economic theorist, but rather as a moral philosopher and scientist of society. Mandeville's recognition, as Hume put it, that pride and humility are not merely human passions but extend themselves over the whole of animal creation, was the cardinal presumption behind the European-wide enterprise in which the *Fable* served as a decisive exemplar. Its aim was to include the entirety of civilized intercourse within the category of the drives of individuals, scientifically considered. In the *Fable*'s anatomy of human motives, the social order could for the first time be analytically isolated and comprehensively understood as a complex, but rule-bound, conjunction of the facts of nature. This science of socialized man would seek to map the unintended consequences of self-interested action and have as its primary objective the discovery of stabilizing social mechanisms inherent in communal expressions of self-regard. Mandeville conceived the goal of this project as the explanation of sociability, and thus of moral standards, in a vocabulary shorn of moralized concepts. His reduction of society to the action of individuals came to be accepted as methodologically prescriptive for an entire program. The *Fable* served in the generations after Mandeville wrote as a fitfully acknowledged, often suppressed, but indelibly inscribed foundation for this enterprise. In so doing, *The Fable of the Bees* became the progenitor of that systematic, though not final, vocabulary for the project of a social science which characterized the European encounter with commercial modernity.

SOURCES

Pierre Nicole, *Of Charity and Self-Love*

I. Although there is nothing so opposed to charity, which relates all to God, as self-love, which relates all to itself, yet there is nothing so resembling the effects of charity as those of self-love. For it proceeds by the same methods, so that one can hardly point out better ways where charity ought to carry us, than in proposing those which self-love takes, which knows its true interests, and inclines by reason to the end it proposes itself.

II. This conformity of effects in principles so different will not appear strange to those who have well considered the nature of self-love. But to know it, he must first consider self-love in itself, and in its first bent, that he may see afterwards what carries him to disguise and hide it from the sight of the world.

III. The name of self-love is not sufficient to make us know its nature, since we may love ourselves diverse ways. We must add other qualities to form a true idea of it. These qualities are, that man does not only love himself, but he loves himself without limits, and without measure; loves only himself, and refers all to himself. He covets all sort of riches, humors, pleasures, and desires, only for or in relation to himself. He makes himself the center of all; he would lord over it, and would have it that all creatures were only employed to content him, to praise him, and to admire him. This tyrannical disposition being stamped in the bottom of all men's hearts, renders them violent, unjust, cruel, ambitious, flatterers, envious, insolent, and quarrelous. In a word, it includes the seeds of all the crimes, and of all the misdemeanors of men, from the smallest to the most detestable ones. See here what a monster we harbor in our bosoms. This monster lives and reigns in us absolutely, except God destroy its empire by putting another love into our hearts. It is the principal of all our actions, which has no other than corrupted nature: and so far it is from terrifying us, that we love, and hate all things which are out of us, only as they conform or are contrary to our inclinations.

IV. But if we love it in ourselves, we are far from using it so when we perceive it in others. It appears then to us, on the contrary, under its natural form, and we hate it by so much more as we love ourselves, because the self-love of other men opposes all the desires of ours. We wish that all others should love us, obey us, and that they should be busied with the care of satisfying us. They have not only no desire to do this, but look upon us as ridiculous in pretending to it, and they are ready to do all, not only to hinder us from succeeding in our desires, but to make us obnoxious to theirs, and require the same things of us. Behold then by this means all men differ one with another; and if he [Hobbes] who has said that men are born in a state and condition of war, and that each man is naturally an enemy to all other men, had a mind only to represent by these words the disposition of the hearts of men, one towards another, without pretense of passing it for legitimate and just; he would have said something conforming to truth and experience, as that which is maintained is contrary to reason and justice.

V. It cannot possibly be imagined how there can be formed societies, commonwealths, and kingdoms out of this multitude of people full of passions, so contrary to union, and who only endeavor the ruin of one another. But self-love, which is the cause of this war, will easily tell the way how to make them live in peace. It loves domination, it loves to enslave all the world to it, but it loves yet more life and conveniences and an easy life more than domination; and sees clearly that others are in no way disposed to suffer themselves to be domineered over, and are sooner ready to take away from it the goods it loves best. Each man sees himself in an impossibility of succeeding by force into the designs which his ambition suggests to him, and understands that he can lose by that violence of others the essential goods he possesses. This obliges us at first to submit to the care of our own preservation, and there is no other way to accomplish this but to unite with others, to beat back by force those who undertake to deprive us both of our lives and fortunes. To strengthen this union, laws are made, and punishments ordered for those who violate them. Thus by the means of tortures and gibbets set up in public are the thoughts and tyrannical designs of every man's self-love restrained.

VI. Fear of death is thus the first tie of civil society, and the first check on self-love. This forces men to obey, whatever aversion they may have to the laws, and that which makes them forget these vast thoughts of domination, so that they rarely appear in the thoughts of most men, for they see that it is impossible to prosper without obedience.

Thus feeling themselves excluded from the open violence, they are constrained to seek other ways, and to substitute craft for force, and they find no other means than to endeavor to content the self-love of those whom they have need of, instead of tyrannizing over them.

Some endeavor to make it fit for their interests, others employ flattery to gain it. Gifts are bestowed to obtain it. This is the source and foundation of all commerce practiced amongst men, and which varies in a thousand ways. For they do not truck merchandises for merchandises or for money, but they mutually traffic, I mean they make a trade also of labors and toils, of services done, of diligence and assiduity, of civility; and men exchange all that, either for things of the same nature, or for real goods, as when by vain politeness we obtain effective commodities.

Thus, by the means and help of this commerce all necessaries for this life are supplied without intermixing charity with it. So that in states where charity has no admittance, because true religion is banished there, men do not cease to live with as much peace, safety, and comfort, as if they lived in a Republic of Saints.

VII. It is not that this tyrannical inclination, which makes desire to rule and govern by force over others, is not always lively in the hearts of men. But as they see themselves unable to prosper, they are forced to dissemble, until they are strengthened by gaining the consent of others by sweet ways in order to have the means to have them submit to their will by force. Everyone therefore is mindful at first to occupy the first rank of the society, and when he sees himself excluded, he thinks of those which follow. In a word, he extols himself the most he can, and he humbles himself only by constraint. In every state and in every condition he endeavors always to acquire some preeminence, authority, intendency, consideration, jurisdiction, and to expand his power as much as he can. Princes wage war with their neighbors so that they may enlarge the limits of their estates. The officers of several companies in one and the same country undertake and intrude upon one another: they strive to supplant them, and to humble each other in all their employments and in all their offices. And if the wars which follow are not so bloody as those which princes make; it is not because the passions are not as quick and sharp, but for the most part because they dread the punishment, which the laws threaten to those who have recourse to violent ways.

IX. What self-love covets particularly in sovereignty is that we be regarded by others as great and powerful, and that we stir up in their hearts motions of respect and submission. But whatever impressions are most agreeable to it, these are not the only ones nourishing self-love, which generally loves all things which are favorable to it, as admiration, respect, constancy, and chiefly love. There are many who scarcely do what they ought to make them beloved, but there are none who do not desire to be beloved, and who do not behold with great pleasure this propensity in others turned towards them, which is that which is called love. What if it appears that we don't strive to obtain this love? It is because we express sentiments of fear and submission under greatness, or because, desiring too passionately to please certain persons, we trouble ourselves very little to please others.

X. When we are carried away by strong passions, we behave in a fashion very improper to make us be beloved; and do not perceive ourselves inconvenienced when we see in the minds of others motions of hatred and aversion. There are likewise many people in whom this inclination of making themselves beloved is stronger than that of domineering and lording over men, and who fear more men's hatred and aversion, and the judgments which produce it, than they love to be rich and powerful. Lastly, whereas there are a few great men, and few likewise who are able to aspire to greatness, on the contrary, there is none who cannot pretend to make himself beloved.

XI. If the desire of being loved is not the strongest passion which springs from self-love, at least it is the most general. The considerations of interest, of ambition, of pleasure, often retard the effects of it, but not effectively. It is always active at the bottom of the heart, and as soon as it is at liberty, it forbears not being active, and makes us desire all that is able to procure us the love of men, as it makes us avoid everything we think may encourage their hatred. We are sometimes deceived in the distinction of things which encourage love or hatred, and that there are some who judge much better than others. But whether we are deceived or not, it is always the same passion which acts, and which flees or seeks the same objects. There is also a common distinction for all men; they know that in every one, at some point, certain actions will excite hatred, and others cause love.

XII. It is not necessary to delve further into the recesses of self-love, or to comprehend how it so imitates charity. It is sufficient to say that self-love, hindering us through fear of chastisement to violate the laws, removes us by this means outwardly from all the crimes, and so renders us like those who avoid them through charity. As charity comforts the necessities of others in the sight of God, we acknowledge his favors in helping our neighbor. Likewise, self-love comforts those in the sight of their proper interest. Lastly, as there is hardly any action motivated by charity that would not please God, self-love engages us to please men.

XIII. But though self-love tends by these means to counterfeit charity, there are many occasions, where neither fear nor interest have any place. We easily distinguish what we do, either through fear or through absolute interest, from what we do by a motive of charity. But it is not the same love and esteem for men. This inclination is so exact and subtle, and at the same time so broad, that there is nothing it cannot enter into; and it knows so well how to trim itself up with the appearances of charity, that it is almost impossible to know precisely what distinguishes it from charity. Because marching in the same steps, and producing the same effects, it defaces with a marvelous subtlety all the signs and characters of self-love from whence it springs, because it sees very well that it could obtain nothing of what it desires if they were noticed. The reason is because nothing so quickly brings the aversion of others upon us as self love, and because it cannot show itself without exciting aversion. We experience this ourselves in regard of the self love of others. We are not able to suffer it as soon as we discover it, and it is easy for us to judge from that, that others are not more favorable to our self-love when they discover it.

Those who understand the hatred of men, and who do not wish to expose themselves to it, endeavor to hide their self-love from the sight of others, to disguise and counterfeit it, never to show it under its natural shape, to imitate the behavior of those who would be entirely exempt from it; that is to say, persons animated with the spirit of charity.

XIV. This suppression of self-love is properly that which makes for civility, and shows in what it consists. And it is this which has caused learned men to say that Christian virtue destroys and annihilates self-love, and that human civility hides and suppresses it.

Thus this civility which has been the idol of the learned pagans is nothing at the bottom but a self-love more intelligent and exact, than that of the generality of the world, which knows how to shun what hurts its designs, which is the esteem and love of men by a more straight and reasonable way, in showing how self-love imitates the principal actions of charity.

XV. It is not difficult to comprehend how charity renders us humble. For making us love justice, which is God himself, it makes us hate injustice, which is contrary to him. Now it is an obvious injustice that, being as we are full of faults, and guilty of so many sins, we should be honored by men, and that we should pretend to deserve their praises, either by human qualities, and so consequently vain and frivolous, or by gifts, which we have received of God, and which do not belong unto us. It is not just that a sinner is honored, but it is just that he be humbled and brought low. The eternal law ordains it, and charity consents to this law. Indeed, charity loves it, and by the love which it bears to it, embraces with joy all humiliations and humblings. Charity makes us hate all that smells of pride and vanity; and as it condemns these motions when they start up in our hearts, it hinders them also from appearing by words and actions, which it reduces to an exact modesty.

XVI. Yet there is nothing in this but what self-love imitates perfectly; for feeling the heart of each man turned absolutely towards itself, and naturally an enemy to the preferring any other: it dares not expose itself to their thought and malignity.

Whoever praises himself, and seeks to promote what he thinks he has that's good, wishes thereby to bring others to him, and this is almost the same thing as if he begged them to give him praises, and to look upon him with esteem and love. Now there is hardly any prayer which appears more uncivil, and more incommodious to self-love, which men bear themselves, than this. It is angry and vexatious, and answers only by scoffing and disdain. Thus those who are cunning enough to know these tricks and devices avoid making these kinds of demands; that is to say, they keep themselves generally at a distance from all that appears vain, from all that tends to make them be taken notice of, and to show these advantages; and they try on the contrary to appear not to notice them, nor to know them. And that is the kind of modesty civility is able to procure.

XVII. Civility does not only shun these means and base vainglories, and the declared commendations which man gives himself; but knowing that self-love of others is extremely subtle in discovering the byways which may be taken to make manifest in us what we desire to show: civility renounces these small crafts, and studies to avoid them. It would force us rather to speak of ourselves directly and publicly, than to make use of these wicked tricks, because civility always fears being surprised, and knows that when men perceive them they take a great delight in making them appear ridiculous. Thus you see there is nothing more simple and humble than these discourses. Civility does not publish nor show itself by any way, and in a word, it has for a general rule never to speak of itself, or if it does, it is with coldness and indifference.

XIX. The fear which civility has of exciting against itself the natural aversion all men have for the vanity of another, has in this conduct a more cunning and delicate sentiment of this pride, which is born with man, and which never abandons him. These people which we see so busied with affairs which have astonished all the world, as Cicero did by his consulship, make it appear that virtue is not at all natural to them, and that they had need of great strength to hoist up their souls to the condition where they are so glad to show themselves. But there is more grandeur in not reflecting upon their great actions, so that they seem to escape us, and that they spring so naturally in the soul that we are not aware of them. This degree of virtue is doubtless much more heroic, and it is of this which human civility, when it is at its height, endeavors, without thinking of it expressly, to give the idea; or which it imitates by cunning and policy, when it is not perfect, and proceeds rather from reason than from nature.

XXII. It is needless to prove that charity is yet more removed from affectation, than mere civility. For loving others but not itself, it has nothing to do but to follow its natural motions, to act with a perfect civility. It does it so much better by how much it does it more sincerely, and that there is nothing counterfeit in it. Whereas this civility of self-love is for the most part not so uniform. If civility represses it in one part, self-love shows itself sometimes in another, and so leaves some little disguise of itself, to those who observe it narrowly. But as that happens but against its intention, it is ashamed being aware of it, or rather perceiving that others did observe it.

Thus it is always true to say, that when self-love follows reason exactly in search of esteem, and the affection of men, it imitates charity perfectly, so that in examining exterior actions it gives us the same answer that charity does, and engages us in the same ways.

XXIII. If for example, one asks charity in what disposition we ought to be concerning the subject of our faults, she will tell us that we ought to condemn ourselves for our own lack of regard for others, that we ought to be sensitive to our selfish blindness, and to dispose us more to believe others in this than ourselves. But in respect of our faults, there would be nothing more unjust than to counterfeit, and destroy in some sort the light of God itself, by pretending to justify what it condemns; and thus the least we can do to escape this pride so criminal, is to acknowledge them sincerely, and to humble ourselves before God and man.

XXIV. Let us now propose the same question to self-love, and we shall see if it does not speak the same language at the bottom of the heart, if it gives yet the same counsel. Though it is hard, it will say, to acknowledge our faults, and desire to deface them, and blot them out of the memory of man, as well as out of our own, it is evident nevertheless that that is impossible. The more we shall strive to disguise them from others, the more ingenious they will be to discover them, and wickedly take notice of them. This same desire of concealing them will pass in their minds for the greatest of faults, and we shall do nothing in striving either to dissemble them or to maintain them, but draw hatred or disdain upon ourselves. We must therefore necessarily steer another course. If we cannot have the glory of being without faults, we must have that of knowing them, and not being cheats to ourselves. Let us take away then from others the pleasure of taking notice of them, in observing them ourselves first, and thereby disarming their wickedness.

It is because of similar considerations that civility forms its conduct, and which encourages it to make an open profession of sincerely acknowledging all its faults, so that others will observe them, and by this strategy gains the reputation of an amiable equity, which makes it judge of itself clearly, and without passion, which knows how to justify itself, and with which one may be untroubled, without being obliged outwardly to admit that one approves of what indeed one does not.

XXV. It is easy to discern from what has been said that some very different considerations and motives serve to unite charity and self-love in the same outward conduct. We know well enough that to which charity sways us; for reflecting upon our behavior as a favorable means to deliver us from out faults, charity responds not only with joy, but with greediness and avidity. The bitterness which accompanies these realizations is agreeable to it, as procuring us the satisfaction of humility, and weakening self-love, which charity esteems as its worst enemy. Thus it is so far from showing any disguise or sharpness of speech to those who procure us this good, that it forgets nothing that may testify its gratefulness; to comfort them in the fear they have of hurting us, to incline them to do us the same favor, and to free them from all doubts which may make them reserved, and to keep them in torment and constraint.

XXVI. Self-love is always inwardly very far removed from this disposition. It does not love that others take notice of our faults, and much less that they admonish us for them. But yet it acts outwardly as charity does. For learning by these admonitions the bad impression men have of us, reason makes self-love conclude that it must be lessened, or at least not augmented. And consulting afterwards other men's minds to learn how we ought to guide ours, self-love easily acknowledges that nothing is a greater stumbling block than the haughtiness of those who are not able to endure to be admonished for any of their faults, who rebel against truth, and who wish that all the world were blind to them, or would suppress their thoughts. On the contrary, nothing is more agreeable to people than to be freed from the resistance of others, and to see that they put a stop to their judgments, and thus in some way submit themselves to their empire. Self-love therefore without hesitating takes this last part, and thereby makes us insinuate ourselves so agreeably into the hearts of those who reprove us, that they love those who humble themselves in that manner much better, whatever faults they have, than those who have none and thus have no opportunity to give them this satisfaction. Because we must observe that our faults are not of themselves contrary to the self-love of others, and likewise that the bravest qualities are not pleasing to it. So that if these faults make us more humble, or if these brave qualities render us more haughty, others will love us with these faults, and hate us with all those brave qualities.

Pierre Bayle, *Miscellaneous Thoughts on the Comet of 1680*

CXXXIII. *Proof that Atheism does not necessarily lead to the corruption of morals.*

(. . .) People are persuaded by a false preconception concerning the light of conscience that atheism is the most abominable state into which anyone may fall, for not having discerned our true motives, they imagine that our beliefs determine our acts. They reason this way: Man is naturally rational, he never desires without a conscious motive, he necessarily seeks happiness and hates unhappiness, and he prefers the objects most agreeable to him. Therefore, if he is convinced that there is a Providence which governs the world, from whose workings nothing is exempt, which rewards the virtuous with an infinite bliss and punishes the wicked with an eternal torment, he will infallibly follow virtue and flee vice. He will renounce all carnal pleasures, knowing on the one hand that these fleeting moments of gratification will procure him an eternity of pain, and feeling on the other hand that in depriving himself of them he will find an eternity of bliss. But if he does not believe in Providence, he will regard his desires as his ultimate end and the rule of all his acts. He will scoff at what others call virtue and integrity and will follow only the movements of his own lusts. If possible, he will do away with all those who displease him. He will perjure himself for the slightest gain, and if his position puts him above human laws, as he has already placed himself above the remorse of conscience, there is no crime which we should not expect of him. He is a monster infinitely more dangerous than those fierce beasts, those lions and mad bulls from which Hercules delivered Greece. Someone else, who had nothing to fear from men, could at least be restrained by the fear of the gods, which has always been a means of bridling the passions of men. And it is certain that many crimes were prevented among the pagans by the care taken to preserve the memory of all the striking punishments visited upon scoundrels for their supposed impiety, or even to invent a few examples, such as the story spread abroad in the time of Augustus when a temple in Asia had been pillaged by the soldiers of Mark Anthony. It was said that the person who first laid his hand upon the altar of the goddess who was worshipped in that temple had immediately been struck blind and had become paralyzed. (Seeking to verify the report, Augustus learned from the old officer who had done the deed that he had not only been sound and healthy ever since, but also that this act had put him in comfortable circumstances for the rest of his life.) . . . People reason that all of these accounts, true or false, which had such a good effect upon the mind of an idolater, have no power over an atheist. He is so impervious to all of these considerations that he must necessarily be the most accomplished and incorrigible scoundrel in the world.

CXXXIV. *Experience opposes the idea that the knowledge of God checks the evil inclinations of men.*

All of this is well and good when we regard that theoretical side of the question and make metaphysical abstractions of it, but unfortunately, the theory does not accord with the findings of experience. Suppose that we asked inhabitants of another world to predict the morals of Christians after telling them that Christians are creatures endowed with reason and good sense, avidly seek happiness, and are persuaded that there is a Paradise for those who obey the law of God and a Hell for those who do not. I admit they would undoubtedly assure us that the Christians strive to excel in observing the precepts of the Gospel and vie to distinguish themselves in works of mercy, in prayer, and in forgiving offenses, if there are any among them capable of offending his neighbor. But why would they make this complimentary judgment? It is because they would have considered only an abstract idea of the Christians, for if they considered them individually and saw everything that makes them act, they would soon reduce the good opinion that they would have formed, and they would not have lived two weeks among us without declaring that in this world people do not conduct themselves according to the light of conscience.

CXXXV. *The reason for the disparity between belief and practice.*

Here we come to the real solution of this question. When we compare the actual morals of a religious man with the abstract idea of what his morals should be, we are surprised not to find any conformity between reality and our expectations. According to our abstract idea, we should expect that a man who believes in a God, a Paradise, and a Hell would do everything that he knew to be pleasing to God and would do nothing he knew to be displeasing to Him; but the life of this man shows us that he does just the opposite. Do you wish to know the cause of this incongruity? Here it is—man does not decide between two possible actions by his abstract knowledge of duty, but by the particular judgment he makes of each one when he is at the point of acting. Now this decision may well be in conformity with his abstract idea of duty, but most often it is not. It is almost always determined by the dominant passion of the heart, the inclination of his temperament, the force of habit, and the taste and sensitivity which he has for certain things. The poet [Euripides] who has Medea say, "I see and approve the good, but I do evil," has perfectly depicted the difference between the light of conscience and the particular judgment which moves us to act. Conscience recognizes the beauty of virtue in the abstract and forces us to agree that nothing is more praiseworthy than to live virtuously. But once the heart is possessed by an unlawful love, when one sees that he will experience pleasure in satisfying it and will be plunged into despair and unbearable anxiety if he does not satisfy it, no light of conscience is of any avail. Nothing is consulted except passion, and judgment is rendered in favor of acting here and now against the abstract idea of duty. All of these observations only go to show that nothing is more illusory than to judge the moral character of a man by the general opinions with which he is imbued. . . . (. . .)

CXXXVI. *Man does not act according to his principles.*

Say what you will about man being a reasonable creature, it is nonetheless true that his conduct is almost never consistent with his principles. In speculative questions he is quite capable of avoiding erroneous conclusions, because in these matters he sins much more by accepting false premises than by drawing false conclusions from them. But it is quite another thing in questions of morals. Here he very seldom adopts false principles and almost never abandons the ideas of natural equity in his conscience, and yet he almost always concludes in favor of his dissolute desires. Why is it, I ask you, that in spite of the prodigious diversity of opinions concerning the way of serving God and living honorably, we see certain passions reigning constantly in all countries and in all ages? Why is it that ambition, avarice, envy, the desire for vengeance, fornication, and all the crimes that can satisfy these passions are seen everywhere? Why is it that the Jew and the Mohammedan, the Turk and the Moor, the Christian and the pagan, the Indian and the Tartar, the islander and the mainlander, the noble and the commoner, all of these kinds of people who in all other things are alike only in their abstract humanity, why is it that they are so alike with respect to these passions that they only seem to copy one another? Where can we find the reason for all of this except in the idea that the true principle of man's actions (I except those in whom the Holy Spirit operates with all of its efficacy) is nothing else than the temperament, the natural inclination for pleasure, the taste acquired for certain objects, the desire to please, a habit contracted through association with one's friends, or some other disposition which results from the essence of our nature, no matter where we were born or what we have been taught?

My explanation must be sound since the ancient pagans, who had an unbelievable collection of superstitions, who were constantly appeasing the wrath of their gods, who were frightened by an endless number of wonders because they believed the gods to be the dispensers of prosperity and adversity according to one's conduct, still did not fail to commit every crime imaginable. And if my explanation were not true, how would it be possible for Christians, who know so clearly by a revelation supported by so many miracles that they must renounce vice to be eternally happy and to avoid eternal misery; who have so many excellent preachers who are paid to compose and deliver the most cogent and compelling exhortations to virtue; who everywhere have so many learned and zealous spiritual advisers; how then would it be possible, I say, for the Christians to live as they do in the most terrible licentiousness and vice?

CXLV. *The pagans, who believed in many gods, were not more virtuous than atheists would be.*

No matter how often you object that the fear of a God is an eminently suitable means of correcting the natural corruption of man, I will always invoke the testimony of experience and ask why the pagans, who carried the fear of their gods to excessive superstitions, were so lax in correcting this corruption that every abominable vice reigned among them. In spite of the ever present memory of spectacular retribution visited by the heavens upon blasphemers and perjurers and those guilty of sacrilege; in spite of the tales forged to make the wicked tremble; in spite of the pompous descriptions of the Furies, Hell, and the Elysian Fields, temples were still pillaged when the occasion was favorable and false witnesses were found in great profusion. Juvenal is inimitable in his picture of false witnesses who have no religion and false witnesses who believe in a God. He says that the former perjure themselves without hesitation, whereas the other reason for some time and then perjure themselves with extreme confidence. They subsequently feel remorse and imagine that the vengeance of God pursues them everywhere. Nonetheless they do not mend their ways, but sin as readily at the next opportunity as they did before.

This picture is an exact copy of Nature. We still see this same spirit reigning everywhere and drawing men to sin in spite of the fear of Hell and the remorse of conscience. This observation is so obviously true that to argue against my thesis is nothing else than pitting metaphysical reasonings against a fact, in the manner of that philosopher [Zeno] who attempted to prove that there was no movement. No one, I am sure, will object to my use of the method of Diogenes, who without answering the subtleties of Zeno point by point merely walked in his presence. Indeed, nothing is more efficacious in convincing an honest man that he reasons upon false hypotheses than to show him that he argues against experience. . . . (. . .)

As I have already said, there are no records informing us of the morals and customs of a nation completely immersed in atheism. We cannot therefore refute by established fact that atheists are incapable of any moral virtue and that they are ferocious beasts to be feared more than lions and tigers. But it is not difficult to show that this conjecture is highly uncertain. For since experience shows us that those who believe in a Paradise and a Hell are capable of committing all sorts of crimes, it is evident that the inclination to do evil does not come from the ignorance of God's existence, and that it is not corrected by acquiring the knowledge of a God who punishes and rewards. One may conclude from this that the inclination to do evil is not any greater in a soul destitute of the knowledge of God than in a soul which knows Him. (. . .)

CLXI. *Conjectures upon the morals of a society of atheists.*

After all these remarks, if you wish to know my conjectures concerning a society of atheists, I will not hesitate to say that with regard to morals and civic affairs, it would be just like a society of pagans. It is true that very strict and well-executed laws would be needed for the punishing of criminals. But are they not needed everywhere? Would we dare to leave our houses if theft, murder, and other acts of violence were permitted by the laws of the sovereign? Is it not the case that in the streets of Paris, both day and night, we are protected from thieves and pickpockets by nothing more than the strict enforcement of the king's laws? Without his laws, would we not be exposed to the same kinds of violence as in former reigns, even though our teachers and confessors discharged their duties even better than they formerly did? In spite of the rack, the zeal of the magistrate, and the diligence of provosts, how many murders and thefts are committed, even in the places of public execution and at the moment when criminals are being executed? We can say without indulging in false oratory that human justice is the cause of the virtue of most people, for as soon as it fails to punish the sinner, few people keep themselves from the sin.

CLXXII. *Whether in a society of atheists there would be laws of propriety and honor.*

We can now see how apparent it is that a society of atheists would practice both civic and moral actions just as other societies practice them, provided that crimes were severely punished and that honor and shame were associated with certain acts. Just as ignorance of a Supreme Being, the Creator and Preserver of the world, would not make the members of this society impervious to glory and scorn, to reward and punishment, and to all the passions which are seen in other men, so too would it not extinguish in them the light of reason. In a society of atheists, therefore, we should expect to see people who would be honest in their business dealings, who would help the poor, who would oppose injustice, who would be faithful to their friends, who would scorn insults addressed to them, who would restrain their carnal appetites and who would do harm to no one. Their motives, it is true, would vary, for some would desire to be praised for all these splendid actions which the public would surely approve, while others would do them with the intention of acquiring the support of friends and protectors when in need. Women would pride themselves on their chastity, because this quality infallibly procures them the love and esteem of men. I do not doubt that there would be crimes of every kind, but no more than are committed in societies of idolaters, because everything which motivates pagans, whether to good or evil, would be found in a society of atheists, that is, rewards and punishments, glory and shame, temperament and education. For concerning this sanctifying grace which fills us with the love of God and which enables us to triumph over our evil habits, the pagans are just as bereft of it as atheists.

If you wish to be fully convinced that a people deprived of the knowledge of God would make rules of honor for themselves and observe them scrupulously, you have only to look among the Christians to see a certain worldly honor which is directly contrary to the spirit of the Gospel. I would be curious to know the origin of this system of honor of which the Christians are so idolatrous and to which they sacrifice everything. When they believe that it is dishonorable to leave an offense unpunished, or to yield first place to another, or to have less ambition or pride than their equals, is it because they believe in a God, a Gospel, a resurrection, a Paradise, and a Hell? Surely not. Examine all of the ideas of propriety which are found among the Christians, and you will scarcely find two which have been borrowed from religion. Moreover, when improper actions become proper, it is not at all because people have consulted the morality of the Gospel. Some time ago women got it into their heads that it was more fashionable to dress in public and in the presence of others than in private, to ride horseback, to chase some wild animal during the hunt, etc., and because these actions have become common, we no longer look upon them as immodest. Is it religion which changed our ideas in this respect? Compare the manners of several nations which profess Christianity; compare them, I say, one with another, and you will see that what is accounted improper in one country is not at all improper elsewhere. It must then be that the ideas of propriety among Christians do not come from the religion that they profess. I admit that some of their ideas are universal, for we have no example of a Christian nation where it is shameful for women to be chaste. But to act in good faith we must confess that this idea is older than both the Gospel and Moses: it is a certain impression which is as old as the world. . . . (. . .) Let us admit, then, that there are ideas of honor in the human race implanted there by nature, that is, by a general Providence. Let us especially admit that such is the case of that honor of which the brave among us are so jealous and which is so in opposition to the law of God. And after that, how can we doubt that nature could do among the atheists, where the knowledge of the Gospel would not oppose it, that which it does among the Christians?

CLXXIII. *Belief in the mortality of the soul does not prevent people from desiring to immortalize their name.*

Perhaps people imagine that the desire to immortalize one's name, which has so much power over the minds of other men, has no effect on an atheist, who is persuaded that his soul dies with his body. But this thought is quite false, since it is certain that those who have done great deeds in order to be praised by posterity were not flattered by the hope of knowing in the next world what people would say about them after their death. Even today we find examples of our brave warriors who expose themselves to so many perils and hardships in order to have their name mentioned in history. Do they imagine that the monuments which will be erected in their honor, and which will inform their most distant posterity of everything great and magnificent which they have done, do they imagine, I say, that these monuments will cause them to feel any pleasure? Do they believe that they will be informed in the next world of what is happening in this one? And don't they know that whether they enjoy the bliss of Paradise or burn in Hell, it would be quite useless to learn that men admire them? Therefore, it is not the belief in the immortality of the soul which causes people to love glory, and consequently atheists are quite capable of desiring an eternal reputation. The most substantial part of the love of glory is a pleasant image which one caresses in his mind during this life of many successive centuries filled with admiration for one's deeds. And after one is dead? This thought is of no further use, for there are many other things to do besides thinking of the reputation which one has left in this world. . . . (. . .)

CLXXIV. *Examples which show that atheists have not been distinguished by the impurity of their morals.*

Perhaps I will be told that it would nonetheless be a strange thing for an atheist to live virtuously. It would be a veritable prodigy beyond the forces of nature. I answer that it is not any stranger for an atheist to live virtuously than it is for a Christian to commit all sorts of crimes. If we see the latter prodigy every day, why should we believe that the other is impossible? But I will put forth some even stronger reasons to show you that what I have said concerning the morals of a society of atheists is more than mere conjecture. I will point out that those few persons among the ancients who made an open profession of atheism, such as Diagoras, Theodorus . . . , and several others, caused no general outcry by their libertinism. Although they have been accused of dreadful aberrations in their reason, I am not aware that they have the reputation of extraordinary licentiousness in their conduct. On the contrary, I find that their conduct appeared so admirable to Clement of Alexandria that he felt obliged to protest against the accusation of atheism that was leveled at them. He maintained that their reputation for impiety was due only to their great zeal and discrimination in pointing out the errors of pagan theology, and that they were called atheists only because they refused to recognize the false pagan gods. . . . (. . .)

Epicurus, who denied Providence and the immortality of the soul, was one of the philosophers of antiquity who lived in the most exemplary way, and although his sect has been brought into disrepute, it is nonetheless certain that it was composed of many honorable and upright persons, and those who dishonored it by their vices were not corrupted by this school. They were people who gave themselves over to debauchery by habit and temperament and who were glad to conceal their filthy passions with such a good pretext as that of following the maxims of one of the greatest philosophers in the world. They were the kind of people who imagined that as long as they hid themselves under the mantle of philosophy they could mock the scandal they caused. They did not become inclined to vice because they had embraced the doctrine of Epicurus, but they embraced the doctrine of Epicurus, which they did not understand, because they were already debauched. At least this is what Seneca says, and although he belonged to a sect which detested the memory of Epicurus, he does not hesitate to voice his belief that the pleasures of this philosopher were very sober and restrained. St. Jerome speaks very advantageously of the frugality of the same Epicurus and holds him up in sharp contrast to the licentiousness of the Christians, in order to shame the latter.

Among the Jews there was a sect which frankly denied the immortality of the soul. I speak of the Sadducees [a Jewish sect ca. 200 B.C. which upheld the authority of written law]. I am not aware that with such a detestable opinion they led a life any more corrupt than the other Jews; and on the contrary it is very likely that they were more upright than the

Pharisees, who prided themselves so much on their observation of the law of God.

Mr. [Guise] de Balzac informs us in *The Christian Socrates* of the last words of a prince who had lived and died an atheist and he testifies that he lacked no moral virtues, swore only by "certainly," drank only herb tea, and was extremely circumspect in every outward appearance.

The detestable Vanini, who was burned in Toulouse for his atheism in 1619, had always lived moderately, and whoever would have accused him of any criminal deviation, except in his dogmas, would have run a great risk of being convicted of slander.

Under the reign of Charles IX in 1573, a man who had secretly affirmed his atheism was burned in Paris. He maintained that there was no other god in the world except the purity of his body. He was therefore reported to be yet a virgin. He had as many shirts as there are days of the year, and he sent them to Flanders to be washed in a fountain famed for the purity of its water and its property of making clothes admirably white. He had an aversion for all kinds of impurities, whether in acts or in words, and although he upheld his blasphemies with a stubbornness which he retained until his death, he always stated them in an extremely mild way.

You cannot be unaware of the account given by Mr. Ricaut, Secretary of the Count of Winchelsey, the English ambassador at Constantinople. I need not comment upon the diligence and exactitude of this author. I will say only that after giving the account of a numerous sect of atheists formed in Turkey, composed mostly of . . . people versed in Arabic literature, he adds that the partisans of this sect have an extraordinary affection for one another, that they render each other all kinds of good services, that they are civil and hospitable, and that if a guest of their persuasion arrives they provide him with the best food they have. I do not deny that their civilities go too far, since they provide their guest with a most improper recreation during the night, but in that they do nothing of which the other Turks are not guilty. Therefore, if we compare the life of the other Turks with that of these atheists, we will find either that there is no difference between the two or that the former are less virtuous than the latter. . . .

The Fable of the Bees:
or,
Private Vices, Public Benefits
(Volume I)

The Preface

Laws and government are to the political bodies of civil societies what the vital spirits and life itself are to the natural bodies of animated creatures; and as those that study the anatomy of dead carcasses may see, that the chief organs and nicest springs more immediately required to continue the motion of our machine are not hard bones, strong muscles and nerves, nor the smooth white skin that so beautifully covers them, but small trifling films and little pipes that are either overlooked, or else seem inconsiderable to vulgar eyes; so they that examine into the nature of man, abstract from art and education, may observe, that what renders him a sociable animal consists not in his desire of company, good nature, pity, affability, and other graces of a fair outside; but that his vilest and most hateful qualities are the most necessary accomplishments to fit him for the largest and, according to the world, the happiest and most flourishing societies.

The following fable, in which what I have said is set forth at large, was printed above eight years ago in a six-penny pamphlet called *The Grumbling Hive; or Knaves turn'd Honest*; and being soon after pirated, cried about the streets in a half-penny sheet. Since the first publishing of it I have met with several that either wilfully or ignorantly mistaking the design, would have it, that the scope of it was a satire upon virtue and morality, and the whole wrote for the encouragement of vice. This made me resolve, whenever it should be reprinted, some way or other to inform the reader of the real intent this little poem was wrote with. I do not dignify these few loose lines with the name of poem, that I would have the reader expect any poetry in them, but barely because they are rhyme, and I am in reality puzzled what name to give them; for they are neither heroic nor pastoral, satire, burlesque nor heroic-comic; to be a tale they want probability, and the whole is rather too long for a fable. All I can say of them is, that they are a story told in doggerel, which without the least design of being witty, I have endeavored to do in as easy and familiar a manner as I was able: the reader shall be welcome to call them what he pleases. It was said of Montaigne, that he was pretty well versed in the defects of mankind, but unacquainted with the excellencies of human nature: if I fare no worse, I shall think myself well used.

What country soever in the universe is to be understood by the bee-hive represented here, it is evident from what is said of the laws and con-stitution of it, the glory, wealth, power and industry of its inhabitants, that it must be a large, rich and warlike nation, that is happily governed by a limited monarchy. The satire therefore to be met with in the following lines upon the several professions and callings, and almost every degree and station of people, was not made to injure and point to particular per-sons, but only to show the vileness of the ingredients that all together compose the wholesome mixture of a well-ordered society; in order to extol the wonderful power of political wisdom, by the help of which so beautiful a machine is raised from the most contemptible branches. For the main design of the fable (as it is briefly explained in the moral) is to show the impossibility of enjoying all the most elegant comforts of life that are to be met with in an industrious, wealthy and powerful nation, and at the same time be blessed with all the virtue and innocence that can be wished for in a golden age; from thence to expose the unreasonableness and folly of those, that desirous of being an opulent and flourishing peo-ple, and wonderfully greedy after all the benefits they can receive as such, are yet always murmuring at and exclaiming against those vices and inconveniences that from the beginning of the world to this present day, have been inseparable from all kingdoms and states that ever were famed for strength, riches, and politeness, at the same time.

To do this, I first slightly touch upon some of the faults and corrup-tions the several professions and callings are generally charged with. After that I show that those very vices of every particular person by skillful management were made subservient to the grandeur and worldly happi-ness of the whole. Lastly, by setting forth what of necessity must be the consequence of general honesty and virtue, and national temperance, innocence and content, I demonstrate that if mankind could be cured of the failings they are naturally guilty of, they would cease to be capable of being raised into such vast, potent and polite societies, as they have been under the several great commonwealths and monarchies that have flour-ished since the creation. If you ask me, why I have done all this, *cui bono* [who benefits]? and what good these notions will produce? Truly, besides the reader's diversion, I believe none at all; but if I was asked, what naturally ought to be expected from them, I would answer, that in the first place the people, who continually find fault with others, by reading them, would be taught to look at home, and examining their own consciences, be made ashamed of always railing at what they are more or less guilty of themselves; and that in the next, those who are so fond of the ease and comforts, and reap all the benefits that are the consequence of a great and flourishing nation, would learn more patiently to submit to those inconveniences, which no government upon earth can remedy, when they should see the impossibility of enjoying any great share of the first, without partaking likewise of the latter.

This I say ought naturally to be expected from the publishing of these notions, if people were to be made better by anything that could be said to them; but mankind having for so many ages remained still the same, notwithstanding the many instructive and elaborate writings, by which their amendment has been endeavored, I am not so vain as to hope for better success from so inconsiderable a trifle.

Having allowed the small advantage this little whim is likely to produce, I think myself obliged to show that it cannot be prejudicial to any; for what is published, if it does no good, ought at least to do no harm: in order to do this I have made some explanatory notes, to which the reader will find himself referred in those passages that seem to be most liable to exceptions.

The censorious that never saw the *Grumbling Hive* will tell me, that whatever I may talk of the fable, it not taking up a tenth part of the book, was only contrived to introduce the remarks that instead of clearing up the doubtful or obscure places, I have only pitched upon such as I had a mind to expatiate upon; and that far from striving to extenuate the errors committed before, I have made bad worse, and shown myself a more barefaced champion for vice, in the rambling digressions, than I had done in the fable itself.

I shall spend no time in answering these accusations; where men are prejudiced, the best apologies are lost; and I know that those who think it criminal to suppose a necessity of vice in any case whatever will never be reconciled to any part of the performance; but if this be thoroughly examined, all the offense it can give must result from the wrong inferences that may perhaps be drawn from it, and which I desire nobody to make. When I assert, that vices are inseparable from great and potent societies, and that it is impossible their wealth and grandeur should subsist without, I do not say that the particular members of them who are guilty of any should not be continually reproved, or not be punished for them when they grow into crimes.

There are, I believe, few people in London, of those that are at any time forced to go afoot, but what could wish the streets of it much cleaner than generally they are; while they regard nothing but their own clothes and private convenience: but when once they come to consider, that what offends them is the result of the plenty, great traffic and opulence of that mighty city, if they have any concern in its welfare, they will hardly ever wish to see the streets of it less dirty. For if we mind the materials of all sorts that must supply such an infinite number of trades and handicrafts, as are always going forward; the vast quantity of victuals, drink and fuel that are daily consumed in it, the waste and superfluities that must be produced from them; the multitudes of horses and other cattle that are always daubing the streets, the carts, coaches and more heavy carriages that are perpetually wearing and breaking the pavement of them, and above all the numberless swarms of people that are continually harassing and trampling through every part of them. If, I say, we mind all these, we shall find that every moment must produce new filth. And considering how far distant the great streets are from the riverside, what cost and care soever be bestowed to remove the nastiness almost as fast as it is made, it is impossible London should be more cleanly before it is less flourishing. Now would I ask if a good citizen, in consideration of what has been said, might not assert, that dirty streets are a necessary evil inseparable from the felicity of London, without being the least hindrance to the cleaning of shoes, or sweeping of streets, and consequently without any prejudice either to the blackguard or the scavengers.

But if, without any regard to the interest or happiness of the city, the question was put, what place I thought most pleasant to walk in? Nobody can doubt but, before the stinking streets of London, I would esteem a fragrant garden, or a shady grove in the country. In the same manner, if laying aside all worldly greatness and vainglory, I should be asked where I thought it was most probable that men might enjoy true happiness, I would prefer a small peaceable society, in which men, neither envied nor esteemed by neighbors, should be contented to live upon the natural product of the spot they inhabit, to a vast multitude abounding in wealth and power, that should always be conquering others by their arms abroad, and debauching themselves by foreign luxury at home.

Thus much I had said to the reader in the first edition; and have added nothing by way of preface in the second. But since that, a violent outcry has been made against the book, exactly answering the expectation I always had of the justice, the wisdom, the charity, and fair-dealing of those whose goodwill I despaired of. It has been presented by the grand jury, and condemned by thousands who never saw a word of it. It has been preached against before my lord mayor; and an utter refutation of it is daily expected from a reverend divine, who has called me names in the advertisements, and threatened to answer me in two months' time for above five months together. What I have to say for myself, the reader will see in my vindication at the end of the book, where he will likewise find the grand jury's presentment. . . .

Considering the length of this epistle, and that it is not wholly leveled at me only, I thought at first to have made some extracts from it of what related to myself; but finding, on a nearer enquiry, that what concerned me was so blended and interwoven with what did not, I was obliged to trouble the reader with it entire, not without hopes that, prolix as it is, the extravagance of it will be entertaining to those who have perused the treatise it condemns with so much horror.

THE GRUMBLING HIVE,
OR *KNAVES turn'd Honest.*

A Spacious Hive well stockt with Bees,
That liv'd in Luxury and Ease;
And yet as fam'd for Laws and Arms,
As yielding large and early Swarms;
Was counted the great Nursery
Of Sciences and Industry.
No Bees had better Government,
More Fickleness, or less Content:
They were not Slaves to Tyranny,
Nor rul'd by wild *Democracy;*
But Kings, that could not wrong, because
Their Power was circumscrib'd by Laws.

THESE Insects liv'd like Men, and all
Our Actions they perform'd in small:
They did whatever's done in Town,
And what belongs to Sword or Gown:
Tho' th' Artful Works, by nimble Slight
Of minute Limbs, 'scap'd Human Sight;

Yet we've no Engines, Labourers,
Ships, Castles, Arms, Artificers,
Craft, Science, Shop, or Instrument,
But they had an Equivalent:
Which, since their Language is unknown,
Must be call'd, as we do our own.
As grant, that among other Things,
They wanted Dice, yet they had Kings;
And those had Guards; from whence we may
Justly conclude, they had some Play;
Unless a Regiment be shewn
Of Soldiers, that make use of none.

VAST Numbers throng'd the fruitful Hive;
Yet those vast Numbers made 'em thrive;
Millions endeavouring to supply
Each other's Lust and Vanity;
While other Millions were employ'd,
To see their Handy-works destroy'd;
They furnish'd half the Universe;
Yet had more Work than Labourers.
Some with vast Stocks, and little Pains,
Jump'd into Business of great Gains;
And some were damn'd to Sythes and Spades,
And all those hard laborious Trades;
Where willing Wretches daily sweat,
And wear out Strength and Limbs to eat:
(*A*.) While others follow'd Mysteries,
To which few Folks bind 'Prentices;
That want no Stock, but that of Brass,
And may set up without a Cross;
As Sharpers, Parasites, Pimps, Players,
Pick-pockets, Coiners, Quacks, South-sayers,
And all those, that in Enmity,
With downright Working, cunningly
Convert to their own Use the Labour
Of their good-natur'd heedless Neighbour.
(*B*.) These were call'd Knaves, but bar the Name,
The grave Industrious were the same:

All Trades and Places knew some Cheat,
No Calling was without Deceit.

THE Lawyers, of whose Art the Basis
Was raising Feuds and splitting Cases,
Oppos'd all Registers, that Cheats
Might make more Work with dipt Estates;
As wer't unlawful, that one's own,
Without a Law-Suit, should be known.
They kept off Hearings wilfully,
To finger the refreshing Fee;
And to defend a wicked Cause,
Examin'd and survey'd the Laws,
As Burglars Shops and Houses do,
To find out where they'd best break through.

PHYSICIANS valu'd Fame and Wealth
Above the drooping Patient's Health,
Or their own Skill: The greatest Part
Study'd, instead of Rules of Art,
Grave pensive Looks and dull Behaviour,
To gain th' Apothecary's Favour;
The Praise of Midwives, Priests, and all
That serv'd at Birth or Funeral.
To bear with th' ever-talking Tribe,
And hear my Lady's Aunt prescribe;
With formal Smile, and kind How d'ye,
To fawn on all the Family;
And, which of all the greatest Curse is,
T' endure th' Impertinence of Nurses.

AMONG the many Priests of *Jove*,
Hir'd to draw Blessings from Above,
Some few were Learn'd and Eloquent,
But thousands Hot and Ignorant:
Yet all pass'd Muster that could hide
Their Sloth, Lust, Avarice and Pride;
For which they were as fam'd as Tailors
For Cabbage, or for Brandy Sailors:
Some, meagre-look'd, and meanly clad,

Would mystically pray for Bread,
Meaning by that an ample Store,
Yet lit'rally received no more;
And, while these holy Drudges starv'd,
The lazy Ones, for which they serv'd,
Indulg'd their Ease, with all the Graces
Of Health and Plenty in their Faces.

(*C.*) THE Soldiers, that were forc'd to fight,
If they surviv'd, got Honour by't;
Tho' some, that shunn'd the bloody Fray,
Had Limbs shot off, that ran away:
Some valiant Gen'rals fought the Foe;
Others took Bribes to let them go:
Some ventur'd always where 'twas warm,
Lost now a Leg, and then an Arm;
Till quite disabled, and put by,
They liv'd on half their Salary;
While others never came in Play,
And staid at Home for double Pay.

THEIR Kings were serv'd, but Knavishly,
Cheated by their own Ministry;
Many, that for their Welfare slaved,
Robbing the very Crown they saved:
Pensions were small, and they liv'd high,
Yet boasted of their Honesty.
Calling, whene'er they strain'd their Right,
The slipp'ry Trick a Perquisite;
And when Folks understood their Cant,
They chang'd that for Emolument;
Unwilling to be short or plain,
In any thing concerning Gain;
(*D.*) For there was not a Bee but would
Get more, I won't say, than he should;
But than he dar'd to let them know,
(*E.*) That pay'd for't; as your Gamesters do,
That, tho' at fair Play, ne'er will own
Before the Losers what they've won.

BUT who can all their Frauds repeat ?
The very Stuff, which in the Street
They sold for Dirt t'enrich the Ground,
Was often by the Buyers found
Sophisticated with a quarter
Of good-for-nothing Stones and Mortar;
Tho' *Flail* had little Cause to mutter,
Who sold the other Salt for Butter.

JUSTICE her self, fam'd for fair Dealing,
By Blindness had not lost her Feeling;
Her Left Hand, which the Scales should hold,
Had often dropt 'em, brib'd with Gold;
And, tho' she seem'd Impartial,
Where Punishment was corporal,
Pretended to a reg'lar Course,
In Murther, and all Crimes of Force;
Tho' some, first pillory'd for Cheating,
Were hang'd in Hemp of their own beating;
Yet, it was thought, the Sword she bore
Check'd but the Desp'rate and the Poor;
That, urg'd by meer Necessity,
Were ty'd up to the wretched Tree
For Crimes, which not deserv'd that Fate,
But to secure the Rich and Great.

THUS every Part was full of Vice,
Yet the whole Mass a Paradise;
Flatter'd in Peace, and fear'd in Wars,
They were th' Esteem of Foreigners,
And lavish of their Wealth and Lives,
The Balance of all other Hives.
Such were the Blessings of that State;
Their Crimes conspir'd to make them Great:
(*F.*) And Virtue, who from Politicks
Had learn'd a Thousand Cunning Tricks,
Was, by their happy Influence,
Made Friends with Vice: And ever since,
(*G.*) The worst of all the Multitude
Did something for the Common Good.

THIS was the State's Craft, that maintain'd
The Whole of which each Part complain'd:
This, as in Musick Harmony,
Made Jarrings in the main agree;
(*H.*) Parties directly opposite,
Assist each other, as 'twere for Spight;
And Temp'rance with Sobriety,
Serve Drunkenness and Gluttony.

(*I.*) THE Root of Evil, Avarice,
That damn'd ill-natur'd baneful Vice,
Was Slave to Prodigality,
(*K.*) That noble Sin; (*L.*) whilst Luxury
Employ'd a Million of the Poor,
(*M.*) And odious Pride a Million more:
(*N.*) Envy it self, and Vanity,
Were Ministers of Industry;
Their darling Folly, Fickleness,
In Diet, Furniture and Dress,
That strange ridic'lous Vice, was made
The very Wheel that turn'd the Trade.
Their Laws and Clothes were equally
Objects of Mutability;
For, what was well done for a time,
In half a Year became a Crime;
Yet while they alter'd thus their Laws,
Still finding and correcting Flaws,
They mended by Inconstancy
Faults, which no Prudence could foresee.

THUS Vice nurs'd Ingenuity,
Which join'd with Time and Industry,
Had carry'd Life's Conveniencies,
(*O.*) It's real Pleasures, Comforts, Ease,
(*P.*) To such a Height, the very Poor
Liv'd better than the Rich before,
And nothing could be added more.

HOW Vain is Mortal Happiness!
Had they but known the Bounds of Bliss;

And that Perfection here below
Is more than Gods can well bestow;
The Grumbling Brutes had been content
With Ministers and Government.
But they, at every ill Success,
Like Creatures lost without Redress,
Curs'd Politicians, Armies, Fleets;
While every one cry'd, *Damn the Cheats*
And would, tho' conscious of his own,
In others barb'rously bear none.

ONE, that had got a Princely Store,
By cheating Master, King and Poor,
Dar'd cry aloud, *The Land must sink
For all its Fraud;* And whom d'ye think
The Sermonizing Rascal chid?
A Glover that sold Lamb for Kid.

The least thing was not done amiss,
Or cross'd the Publick Business;
But all the Rogues cry'd brazenly,
Good Gods, Had we but Honesty!
Merc'ry smil'd at th' Impudence,
And others call'd it want of Sense,
Always to rail at what they lov'd:
But *Jove* with Indignation mov'd,
At last in Anger swore, *He'd rid
The bawling Hive of Fraud;* and did.
The very Moment it departs,
And Honesty fills all their Hearts;
There shews 'em, like th' Instructive Tree,
Those Crimes which they're asham'd to see;
Which now in Silence they confess,
By blushing at their Ugliness:
Like Children, that would hide their Faults,
And by their Colour own their Thoughts:
Imag'ning, when they're look'd upon,
That others see what they have done.

BUT, Oh ye Gods! What Consternation,
How vast and sudden was th' Alteration!
In half an Hour, the Nation round,
Meat fell a Peny in the Pound.
The Mask Hypocrisy's flung down,
From the great Statesman to the Clown:
And some in borrow'd Looks well known,
Appear'd like Strangers in their own.
The Bar was silent from that Day;
For now the willing Debtors pay,
Ev'n what's by Creditors forgot;
Who quitted them that had it not.
Those, that were in the Wrong, stood mute,
And dropt the patch'd vexatious Suit:
On which since nothing less can thrive,
Than Lawyers in an honest Hive,
All, except those that got enough,
With Inkhorns by their sides troop'd off.

JUSTICE hang'd some, set others free;
And after Goal delivery,
Her Presence being no more requir'd,
With all her Train and Pomp retir'd.
First march'd some Smiths with Locks and Grates,
Fetters, and Doors with Iron Plates:
Next Goalers, Turnkeys and Assistants:
Before the Goddess, at some distance,
Her chief and faithful Minister,
'Squire CATCH, the Law's great Finisher,
Bore not th' imaginary Sword,
But his own Tools, an Ax and Cord:
Then on a Cloud the Hood-wink'd Fair,
JUSTICE her self was push'd by Air:
About her Chariot, and behind,
Were Serjeants, Bums of every kind,
Tip-staffs, and all those Officers,
That squeeze a Living out of Tears.

THO' Physick liv'd, while Folks were ill,
None would prescribe, but Bees of skill,

Which through the Hive dispers'd so wide,
That none of them had need to ride;
Wav'd vain Disputes, and strove to free
The Patients of their Misery;
Left Drugs in cheating Countries grown,
And us'd the Product of their own;
Knowing the Gods sent no Disease
To Nations without Remedies.

THEIR Clergy rous'd from Laziness,
Laid not their Charge on Journey-Bees;
But serv'd themselves, exempt from Vice,
The Gods with Pray'r and Sacrifice;
All those, that were unfit, or knew
Their Service might be spar'd, withdrew:
Nor was there Business for so many,
(If th' Honest stand in need of any,)
Few only with the High-Priest staid,
To whom the rest Obedience paid:
Himself employ'd in Holy Cares,
Resign'd to others State-Affairs.
He chas'd no Starv'ling from his Door,
Nor pinch'd the Wages of the Poor;
But at his House the Hungry's fed,
The Hireling finds unmeasur'd Bread,
The needy Trav'ler Board and Bed.

AMONG the King's great Ministers,
And all th' inferior Officers
The Change was great; (*Q.*) for frugally
They now liv'd on their Salary:
That a poor Bee should ten times come
To ask his Due, a trifling Sum,
And by some well-hir'd Clerk be made
To give a Crown, or ne'er be paid,
Would now be call'd a downright Cheat,
Tho' formerly a Perquisite.
All Places manag'd first by Three,
Who watch'd each other's Knavery,
And often for a Fellow-feeling,

Promoted one another's stealing,
Are happily supply'd by One,
By which some thousands more are gone.

(*R.*) No Honour now could be content,
To live and owe for what was spent;
Liv'ries in Brokers Shops are hung,
They part with Coaches for a Song;
Sell stately Horses by whole Sets;
And Country-Houses, to pay Debts.

VAIN Cost is shunn'd as much as Fraud;
They have no Forces kept Abroad;
Laugh at th' Esteem of Foreigners,
And empty Glory got by Wars;
They fight, but for their Country's sake,
When Right or Liberty's at Stake.

NOW mind the glorious Hive, and see
How Honesty and Trade agree.
The Shew is gone, it thins apace;
And looks with quite another Face.
For 'twas not only that They went,
By whom vast Sums were Yearly spent;
But Multitudes that liv'd on them,
Were daily forc'd to do the same.
In vain to other Trades they'd fly;
All were o'er-stock'd accordingly.

THE Price of Land and Houses falls;
Mirac'lous Palaces, whose Walls,
Like those of *Thebes*, were rais'd by Play,
Are to be let; while the once gay,
Well-seated Houshold Gods would be
More pleas'd to expire in Flames, than see
The mean Inscription on the Door
Smile at the lofty ones they bore.
The building Trade is quite destroy'd,
Artificers are not employ'd;

(*S.*) No Limner for his Art is fam'd,
Stone-cutters, Carvers are not nam'd.

THOSE, that remain'd, grown temp'rate, strive,
Not how to spend, but how to live,
And, when they paid their Tavern Score,
Resolv'd to enter it no more:
No Vintner's Jilt in all the Hive
Could wear now Cloth of Gold, and thrive;
Nor *Torcol* such vast Sums advance,
For *Burgundy* and *Ortelans;*
The Courtier's gone, that with his Miss
Supp'd at his House on *Christmas* Peas;
Spending as much in two Hours stay,
As keeps a Troop of Horse a Day.

THE haughty *Chloe*, to live Great,
Had made her (*T.*) Husband rob the State:
But now she sells her Furniture,
Which th' *Indies* had been ransack'd for;
Contracts th' expensive Bill of Fare,
And wears her strong Suit a whole Year:
The slight and fickle Age is past;
And Clothes, as well as Fashions, last.
Weavers, that join'd rich Silk with Plate,
And all the Trades subordinate,
Are gone. Still Peace and Plenty reign,
And every Thing is cheap, tho' plain:
Kind Nature, free from Gard'ners Force,
Allows all Fruits in her own Course;
But Rarities cannot be had,
Where Pains to get them are not paid.

AS Pride and Luxury decrease,
So by degrees they leave the Seas.
Not Merchants now, but Companies
Remove whole Manufactories.
All Arts and Crafts neglected lie;
(*V.*) Content, the Bane of Industry,

Makes 'em admire their homely Store,
And neither seek nor covet more.

SO few in the vast Hive remain,
The hundredth Part they can't maintain
Against th' Insults of numerous Foes;
Whom yet they valiantly oppose:
'Till some well-fenc'd Retreat is found,
And here they die or stand their Ground.
No Hireling in their Army's known;
But bravely fighting for their own,
Their Courage and Integrity
At last were crown'd with Victory.
They triumph'd not without their Cost,
For many Thousand Bees were lost.
Hard'ned with Toils and Exercise,
They counted Ease it self a Vice;
Which so improv'd their Temperance;
That, to avoid Extravagance,
They flew into a hollow Tree,
Blest with Content and Honesty.

THE MORAL

T*HEN leave Complaints: Fools only strive*
(X.) *To make a Great an Honest Hive*
(Y.) *T' enjoy the World's Conveniencies,*
Be fam'd in War, yet live in Ease,
Without great Vices, is a vain
EUTOPIA *seated in the Brain.*
Fraud, Luxury and Pride must live,
While we the Benefits receive:
Hunger's a dreadful Plague, no doubt,
Yet who digests or thrives without?
Do we not owe the Growth of Wine
To the dry shabby crooked Vine?
Which, while its Shoots neglected stood,
Chok'd other Plants, and ran to Wood;
But blest us with its noble Fruit,

As soon as it was ty'd and cut:
So Vice is beneficial found,
When it's by Justice lopt and bound;
Nay, where the People would be great,
As necessary to the State,
As Hunger is to make 'em eat.
Bare Virtue can't make Nations live
In Splendor; they, that would revive
A Golden Age, must be as free,
For Acorns, as for Honesty.

FINIS.

The Introduction

One of the greatest reasons why so few people understand themselves is that most writers are always teaching men what they should be, and hardly ever trouble their heads with telling them what they really are. As for my part, without any compliment to the courteous reader, or myself, I believe man (besides skin, flesh, bones, etc. that are obvious to the eye) to be a compound of various passions; that all of them, as they are provoked and come uppermost, govern him by turns, whether he will or no. To show that these qualifications, which we all pretend to be ashamed of, are the great support of a flourishing society has been the subject of the foregoing poem. But there being some passages in it seemingly paradoxical, I have in the Preface promised some explanatory remarks on it, which to render more useful, I have thought fit to enquire, how man, no better qualified, might yet by his own imperfections be taught to distinguish between virtue and vice. And here I must desire the reader once for all to take notice, that when I say men, I mean neither Jews nor Christians, but mere man, in the state of nature and ignorance of the true deity.

An Enquiry into the Origin of Moral Virtue

All untaught animals are only solicitous of pleasing themselves, and naturally follow the bent of their own inclinations, without considering the good or harm that from their being pleased will accrue to others. This is the reason that in the wild state of nature those creatures are fittest to live peaceably together in great numbers that discover the least of understanding, and have the fewest appetites to gratify. And consequently no species of animals is, without the curb of government, less capable of agreeing long together in multitudes than that of man. Yet such are his qualities, whether good or bad, I shall not determine, that no creature besides himself can ever be made sociable: but being an extraordinary selfish and headstrong, as well as [a] cunning animal, however he may be subdued by superior strength, it is impossible by force alone to make him tractable, and receive the improvements he is capable of.

The chief thing, therefore, which lawgivers and other wise men that have labored for the establishment of society have endeavored, has been to make the people they were to govern believe that it was more beneficial for everybody to conquer than indulge his appetites, and much better to mind the public than what seemed his private interest. As this has always been a very difficult task, so no wit or eloquence has been left untried to compass it; and the moralists and philosophers of all ages employed their utmost skill to prove the truth of so useful an assertion. But whether mankind would have ever believed it or not, it is not likely that anybody could have persuaded them to disapprove of their natural inclinations, or prefer the good of others to their own, if at the same time he had not shown them an equivalent to be enjoyed as a reward for the violence, which by so doing they of necessity must commit upon themselves. Those that have undertaken to civilize mankind were not ignorant of this. But being unable to give so many real rewards as would satisfy all persons for every individual action, they were forced to contrive an imaginary one, that as a general equivalent for the trouble of self-denial should serve on all occasions, and without costing anything either to themselves or others, be yet a most acceptable recompense to the receivers.

They thoroughly examined all the strength and frailties of our nature, and observing that none were either so savage as not to be charmed with praise, or so despicable as patiently to bear contempt, justly concluded, that flattery must be the most powerful argument that could be used to human creatures. Making use of this bewitching engine, they extolled the excellency of our nature above other animals, and setting forth with unbounded praises the wonders of our sagacity and vastness of understanding, bestowed a thousand encomiums on the rationality of our souls, by the help of which we were capable of performing the most noble achievements. Having by this artful way of flattery insinuated themselves into the hearts of men, they began to instruct them in the notions of honor and shame, representing the one as the worst of all evils, and the other as the highest good to which mortals could aspire. Which being done, they laid before them how unbecoming it was the dignity of such sublime creatures to be solicitous about gratifying those appetites, which they had in common with brutes, and at the same time unmindful of those higher qualities that gave them the preeminence over all visible beings. They indeed confessed, that those impulses of nature were very pressing; that it was troublesome to resist, and very difficult wholly to subdue them. But this they only used as an argument to demonstrate how glorious the conquest of them was on the one hand, and how scandalous on the other not to attempt it.

To introduce, moreover, an emulation amongst men, they divided the whole species into two classes, vastly differing from one another. The one consisted of abject, low-minded people, that always hunting after immediate enjoyment, were wholly incapable of self-denial, and without regard to the good of others, had no higher aim than their private advantage.

Such as being enslaved by voluptuousness, [they] yielded without resistance to every gross desire, and made no use of their rational faculties but to heighten their sensual pleasure. These vile groveling wretches, they said, were the dross of their kind, and having only the shape of men, differed from brutes in nothing but their outward figure. But the other class was made up of lofty high-spirited creatures, that free from sordid selfishness, esteemed the improvements of the mind to be their fairest possessions. And setting a true value upon themselves, took no delight but in embellishing that part in which their excellency consisted, such as despising whatever they had in common with irrational creatures, opposed by the help of reason their most violent inclinations. And making a continual war with themselves to promote the peace of others, [they] aimed at no less than the public welfare and the conquest of their own passion. . . . These they called the true representatives of their sublime species, exceeding in worth the first class by more degrees, than that itself was superior to the beasts of the field.

As in all animals that are not too imperfect to discover pride, we find that the finest and such as are the most beautiful and valuable of their kind have generally the greatest share of it. So in man, the most perfect of animals, it is so inseparable from his very essence (how cunningly soever some may learn to hide or disguise it) that without it the compound he is made of would want one of the chiefest ingredients. Which, if we consider, it is hardly to be doubted but lessons and remonstrances, so skillfully adapted to the good opinion man has of himself, as those I have mentioned, must, if scattered amongst a multitude not only gain the assent of most of them, as to the speculative part, but likewise induce several, especially the fiercest, most resolute, and best among them, to endure a thousand inconveniences, and undergo as many hardships, that they may have the pleasure of counting themselves men of the second class, and consequently appropriating to themselves all the excellences they have heard of it.

From what has been said, we ought to expect in the first place that the heroes who took such extraordinary pains to master some of their natural appetites, and preferred the good of others to any visible interest of their own, would not recede an inch from the fine notions they had received concerning the dignity of rational creatures. And having ever the authority of the government on their side, with all imaginable vigor assert the esteem that was due to those of the second class, as well as their superiority over the rest of their kind. In the second, that those who wanted a sufficient stock of either pride or resolution to buoy them up in mortifying of what was dearest to them, followed the sensual dictates of nature, would yet be ashamed of confessing themselves to be those despicable wretches that belonged to the inferior class, and were generally reckoned to be so little removed from brutes. And that therefore in their own defense they would say, as others did, and hiding their own imperfections as well as they could, cry up self-denial and public-spiritedness as much as any. For it is highly probable that some of them, convinced by the real proofs of fortitude and self-conquest they had seen, would admire in others what they found wanting in themselves; others be afraid of the resolution and prowess of those of the second class, and that all of them were kept in awe by the power of their rulers. Wherefore it is reasonable to think, that none of them (whatever they thought in themselves) would dare openly contradict, what by everybody else was thought criminal to doubt of.

This was (or at least might have been) the manner after which savage man was broke. From whence it is evident that the first rudiments of morality, broached by skillful politicians, to render men useful to each other as well as tractable, were chiefly contrived that the ambitious might reap the more benefit from, and govern vast numbers of them with the greater ease and security. This foundation of politics being once laid, it is impossible that man should long remain uncivilized. For even those who only strove to gratify their appetites, being continually crossed by others of the same stamp, could not but observe, that whenever they checked their inclinations or but followed them with more circumspection, they avoided a world of troubles, and often escaped many of the calamities that generally attended the too eager pursuit after pleasure.

First, they received, as well as others, the benefit of those actions that were done for the good of the whole society, and consequently could not forbear wishing well to those of the superior class that performed them. Secondly, the more intent they were in seeking their own advantage, without regard to others, the more they were hourly convinced, that none stood so much in their way as those that were most like themselves.

It being the interest then of the very worst of them, more than any, to preach up public-spiritedness, that they might reap the fruits of the labor and self-denial of others, and at the same time indulge their own appetites with less disturbance, they agreed with the rest to call everything which, without regard to the public, man should commit to gratify any of his appetites, vice; if in that action there could be observed the least prospect, that it might either be injurious to any of the society, or ever render himself less serviceable to others. And to give the name of virtue to every performance, by which man, contrary to the impulse of nature, should endeavor the benefit of others, or the conquest of his own passions out of a rational ambition of being good.

It shall be objected that no society was ever any ways civilized before the major part had agreed upon some worship or other of an over-ruling power, and consequently that the notions of good and evil, and the distinction between virtue and vice, were never the contrivance of politicians, but the pure effect of religion. Before I answer this objection, I must repeat what I have said already, that in this *Enquiry into the Origin of Moral Virtue* I speak neither of Jews or Christians, but man in his state of nature and ignorance of the true deity. And then I affirm that the idolatrous superstitions of all other nations, and the pitiful notions they had of the supreme being, were incapable of exciting man to virtue, and good for nothing but to awe and amuse a rude and unthinking multitude. It is evident from history that in all considerable societies, how stupid or ridiculous soever people's received notions have been as to the deities they worshipped, human nature has ever exerted itself in all its branches, and that there is no earthly wisdom or moral virtue but at one time or other men have excelled in it in all monarchies and commonwealths, that for riches and power have been any ways remarkable.

The Egyptians, not satisfied with having deified all the ugly monsters they could think on, were so silly as to adore the onions of their own sowing. Yet at the same time their country was the most famous nursery of arts and sciences in the world, and themselves more eminently skilled in the deepest mysteries of nature than any nation has been since.

No states or kingdoms under Heaven have yielded more or greater patterns in ail sorts of moral virtues than the Greek and Roman empires, more especially the latter. And yet how loose, absurd and ridiculous were their sentiments as to sacred matters? For without reflecting on the extravagant number of their deities, if we only consider the infamous stories they fathered upon them, it is not to be denied but that their religion, far from teaching men the conquest of their passions and the way to virtue, seemed rather contrived to justify their appetites, and encourage their vices. But if we would know what made them excel in fortitude, courage and magnanimity, we must cast our eyes on the pomp of their triumphs, the magnificence of their monuments and arches; their trophies, statues, and inscriptions; the variety of their military crowns, their honors decreed to the dead, public encomiums on the living, and other imaginary rewards they bestowed on men of merit. And we shall find that what carried so many of them to the utmost pitch of self-denial was nothing but their policy in making use of the most effectual means that human pride could be flattered with.

It is visible, then, that it was not any heathen religion or other idolatrous superstition that first put man upon crossing his appetites and subduing his dearest inclinations, but the skillful management of wary politicians. And the nearer we search into human nature, the more we shall be convinced, that the moral virtues are the political offspring which flattery begot upon pride.

There is no man of what capacity or penetration soever that is wholly proof against the witchcraft of flattery, if artfully performed, and suited to his abilities. Children and fools will swallow personal praise, but those that are more cunning must be managed with greater circumspection. And the more general the flattery is, the less it is suspected by those it is leveled at. What you say in commendation of a whole town is received with pleasure by all the inhabitants. Speak in commendation of letters in general, and every man of learning will think himself in particular obliged to you. You may safely praise the employment a man is of, or the country he was born in, because you give him an opportunity of screening the joy he feels upon his own account, under the esteem which he pretends to have for others.

It is common among cunning men that understand the power which flattery has upon pride, when they are afraid they shall be imposed upon, to enlarge, though much against their conscience, upon the honor, fair dealing and integrity of the family, country, or sometimes the profession of him they suspect; because they know that men often will change their resolution, and act against their inclination, that they may have the pleasure of continuing to appear in the opinion of some, what they are conscious not to be in reality. Thus sagacious moralists draw men like angels, in hopes that the pride at least of some will put them upon copying after the beautiful originals which they are represented to be.

When the incomparable Sir Richard Steele, in the usual elegance of his easy style, dwells on the praises of his sublime species, and with all the embellishments of rhetoric sets forth the excellency of human nature, it is impossible not to be charmed with his happy turns of thought, and the politeness of his expressions. But though I have been often moved by the force of his eloquence, and ready to swallow the ingenious sophistry with pleasure, yet I could never be so serious, but reflecting on his artful encomiums I thought on the tricks made use of by the women that would teach children to be mannerly. When an awkward girl, before she can either speak or go, begins after many intreaties to make the first rude essays of curtsying, the nurse falls in an ecstasy of praise: "There's a delicate curtsy! O fine miss! There's a pretty lady! Mama! Miss can make a better curtsy than her sister Molly!" The same is echoed over by the maids, whilst Mama almost hugs the child to pieces. Only Miss Molly, who being four years older knows how to make a very handsome curtsy, wonders at the perverseness of their judgment, and swelling with indignation, is ready to cry at the injustice that is done her, until, being whispered in the ear that it is only to please the baby, and that she is a woman, she grows proud at being let into the secret, and rejoicing at the superiority of her understanding, repeats what has been said with large additions, and insults over the weakness of her sister, whom all this while she fancies to be the only bubble among them. These extravagant praises would by anyone, above the capacity of an infant, be called fulsome flatteries and, if you will, abominable lies. Yet experience teaches us that by the help of such gross encomiums young misses will be brought to make pretty curtsies, and behave themselves womanly much sooner, and with less trouble, than they would without them. It is the same with boys, whom they'll strive to persuade, that all fine gentlemen do as they are bid, and that none but beggar boys are rude, or dirty their clothes. Nay, as soon as the wild brat with his untaught fist begins to fumble for his hat, the mother, to make him pull it off, tells him before he is two years old, that he is a man. And if he repeats that action when she desires him, he's presently a captain, a lord mayor, a king, or something higher if she can think of it, till egged on by the force of praise, the little urchin endeavors to imitate man as well as he can, and strains all his faculties to appear what his shallow noddle imagines he is believed to be.

The meanest wretch puts an inestimable value upon himself, and the highest wish of the ambitious man is to have all the world, as to that particular, of his opinion. So that the most insatiable thirst after fame that every hero was inspired with, was never more than an ungovernable greediness to engross the esteem and admiration of others in future ages as well as his own. And (what mortification soever this truth might be to the second thoughts of an Alexander or a Caesar) the great recompense in view, for which the most exalted minds have with so much alacrity sacrificed their quiet, health, sensual pleasures, and every inch of themselves, has never been anything else but the breath of man, the aerial coin of praise. Who can forbear laughing when he thinks on all the great men that have been so serious on the subject of that Macedonian madman [Alexander the Great], his capacious soul, that mighty heart, in one corner of which, according to Lorenzo Gratian, the world was so commodiously lodged, that in the whole there was room for six more? Who can forbear laughing, I say, when he compares the fine things that have been said of Alexander with the end he proposed to himself from his vast exploits, to be proved from his own mouth; when the vast pains he took to pass the Hydaspes forced him to cry out? "Oh ye Athenians, could you believe what dangers I expose myself to, to be praised by you!" To define then the reward of glory in the amplest manner, the most that can be said of it is that it consists in a superlative felicity which a man, who is conscious of having performed a noble action, enjoys in self-love, whilst he is thinking on the applause he expects of others.

But here I shall be told, that besides the noisy toils of war and public bustle of the ambitious, there are noble and generous actions that are performed in silence; that virtue being its own reward, those who are really good have a satisfaction in their consciousness of being so, which is all the recompense they expect from the most worthy performances; that among the heathens there have been men who, when they did good to others, were so far from coveting thanks and applause, that they took all imaginable care to be forever concealed from those on whom they bestowed their benefits, and consequently that pride has no hand in spurring man on to the highest pitch of self-denial.

In answer to this I say that it is impossible to judge of a man's performance unless we are thoroughly acquainted with the principle and motive from which he acts. Pity, though it is the most gentle and the least mischievous of all our passions, is yet as much a frailty of our nature as anger, pride, or fear. The weakest minds have generally the greatest share of it, for which reason none are more compassionate than women and children. It must be owned that of all our weaknesses it is the most amiable, and bears the greatest resemblance to virtue. Nay, without a considerable mixture of [pity] the society could hardly subsist. But as it is an impulse of nature that consults neither the public interest nor our own reason, it may produce evil as well as good. It has helped to destroy the honor of virgins, and corrupted the integrity of judges. And whoever acts from it as a principle, what good soever he may bring to the society, has nothing to boast of but that he has indulged a passion that has happened to be beneficial to the public. There is no merit in saving an innocent babe ready to drop into the fire. The action is neither good nor bad, and what benefit soever the infant received, we only obliged ourselves. For to have seen it fall, and not strove to hinder it, would have caused a pain which self-preservation compelled us to prevent. Nor has a rich prodigal, that happens to be of a commiserating temper, and loves to gratify his passions, greater virtue to boast of when he relieves an object of compassion with what to himself is a trifle.

But such men, as without complying with any weakness of their own, can part from what they value themselves and from no other motive but their love to goodness, perform a worthy action in silence. Such men, I confess, have acquired more refined notions of virtue than those I have hitherto spoken of. Yet even in these (with which the world has yet never swarmed) we may discover no small symptoms of pride, and the humblest man alive must confess that the reward of a virtuous action, which is the satisfaction that ensues upon it, consists in a certain pleasure he procures to himself by contemplating on his own worth: which pleasure, together with the occasion of it, are as certain signs of pride, as looking pale and trembling at any imminent danger are the symptoms of fear.

If the too scrupulous reader should at first view condemn these notions concerning the origin of moral virtue, and think them perhaps offensive to Christianity, I hope he'll forbear his censures, when he shall consider, that nothing can render the unsearchable depth of the divine wisdom more conspicuous than that man, whom Providence had designed for society, should not only by his own frailties and imperfections be led into the road to temporal happiness, but likewise receive, from a seeming necessity of natural causes, a tincture of that knowledge, in which he was afterwards to be made perfect by the true religion, to his eternal welfare.

Remark C

The Soldiers that were forc'd to fight,
If they surviv'd, got Honour by 't.

So unaccountable is the desire to be thought well of in men, that though they are dragged into the war against their will, and some of them for their crimes, and are compelled to fight with threats, and often blows, yet they would be esteemed for what they would have avoided, if it had been in their power. Whereas if reason in man was of equal weight with his pride, he could never be pleased with praises, which he is conscious he doesn't deserve.

By honor, in its proper and genuine signification, we mean nothing else but the good opinion of others, which is counted more or less substantial the more or less noise or bustle there is made about the demonstration of it. And when we say the sovereign is the fountain of honor, it signifies that he has the power, by titles or ceremonies, or both together, to stamp a mark upon whom he pleases, that shall be as current as his coin, and procure the owner the good opinion of everybody, whether he deserves it or not.

The reverse of honor is dishonor, or ignominy, which consists in the bad opinion and contempt of others. And as the first is counted a reward for good actions, so this is esteemed a punishment for bad ones; and the more or less public or heinous the manner is in which this contempt of others is shown, the more or less the person so suffering is degraded by it. This ignominy is likewise called shame, from the effect it produces. For though the good and evil of honor and dishonor are imaginary, yet there is a reality in shame, as it signifies a passion that has its proper symptoms, overrules our reason, and requires as much labor and self-denial to be subdued, as any of the rest. And since the most important actions of life often are regulated according to the influence this passion has upon us, a thorough understanding of it must help to illustrate the notions the world has of honor and ignominy. I shall therefore describe it at large.

First, to define the passion of shame, I think it may be called a sorrowful reflection on our own unworthiness, proceeding from an apprehension that others either do, or might, if they knew all, deservedly despise us. The only objection of weight that can be raised against this definition is that innocent virgins are often ashamed, and blush when they are guilty of no crime, and can give no manner of reason for this frailty; and that men

are often ashamed for others for, or with whom, they have neither friendship nor affinity, and consequently that there may be a thousand instances
of shame given, to which the words of the definition are not applicable. To
answer this, I would have it first considered that the modesty of women is
the result of custom and education, by which all unfashionable denudations and filthy expressions are rendered frightful and abominable to
them, and that notwithstanding this, the most virtuous young woman
alive will often, in spite of her teeth, have thoughts and confused ideas of
things arise in her imagination, which she would not reveal to some people for a thousand worlds. Then, I say, that when obscene words are spoken in the presence of an inexperienced virgin, she is afraid that
somebody will reckon her to understand what they mean, and consequently that she understands this and that and several things which she
desires to be thought ignorant of. The reflecting on this, and that
thoughts are forming to her disadvantage, brings upon her that passion
which we call shame; and whatever can fling her, though never so remote
from lewdness, upon that set of thoughts I hinted, and which she thinks
criminal, will have the same effect, especially before men, as long as her
modesty lasts.

To try the truth of this, let them talk as much bawdy as they please in
the room next to the same virtuous young woman, where she is sure that
she is undiscovered, and she will hear, if not hearken to it, without blushing at all, because then she looks upon herself as no party concerned. And
if the discourse should stain her cheeks with red, whatever her innocence
may imagine, it is certain that what occasions her color is a passion not
half so mortifying as that of shame. But if in the same place she hears
something said of herself that must tend to her disgrace, or anything is
named, of which she is secretly guilty, then it is ten to one but she'll be
ashamed and blush, though nobody sees her; because she has room to
fear, that she is or, if all was known, should be thought of contemptibly.

That we are often ashamed and blush for others, which was the second
part of the objection, is nothing else but that sometimes we make the case
of others too nearly our own. So people shriek out when they see others in
danger. Whilst we are reflecting with too much earnest on the effect which
such a blameable action, if it was ours, would produce in us, the spirits,
and consequently the blood, are insensibly moved after the same manner,
as if the action was our own, and so the same symptoms must appear.

The shame that raw, ignorant, and ill-bred people, though seemingly
without a cause, discover before their betters, is always accompanied with
and proceeds from a consciousness of their weakness and inabilities. And

the most modest man, how virtuous, knowing, and accomplished soever he might be, was never yet ashamed without some guilt or diffidence. Such [persons] as out of rusticity and want of education are unreasonably subject to and at every turn overcome by this passion we call bashful; and those who out of disrespect to others and a false opinion of their own sufficiency have learned not to be affected with it, when they should be, are called impudent or shameless. What strange contradictions man is made of! The reverse of shame is pride (see remark M). Yet nobody can be touched with the first that never felt anything of the latter; for that we have such an extraordinary concern in what others think of us can proceed from nothing but the vast esteem we have for ourselves.

That these two passions, in which the seeds of most virtues are contained, are realities in our frame and not imaginary qualities, is demonstrable from the plain and different effects that in spite of our reason are produced in us as soon as we are affected with either.

When a man is overwhelmed with shame, he observes a sinking of the spirits; the heart feels cold and condensed, and the blood flies from it to the circumference of the body. The face glows, the neck and part of the breast partake of the fire: he is heavy as lead; the head is hung down, and the eyes through a mist of confusion are fixed on the ground. No injuries can move him; he is weary of his being, and heartily wishes he could make himself invisible. But when, gratifying his vanity, he exults in his pride, he discovers quite contrary symptoms: his spirits swell and fan the arterial blood; a more than ordinary warmth strengthens and dilates the heart; the extremities are cool; he feels light to himself, and imagines he could tread on air. His head is held up, his eyes rolled about with sprightliness; he rejoices at his being, is prone to anger, and would be glad that all the world could take notice of him.

It is incredible how necessary an ingredient shame is to make us sociable. It is a frailty in our nature. All the world, whenever it affects them, submit to it with regret, and would prevent it if they could. Yet the happiness of conversation depends upon it, and no society could be polished if the generality of mankind were not subject to it. As therefore the sense of shame is troublesome, and all creatures are ever laboring for their own defense, it is probable that man striving to avoid this uneasiness would in a great measure conquer his shame by that [time] he was grown up. But this would be detrimental to the society, and therefore from his infancy throughout his education we endeavor to increase instead of lessening or destroying this sense of shame. And the only remedy prescribed is a strict observance of certain rules to avoid those things that might bring this troublesome sense of shame upon him. But as to rid or cure him of it, the politician would sooner take away his life.

The rules I speak of consist in a dexterous management of ourselves, a stifling of our appetites, and hiding the real sentiments of our hearts before others. Those who are not instructed in these rules long before they come to years of maturity seldom make any progress in them afterwards. To acquire and bring to perfection the accomplishment I hint at, nothing is more assisting than pride and good sense. The greediness we have after the esteem of others, and the raptures we enjoy in the thoughts of being liked, and perhaps admired, are equivalents that overpay the conquest of the strongest passions, and consequently keep us at a great distance from all such words or actions that can bring shame upon us. The passions we chiefly ought to hide for the happiness and embellishment of the society are lust, pride, and selfishness. Therefore, the word modesty has three different acceptations that vary with the passions it conceals.

As to the first, I mean that branch of modesty that has a general pretension to chastity for its object. It consists in a sincere and painful endeavor with all our faculties to stifle and conceal before others that inclination which nature has given us to propagate our species. The lessons of it, like those of grammar, are taught us long before we have occasion for or understand the usefulness of them. For this reason children often are ashamed, and blush out of modesty, before the impulse of nature I hint at makes any impression upon them. A girl who is modestly educated may, before she is two years old, begin to observe how careful the women she converses with are of covering themselves before men. And the same caution being inculcated to her by precept, as well as example, it is very probable that at six she'll be ashamed of showing her leg, without knowing any reason why such an act is blameable, or what the tendency of it is.

To be modest, we ought in the first place to avoid all unfashionable denudations. A woman is not to be found fault with for going with her neck bare, if the custom of the country allows of it; and when the mode orders the stays to be cut very low, a blooming virgin may, without fear of rational censure, show all the world:

> *How firm her pouting Breasts, that white as Snow,*
> *On th' ample Chest at mighty distance grow.*

But to suffer her ankle to be seen, where it is the fashion for women to hide their very feet, is a breach of modesty; and she is impudent, who shows half her face in a country where decency bids her to be veiled. In the second, our language must be chaste and not only free but remote from obscenities, that is, whatever belongs to the multiplication of our species is not to be spoken of, and the least word or expression, that though at a great distance has any relation to that performance, ought never to come from our lips. Thirdly, all postures and motions that can any ways sully the imagination, that is, put us in mind of what I have called obscenities, are to be forebore with great caution.

A young woman, moreover, that would be thought well-bred, ought to be circumspect before men in all her behavior, and never known to receive from, much less to bestow favors upon them, unless the great age of the man, near consanguinity, or a vast superiority on either side plead her excuse. A young lady of refined education keeps a strict guard over her looks, as well as actions, and in her eyes we may read a consciousness that she has a treasure about her, not out of danger of being lost, and which yet she is resolved not to part with at any terms. [A] thousand satires have been made against prudes, and as many encomiums to extol the careless graces and negligent air of virtuous beauty. But the wiser sort of mankind are well assured that the free and open countenance of the smiling fair is more inviting, and yields greater hopes to the seducer, than the ever-watchful look of a forbidding eye.

This strict reservedness is to be complied with by all young women, especially virgins, if they value the esteem of the polite and knowing world. Men may take greater liberty because in them the appetite is more violent and ungovernable. Had equal harshness of discipline been imposed upon both, neither of them could have made the first advances, and propagation must have stood still among all the fashionable people; which being far from the politician's aim, it was advisable to ease and indulge the sex that suffered most by the severity, and make the rules abate of their rigor, where the passion was the strongest, and the burden of a strict restraint would have been the most intolerable.

For this reason the man is allowed openly to profess the veneration and great esteem he has for women, and show greater satisfaction, more mirth and gaiety in their company, than he is used to do out of it. He may not only be complaisant and serviceable to them on all occasions, but it is reckoned his duty to protect and defend them. He may praise the good qualities they are possessed of, and extol their merit with as many exaggerations as his invention will let him, and are consistent with good sense. He may talk of love, he may sigh and complain of the rigors of the fair, and what his tongue must not utter he has the privilege to speak with his eyes, and in that language to say what he pleases, so it be done with decency, and short abrupt glances. But too closely to pursue a woman, and fasten upon her with one's eyes, is counted very unmannerly. The reason is plain: it makes her uneasy and, if she be not sufficiently fortified by art and dissimulation, often throws her into visible disorders. As the eyes are the windows of the soul, so this staring impudence flings a raw, inexperienced woman into panic fears, that she may be seen through; and that the man will discover, or has already betrayed, what passes within her. It keeps her on a perpetual rack that commands her to reveal her secret wishes, and seems designed to extort from her the grand truth, which modesty bids her with all her faculties to deny.

The multitude will hardly believe the excessive force of education, and in the difference of modesty between men and women ascribe that to nature, which is altogether owing to early instruction. Miss is scarcely three years old, but she is spoken to every day to hide her leg, and rebuked in good earnest if she shows it; while Little Master at the same age is bid to take up his coats, and piss like a man. It is shame and education that contains the seeds of all politeness, and he that has neither, and offers to speak the truth of his heart, and what he feels within, is the most contemptible creature upon earth, though he committed no other fault. If a man should tell a woman that he could like nobody so well to propagate his species upon as herself, and that he found a violent desire that moment to go about it, and accordingly offered to lay hold of her for that purpose, the consequence would be that he would be called a brute, the woman would run away, and himself never be admitted in any civil company. There is nobody that has any sense of shame but would conquer the strongest passion rather than be so served. But a man need not conquer his passions; it is sufficient that he conceals them. Virtue bids us subdue, but good breeding only requires we should hide our appetites. A fashionable gentleman may have as violent an inclination to a woman as the brutish fellow; but then he behaves himself quite otherwise. He first addresses the lady's father, and demonstrates his ability splendidly to maintain his daughter. Upon this he is admitted into her company, where, by flattery, submission, presents, and assiduity, he endeavors to procure her liking to his person, which if he can compass, the lady in a little while resigns herself to him before witnesses in a most solemn manner. At night they go to bed together, where the most reserved virgin very tamely suffers him to do what he pleases, and the upshot is that he obtains what he wanted without having ever asked for it.

The next day they receive visits and nobody laughs at them, or speaks a word of what they have been doing. As to the young couple themselves, they take no more notice of one another—I speak of well-bred people—than they did the day before. They eat and drink, divert themselves as usual, and having done nothing to be ashamed of, are looked upon as what in reality they may be, the most modest people upon earth. What I mean by this is to demonstrate that by being well-bred we suffer no abridgment in our sensual pleasures, but only labor for our mutual happiness, and assist each other in the luxurious enjoyment of all worldly comforts. The fine gentleman I spoke of need not practice any greater self-denial than the savage, and the latter acted more according to the laws of nature and sincerity than the first. The man that gratifies his appetites after the manner the custom of the country allows of has no censure to fear. If he is hotter than goats or bulls, as soon as the ceremony is over let him sate and fatigue himself with joy and ecstasies of pleasure, raise and indulge his appetites by turns as extravagantly as his strength and manhood will give him leave. He may with safety laugh at the wise men that should reprove him. All the women and above nine in ten of the men are of his side; nay, he has the liberty of valuing himself upon the fury of his unbridled passion, and the more he wallows in lust and strains every faculty to be abandonedly voluptuous, the sooner he shall have the goodwill and gain the affection of the women, not the young, vain and lascivious only, but the prudent, grave and most sober matrons.

Because impudence is a vice, it does not follow that modesty is a virtue. It is built upon shame, a passion in our nature, and may be either good or bad according to the actions performed from that motive. Shame may hinder a prostitute from yielding to a man before company, and the same shame may cause a bashful good-natured creature, that has been overcome by frailty, to make away with her infant. Passions may do good by chance, but there can be no merit but in the conquest of them.

Was there virtue in modesty, it would be of the same force in the dark as it is in the light, which it is not. This the men of pleasure know very well, who never trouble their heads with a woman's virtue so they can but conquer her modesty. Seducers therefore don't make their attacks at noonday, but cut their trenches at night. . . .

People of substance may sin without being exposed for their stolen pleasure, but servants and the poorer sort of women have seldom an opportunity of concealing a big belly, or at least the consequences of it. It is possible that an unfortunate girl of good parentage may be left destitute, and know no shift for a livelihood than to become a nursery, or a chambermaid. She may be diligent, faithful and obliging, have abundance of modesty, and if you will, be religious: she may resist temptations, and preserve her chastity for years together, and yet at last meet with an unhappy moment in which she gives up her honor to a powerful deceiver, who afterwards neglects her. If she proves with child, her sorrows are unspeakable, and she can't be reconciled with the wretchedness of her condition. The fear of shame attacks her so lively, that every thought distracts her. All the family she lives in have a great opinion of her virtue, and her last mistress took her for a saint. How will her enemies, that envied her character, rejoice! How will her relations detest her! The more modest she is now, and the more violently the dread of coming to shame hurries her away, the more wicked and more cruel her resolutions will be, either against herself or what she bears.

It is commonly imagined that she who can destroy her child, her own flesh and blood, must have a vast stock of barbarity, and be a savage monster, different from other women; but this is likewise a mistake, which we commit for want of understanding nature and the force of passions. The same woman that murders her bastard in the most execrable manner, if she is married afterwards, may take care of, cherish and feel all the tenderness for her infant that the fondest mother can be capable of. All mothers naturally love their children. But as this is a passion, and all passions center in self-love, so it may be subdued by any superior passion, to soothe that same self-love, which if nothing had intervened would have bid her fondle her offspring. Common whores, whom all the world knows to be such, hardly ever destroy their children. Nay, even those who assist in robberies and murders seldom are guilty of this crime; not because they are less cruel or more virtuous, but because they have lost their modesty to a greater degree, and the fear of shame makes hardly any impression upon them.

Our love to what never was within the reach of our senses is but poor and inconsiderable, and therefore women have no natural love to what they bear. Their affection begins after the birth; what they feel before is the result of reason, education, and the thoughts of duty. Even when children first are born the mother's love is but weak, and increases with the sensibility of the child, and grows up to a prodigious height when by signs it begins to express his sorrows and joys, makes his wants known, and discovers his love to novelty and the multiplicity of his desires. What labors and hazards have not women undergone to maintain and save their children, what force and fortitude beyond their sex have they not shown in their behalf! But the vilest women have exerted themselves on this head as violently as the best. All are prompted to it by a natural drift and inclination, without any consideration of the injury or benefit the society receives from it. There is no merit in pleasing ourselves, and the very offspring is often irreparably ruined by the excessive fondness of parents. For though infants for two or three years may be the better for this indulging care of mothers, yet afterwards, if not moderated, it may totally spoil them, and many it has brought to the gallows.

If the reader thinks I have been too tedious on that branch of modesty, by the help of which we endeavor to appear chaste, I shall make him amends in the brevity with which I design to treat of the remaining part, by which we would make others believe that the esteem we have for them exceeds the value we have for ourselves, and that we have no disregard so great to any interest as we have to our own. This laudable quality is commonly known by the name of manners and good-breeding, and consists in a fashionable habit, acquired by precept and example, of flattering the pride and selfishness of others, and concealing our own with judgment and dexterity. This must be only understood of our commerce with our equals and superiors, and while we are in peace and amity with them. For our complaisance must never interfere with the rules of honor, nor the homage that is due to us from servants and others that depend upon us.

With this caution, I believe that the definition will quadrate [equate] with everything that can be alleged as a piece or an example of either good-breeding or ill manners. And it will be very difficult throughout the various accidents of human life and conversation to find out an instance of modesty or impudence that is not comprehended in, and illustrated by it, in all countries and in all ages. A man that asks considerable favors of one who is a stranger to him, without consideration, is called impudent, because he shows openly his selfishness without having any regard to the selfishness of the other. We may see in it likewise the reason why a man ought to speak of his wife and children, and everything that is dear to him, as sparingly as is possible, and hardly ever of himself, especially in commendation of them. A well-bred man may be desirous and even greedy after praise and the esteem of others, but to be praised to his face offends his modesty. The reason is this: all human creatures, before they are yet polished, receive an extraordinary pleasure in hearing themselves praised. This we are all conscious of, and therefore when we see a man openly enjoy and feast on this delight, in which we have no share, it rouses our selfishness, and immediately we begin to envy and hate him. For this reason the well-bred man conceals his joy, and utterly denies that he feels any, and by this means consulting and soothing our selfishness, he averts that envy and hatred, which otherwise he would have justly to fear. When from our childhood we observe how those are ridiculed who calmly can hear their own praises, it is possible that we may so strenuously endeavor to avoid that pleasure, that in [a] tract of time we grow uneasy at the approach of it. But this is not following the dictates of nature, but warping her by education and custom. For if the generality of mankind took no delight in being praised, there could be no modesty in refusing to hear it.

The man of manners picks not the best but rather takes the worst out of the dish, and gets of everything, unless it be forced upon him, always the most indifferent share. By this civility the best remains for others, which being a compliment to all that are present, everybody is pleased with it. The more they love themselves, the more they are forced to approve of his behavior, and gratitude stepping in, they are obliged almost whether they will or not to think favorably of him. After this manner it is that the well-bred man insinuates himself in the esteem of all the companies he comes in, and if he gets nothing else by it, the pleasure he receives in reflecting on the applause which he knows is secretly given him is to a proud man more than an equivalent for his former self-denial, and over-pays to self-love with interest, the loss it sustained in his complaisance to others.

If there are seven or eight apples or peaches among six people of ceremony, that are pretty near equal, he who is prevailed upon to choose first, will take that, which, if there be any considerable difference, a child would know to be the worst. This he does to insinuate, that he looks upon those he is with to be of superior merit, and that there is not one whom he wishes not better to than he does to himself. It is custom and a general practice that makes this modish deceit familiar to us, without being shocked at the absurdity of it. For if people had been used to speak[ing] from the sincerity of their hearts, and act[ing] according to the natural sentiments they felt within, till they were three or four and twenty, it would be impossible for them to assist at this comedy of manners, without either loud laughter or indignation. And yet it is certain that such behavior makes us more tolerable to one another than we could be otherwise.

It is very advantageous to the knowledge of ourselves to be able well to distinguish between good qualities and virtues. The bond of society exacts from every member a certain regard for others, which the highest is not exempt from in the presence of the meanest, even in an empire. But when we are by ourselves, and so far removed from company as to be beyond the reach of their senses, the words modesty and impudence lose their meaning. A person may be wicked, but he cannot be immodest while he is alone, and no thought can be impudent that never was communicated to another. A man of exalted pride may so hide it that nobody shall be able to discover that he has any; and yet receive greater satisfaction from that passion than another, who indulges himself in the declaration of it before all the world. Good manners have nothing to do with virtue or religion. Instead of extinguishing, they rather inflame the passions. The man of sense and education never exults more in his pride than when he hides it with the greatest dexterity. And in feasting on the applause, which he is sure all good judges will pay to his behavior, he enjoys a pleasure altogether unknown to the short-sighted, surly alderman, that shows his haughtiness glaringly in his face, pulls off his hat to nobody, and hardly deigns to speak to an inferior.

A man may carefully avoid everything that in the eye of the world is esteemed to be the result of pride, without mortifying himself, or making the least conquest of his passion. It is possible that he only sacrifices the insipid outward part of his pride which none but silly ignorant people take delight in, to that part we all feel within, and which the men of the highest spirit and most exalted genius feed on with so much ecstasy in silence. The pride of great and polite men is nowhere more conspicuous than in the debates about ceremony and precedence, where they have an opportunity of giving their vices the appearance of virtues, and can make the world believe that it is their care, their tenderness for the dignity of their office, or the honor of their masters, what is the result of their own personal pride and vanity. This is most manifest in all negotiations of ambassadors and plenipotentiaries, and must be known by all that observe what is transacted at public treaties. And it will ever be true, that men of the best taste have no relish in their pride as long as any mortal can find out that they are proud.

Remark F

And Virtue, who from Politicks
Had learn'd a thousand cunning Tricks,
Was, by their happy Influence,
Made Friends with Vice.———

It may be said that virtue is made friends with vice when industrious good people, who maintain their families and bring up their children handsomely, pay taxes, and are several ways useful members of the society, get a livelihood by something that chiefly depends on, or is very much influenced by the vices of others, without being themselves guilty of, or accessory to them, any otherwise than by way of trade, as a druggist may be to poisoning, or a sword-cutler to bloodshed.

Thus the merchant that sends corn or cloth into foreign parts to purchase wines and brandies encourages the growth or manufacture of his own country. He is a benefactor to navigation, increases the customs, and is in many ways beneficial to the public. Yet it is not to be denied but that his greatest dependence is lavishness and drunkenness. For if none were to drink wine but such only as stand in need of it, nor anybody more than his health required, that multitude of wine merchants, vintners, coopers, etc. that make such a considerable show in this flourishing city would be in a miserable condition. The same may be said not only of card and dice-makers, that are the immediate ministers to a legion of vices, but of mercers, upholsterers, tailors, and many others, that would be starved in half a year's time if pride and luxury were at once to be banished from the nation.

Remark G

The worst of all the Multitude
Did something for the Common Good.

This, I know, will seem to be a strange paradox to many; and I shall be asked what benefit the public receives from thieves and house-breakers. They are, I own, very pernicious to human society, and every government ought to take all imaginable care to root out and destroy them. Yet if all people were strictly honest, and nobody would meddle with or pry into anything but his own, half the smiths of the nation would want employment; and abundance of workmanship (which now serves for ornament as well as defense) is to be seen everywhere both in town and country, that would never have been thought of, but to secure us against the attempts of pilferers and robbers.

If what I have said be thought farfetched, and my assertion seems still a paradox, I desire the reader to look upon the consumption of things, and he'll find that the laziest and most inactive, the profligate and most mischievous, are all forced to do something for the common good. And while their mouths are not sewn up, and they continue to wear and otherwise destroy what the industrious are daily employed about to make, fetch and procure, in spite of their teeth [are] obliged to help maintain the poor and the public charges. The labor of millions would soon be at an end, if there were not other millions, as I say, in the fable,

—————*Employ'd,*
To see their Handy-works destroy'd.

But men are not to be judged by the consequences that may succeed their actions, but the facts themselves, and the motives which it shall appear they acted from. If an ill-natured miser who is almost a plumb [worth almost £100,000] and spends but fifty pounds a year, though he has no relation to inherit his wealth, should be robbed of five hundred or a thousand guineas, it is certain that as soon as this money should come to circulate the nation would be the better for the robbery, and receive the same and as real a benefit from it, as if an archbishop had left the same sum to the public. Yet justice and the peace of the society require that he or they who robbed the miser should be hanged, though there were half a dozen of them concerned.

Thieves and pickpockets steal for a livelihood, and either what they can get honestly is not sufficient to keep them, or else they have an aversion to constant working. They want to gratify their senses, have victuals, strong drink, lewd women, and to be idle when they please. The victualler, who entertains them and takes their money, knowing which way they come at it, is very near as great a villain as his guests. But if he fleeces them well, minds his business and is a prudent man, he may get money and be punctual with them he deals with. The trusty out-clerk, whose chief aim is his master's profit, sends him in what beer he wants, and takes care not to lose his custom; while the man's money is good, he thinks it no business of his to examine whom he gets it by. In the meantime the wealthy brewer, who leaves all the management to his servants, knows nothing of the matter, but keeps his coach, treats his friends, and enjoys his pleasure with ease and a good conscience. He gets an estate, builds houses, and educates his children in plenty, without ever thinking of the labor which wretches perform, the shifts fools make, and the tricks knaves play to come at the commodity, by the vast sale of which he amasses his great riches.

A highwayman, having met with a considerable booty, gives a poor common harlot he fancies ten pounds to new-rig her from top to toe. Is there a spruce mercer so conscientious that he will refuse to sell her a thread satin, though he knew who she was? She must have shoes and stockings, gloves, the stay and mantua-maker [a loose silk gown worn by fashionable women], the seamstress, the linen draper, all must get something by her, and a hundred different tradesmen dependent on those she laid her money out with may touch part of it before a month is at an end. The generous gentleman, in the meantime, his money being near spent, ventured again on the road, but the second day having committed a robbery near Highgate, he was taken with one of his accomplices, and the next [court] sessions both were condemned, and suffered the law. The money due on their conviction fell to three country fellows, on whom it was admirably well bestowed. One was an honest farmer, a sober painstaking man, but reduced by misfortunes. The summer before, by the mortality among the cattle, he had lost six cows out of ten, and now his landlord, to whom he owed thirty pounds, had seized on all his stock. The other was a day-laborer, who struggled hard with the world, had a sick wife at home and several small children to provide for. The third was a gentleman's gardener, who maintained his father in prison, where being bound for a neighbor he had lain for twelve pounds almost a year and a half. This act of filial duty was the more meritorious, because he had for some time been engaged to a young woman whose parents lived in good circumstances, but would not give their consent before our gardener had fifty guineas of his own to show. They received above fourscore pounds each, which extricated every one of them out of the difficulties they labored under, and made them in their opinion the happiest people in the world.

Nothing is more destructive, either in regard to the health or the vigilance and industry of the poor, than the infamous liquor, the name of which, derived from juniper in Dutch, is now by frequent use and the laconic spirit of the nation, from a word of middling length shrunk into a monosyllable, intoxicating gin, that charms the inactive, the desperate and crazy of either sex, and makes the starving sot behold his rags and nakedness with stupid indolence, or banter both in senseless laughter, and more insipid jests. It is a fiery lake that sets the brain in flame, burns up the entrails, and scorches every part within; and at the same time a Lethe of oblivion, in which the wretch immersed drowns his most pinching cares, and with his reason all anxious reflection on brats that cry for food, hard winters' frosts, and horrid empty home.

In hot and adust [dried up] tempers it makes men quarrelsome, renders them brutes and savages, sets them on to fight for nothing, and has often been the cause of murder. It has broken and destroyed the strongest constitutions, thrown them into consumptions, and been the fatal and immediate occasion of apoplexies, frenzies and sudden death. But as these latter mischiefs happen but seldom, they might be overlooked and connived at; but this cannot be said of the many diseases that are familiar to the liquor, and which are daily and hourly produced by it, such as loss of appetite, fevers, black and yellow jaundice, convulsions, stone and gravel, dropsies, and leuco-phlegmacies [a pale and flabby body, the symptoms of dropsy].

Among the doting admirers of this liquid poison, many of the meanest rank, from a sincere affection to the commodity itself, become dealers in it, and take delight to help others to what they love themselves, as whores commence bawds to make the profits of one trade subservient to the pleasures of the other. But as these starvelings commonly drink more than their gains, they seldom by selling mend the wretchedness of condition they labored under while they were only buyers. In the fag-end and outskirts of the town, and all places of the vilest resort, it is sold in some part or other of almost every house, frequently in cellars, and sometimes in the garret. The petty traders in this Stygian comfort are supplied by others in somewhat higher station, that keep professed brandy shops, and are as little to be envied as the former. And among the middling people, I know not a more miserable shift for a livelihood than their calling. Whoever would thrive in it must in the first place be of a watchful and suspicious as well as a bold and resolute temper, that he may not be imposed upon by cheats and sharpers, nor out-bullied by the oaths and imprecations of hackney-coachmen and foot-soldiers. In the second, he ought to be a dabster at gross jokes and loud laughter, and have all the winning ways to allure customers and draw out their money, and be well versed in the low jests and railleries the mob make use of to banter prudence and frugality. He must be affable and obsequious to the most despicable, always ready and officious to help a porter down with his load, shake hands with a basket-woman, pull off his hat to an oyster-wench, and be familiar with a beggar. With patience and good humor he must be able to endure the filthy actions and viler language of nasty drabs, and the lewdest rakehells, and without a frown or the least aversion bear with all the stench and squalor, noise and impertinence that the utmost indigence, laziness and ebriety can produce in the most shameless and abandoned vulgar.

The vast number of the shops I speak of throughout the city and suburbs are an astonishing evidence of the many seducers, that in a lawful occupation are accessory to the introduction and increase of all the sloth, sottishness, want and misery, which the abuse of strong waters is the immediate cause of, to lift above mediocrity perhaps half a score men that deal in the same commodity by wholesale. While among the retailers, though qualified as I required, a much greater number are broke and ruined, for not abstaining from the Circean cup they hold out to others, and the more fortunate are their whole lifetime obliged to take the uncommon pains, endure the hardships, and swallow all the ungrateful and shocking things I named, for little or nothing beyond a bare sustenance, and their daily bread.

The short-sighted vulgar in the chain of causes seldom can see further than one link. But those who can enlarge their view, and will give themselves the leisure of gazing on the prospect of concatenated events may, in a hundred places, see good spring up and pullulate from evil, as naturally as chickens do from eggs. The money that arises from the duties upon malt is a considerable part of the national revenue, and should no spirits be distilled from it, the public treasure would prodigiously suffer on that head. But if we would set in a true light the many advantages, and large catalogue of solid blessings that accrue from, and are owing to the evil I treat of, we are to consider the rents that are received, the ground that is tilled, the tools that are made, the cattle that are employed, and above all, the multitude of poor that are maintained, by the variety of labor, required in husbandry, in malting, in carriage and distillation, before we can have the product of malt, which we call low wines, and is but the beginning from which the various spirits are afterwards to be made.

Besides this, a sharp-sighted good-humored man might pick up abundance of good from the rubbish, which I have all flung away for evil. He would tell me that whatever sloth and sottishness might be occasioned by the abuse of malt-spirits, the moderate use of it was of inestimable benefit to the poor, who could purchase no cordials of higher prices, that it was a universal comfort, not only in cold and weariness, but most of the afflictions that are peculiar to the necessitous, and had often to the most destitute supplied the places of meat, drink, clothes, and lodging. That the stupid indolence in the most wretched condition occasioned by those composing draughts, which I complained of, was a blessing to thousands, for that certainly those were the happiest, who felt the least pain. As to diseases, he would say that as it caused some, so it cured others, and that if the excess in those liquors had been sudden death to some few, the habit of drinking them daily prolonged the lives of many, whom once it agreed with; that for the loss sustained from the insignificant quarrels it created at home, we were overpaid in the advantage we received from it abroad, by upholding the courage of soldiers, and animating the sailors to the combat; and that in the two last wars no considerable victory had been obtained without.

To the dismal account I have given of the retailers, and what they are forced to submit to, he would answer, that not many acquired more than middling riches in any trade, and that what I had counted so offensive and intolerable in the calling, was trifling to those who were used to it; that what seemed irksome and calamitous to some, was delightful and often ravishing to others, as men differed in circumstances and education. He would put me in mind that the profit of an employment ever made amends for the toil and labor that belonged to it, nor forget, *Dulcis odor lucri è re qualibet;* [that is,] to tell me that the smell of gain was fragrant even to night-workers [waste removers].

If I should ever urge to him that to have here and there one great and eminent distiller was a poor equivalent for the vile means, the certain want, and lasting misery of so many thousand wretches as were necessary to raise them, he would answer that of this I could be no judge, because I don't know what vast benefit they might afterwards be of to the common-wealth. Perhaps, would he say, the man thus raised will exert himself in the commission of the peace, or other station, with vigilance and zeal against the dissolute and I disaffected, and retaining his stirring temper, be as industrious in spreading loyalty and the reformation of manners throughout every cranny of the wide populous town, as once he was in filling it with spirits; until he becomes at last the scourge of whores, of vagabonds and beggars, the terror of rioters and discontented rabbles, and constant plague to Sabbath-breaking butchers. Here my good-humored antagonist would exult and triumph over me, especially if he could instance to me such a bright example. What an uncommon blessing, would he cry out, is this man to his country! How shining and illustrious his virtue!

To justify his exclamation he would demonstrate to me that it was impossible to give a fuller evidence of self-denial in a grateful mind than to see him at the expense of his quiet and hazard of his life and limbs, be always harassing, and even for trifles persecuting that very class of men to whom he owes his fortune, from no other motive than his aversion to idleness, and great concern for religion and the public welfare.

Remark I

The Root of Evil, Avarice,
That damn'd ill-natur'd baneful Vice,
Was Slave to Prodigality.

I have joined so many odious epithets to the word avarice, in compliance to the vogue of mankind, who generally bestow more ill language upon this than upon any other vice, and indeed not undeservedly; for there is hardly a mischief to be named which it has not produced at one time or other. But the true reason why everybody exclaims so much against it is that almost everybody suffers by it. For the more the money is hoarded up by some, the scarcer it must grow among the rest, and therefore when men rail very much at misers there is generally self-interest at bottom.

As there is no living without money, so those that are unprovided, and have nobody to give them any, are obliged to do some service or other to the society, before they can come at it. But everybody esteeming his labor as he does himself, which is generally not under the value, most that want money only to spend it again presently imagine they do more for it than it is worth. Men can't forbear looking upon the necessities of life as their due, whether they work or not; because they find that nature, without consulting whether they have victuals or not bids them eat whenever they are hungry. For which reason everybody endeavors to get what he wants with as much ease as he can; and therefore when men find that the trouble they are put to in getting money is either more or less, according as those they would have it from are more or less tenacious, it is very natural for them to be angry at covetousness in general, for it obliges them either to go without what they have occasion for, or else to take greater pains for it than they are willing.

Avarice, notwithstanding [that] it is the occasion of so many evils, is yet very necessary to the society to glean and gather what has been dropped and scattered by the contrary vice. Was it not for avarice, spendthrifts would soon want materials; and if none would lay up and get faster than they spend, very few could spend faster than they get. That it is a slave to prodigality, as I have called it, is evident from so many misers as we daily see toil and labor, pinch and starve themselves to enrich a lavish heir. Though these two vices appear very opposite, yet they often assist each other. Florio is an extravagant young blade, of a very profuse temper. As he is the only son of a very rich father, he wants to live high, keep horses and dogs, and throw his money about, as he sees some of his companions do. But the old hunks will part with no money, and hardly allows him necessities. Florio would have borrowed money upon his own credit long ago; but as all would be lost if he died before his father, no prudent man would lend him any. At last he has met with the greedy Cornaro, who lets him have money at thirty percent, and now Florio thinks himself happy, and spends a thousand a year. Where would Cornaro ever have got such a prodigious interest if it was not for such a fool as Florio, who will give so great a price for money to fling it away? And how would Florio get it to spend, if he had not lit of such a greedy usurer as Cornaro, whose excessive covetousness makes him overlook the great risk he runs in venturing such great sums upon the life of a wild debauchee?

Avarice is no longer the reverse of profuseness than while it signifies that sordid love of money and narrowness of soul that hinders misers from parting with what they have, and makes them covet only to hoard up. But there is a sort of avarice which consists in a greedy desire of riches in order to spend them, and this often meets with prodigality in the same persons, as is evident in most courtiers and great officers, both civil and military. In their buildings and furniture, equipment and entertainment, their gallantry is displayed with the greatest profusion, while the base actions they submit to for lucre and the many frauds and impositions they are guilty of discover the utmost avarice. This mixture of contrary vices comes up exactly to the character of Catiline, of whom it is said, that he was *appertens alieni & sui profusus,* [that is,] greedy after the goods of others and lavish of his own.

Remark K

That noble Sin

The prodigality I call a noble sin is not that which has avarice for its companion, and makes men unreasonably profuse to some of what they unjustly extort from others, but that agreeable good-natured vice that makes the chimney smoke, and all the tradesmen smile. I mean the unmixed prodigality of heedless and voluptuous men, that being educated in plenty, abhor the vile thoughts of lucre, and lavish away only what others took pains to scrape together. Such [men] indulge their inclinations at their own expense, have the continual satisfaction of bartering old gold for new pleasures, and from the excessive largeness of a diffusive soul are made guilty of despising too much what most people overvalue.

When I speak thus honorably of this vice, and treat it with so much tenderness and good manners as I do, I have the same thing at heart that made me give so many ill names to the reverse of it, the interest of the public. For as the avaricious does no good to himself, and is injurious to all the world besides, except his heir, so the prodigal is a blessing to the whole society, and injures nobody but himself. It is true, that as most of the first are knaves, so the latter are all fools. Yet they are delicious morsels for the public to feast on, and may with as much justice as the French call the monks the partridges of the women, be styled the woodcocks of the society. Was it not for prodigality, nothing could make us amends for the rapine and extortion of avarice in power. When a covetous statesman is gone, who spent his whole life in fattening himself with the spoils of the nation, and had by pinching and plundering heaped up an immense treasure, it ought to fill every good member of the society with joy, to behold the uncommon profuseness of his son. This is refunding to the public what was robbed from it. Resuming of grants is a barbarous way of stripping, and it is ignoble to ruin a man faster than he does it himself, when he sets about it in such good earnest. Does he not feed an infinite number of dogs of all sorts and sizes, though he never hunts; keep more horses than any nobleman in the kingdom, though he never rides them, and give as large an allowance to an ill-favored whore as would keep a duchess, though he never lies with her? Is he not still more extravagant in those things he makes use of? Therefore let him alone, or praise him, call him public-spirited lord, nobly bountiful and magnificently generous, and in a few years he'll suffer himself to be stripped his own way. As long as the nation has its own back again we ought not to quarrel with the manner in which the plunder is repaid.

Abundance of moderate men I know that are enemies to extremes will tell me that frugality might happily supply the place of the two vices I speak of, that, if men had not so many profuse ways of spending wealth, they would not be tempted to so many evil practices to scrape it together, and consequently that the same number of men by equally avoiding both extremes, might render themselves more happy, and be less vicious without than they could with them. Whoever argues thus shows himself a better man than he is a politician. Frugality is like honesty, a mean starving virtue, that is only fit for small societies of good peaceable men, who are contented to be poor so they may be easy; but in a large stirring nation you may have soon enough of it.

It is an idle dreaming virtue that employs no hands, and therefore very useless in a trading country, where there are vast numbers that one way or other must be all set to work. Prodigality has a thousand inventions to keep people from sitting still, that frugality would never think of; and as this must consume a prodigious wealth, so avarice again knows innumerable tricks to rake it together, which frugality would scorn to make use of.

Authors are always allowed to compare small things to great ones, especially if they ask leave first. *Si licet exemplis* [if you wish an example], etc. but to compare great things to mean trivial ones is insufferable, unless it be in burlesque; otherwise I would compare the body politic (I confess the simile is very low) to a bowl of punch. Avarice should be the souring and prodigality the sweetening of it. The water I would call the ignorance, folly and credulity of the floating insipid multitude. While wisdom, honor, fortitude and the rest of the sublime qualities of men, which separated by art from the dregs of nature the fire of glory has exalted and refined into a spiritual essence, should be an equivalent to brandy. I don't doubt but a Westphalian, Laplander, or any other dull stranger that is unacquainted with the wholesome composition, if he was to taste the several ingredients apart, would think it impossible they should make any tolerable liquor. The lemons would be too sour, the sugar too luscious, the brandy he'll say is too strong ever to be drunk in any quantity, and the water he'll call a tasteless liquor only fit for cows and horses. Yet experience teaches us that the ingredients I named, judiciously mixed, will make an excellent liquor, liked of and admired by men of exquisite palates. . . .

Remark L

―――*While Luxury*
Employ'd a Million of the Poor, &c.

If everything is to be luxury (as in strictness it ought) that is not immediately necessary to make man subsist as he is a living creature, there is nothing else to be found in the world, no, not even among the naked savages; of which it is not probable that there are any but what by this time have made some improvements upon their former manner of living, and either in the preparation of their eatables, the ordering of their huts, or otherwise, added something to what once sufficed them. This definition everybody will say is too rigorous. I am of the same opinion, but if we are to abate one inch of this severity, I am afraid we shan't know where to stop. When people tell us they only desire to keep themselves sweet and clean, there is no understanding what they would be at. If they made use of these words in their genuine proper literal sense, they might soon be satisfied without much cost or trouble, if they did not want water. But these two little adjectives are so comprehensive, especially in the dialect of some ladies, that nobody can guess how far they may be stretched. The comforts of life are likewise so various and extensive that nobody can tell what people mean by them, except he knows what sort of life they lead.

The same obscurity I observe in the words "decency" and "convenience," and I never understand them unless I am acquainted with the quality of the persons that make use of them. People may go to church together, and be all of one mind as much as they please. I am apt to believe that when they pray for their daily bread, the bishop includes several things in that · petition which the sexton does not think on.

By what I have said hitherto I would only show that if once we depart from calling everything luxury that is not absolutely necessary to keep a man alive, that then there is no luxury at all. For if the wants of men are innumerable, then what ought to supply them has no bounds. What is called superfluous to some degree of people will be thought requisite to those of higher quality; and neither the world nor the skill of man can produce anything so curious or extravagant, but some most gracious sovereign or other, if it either eases or diverts him, will reckon it among the necessities of life; not meaning everybody's life, but that of his sacred person.

It is a received notion that luxury is as destructive to the wealth of the whole body politic as it is to that of every individual person who is guilty of it, and that a national frugality enriches a country in the same manner as that which is less general increases the estates of private families. I confess that though I have found men of much better understanding than myself of this opinion, I cannot help dissenting from them in this point. They argue thus: we send, say they, for example, to Turkey of woollen manufacture, and other things of our own growth, a million's worth every year. For this we bring back silk, mohair, drugs, etc. to the value of twelve hundred thousand pounds, that are all spent in our own country. By this, say they, we get nothing. But if most of us would be content with our own growth, and so consume but half the quantity of those foreign commodities than those in Turkey, who would still want the same quantity of our manufactures, would be forced to pay ready money for the rest, and so by the balance of that trade only the nation should get six hundred thousand pounds per annum.

To examine the force of this argument, we'll suppose (what they would have) that but half the silk, etc. shall be consumed in England of what there is now. We'll suppose likewise, that those in Turkey, though we refuse to buy above half as much of their commodities as we used to do, either can or will not be without the same quantity of our manufactures they had before, and that they'll pay the balance in money; that is to say, that they shall give us as much gold or silver, as the value of what they buy from us exceeds the value of what we buy from them. Though what we suppose might perhaps be done for one year, it is impossible it should last.

Buying is bartering, and no nation can buy goods of others that has none of her own to purchase them with. Spain and Portugal, that are yearly supplied with new gold and silver from their mines, may forever buy for ready money as long as their yearly increase of gold or silver continues, but then money is their growth and the commodity of the country. We know that we could not continue long to purchase the goods of other nations if they would not take our manufactures in payment for them. And why should we judge otherwise of other nations? If those in Turkey then had no more money fall from the skies than we, let us see what would be the consequence of what we supposed. The six hundred thousand pounds in silk, mohair, etc. that are left upon their hands the first year, must make those commodities fall considerably. Of this the Dutch and French will reap the benefit as much as ourselves and if we continue to refuse taking their commodities in payment for our manufactures, they can trade no longer with us, but must content themselves with buying what they want of such nations as are willing to take what we refuse, though their goods are much worse than ours. Thus our commerce with Turkey must in few years be infallibly lost.

But they'll say, perhaps, that to prevent the ill consequence I have shown, we shall take the Turkish merchandises as formerly, and only be so frugal as to consume but half the quantity of them ourselves, and send the rest abroad to be sold to others. Let us see what this will do, and whether it will enrich the nation by the balance of that trade with six hundred thousand pounds. In the first place, I'll grant them that our people at home making use of so much more of our own manufactures, those who were employed in silk, mohair, etc. will get a living by the various preparations of woollen goods. But in the second, I cannot allow that the goods can be sold as formerly. For suppose the half that is worn at home to be sold at the same rate as before: certainly the other half that is sent abroad will want very much of it. For we must send those goods to markets already supplied; and besides that there must be freight, insurance, provision, and all other charges deducted, and the merchants in general must lose much more by this half that is re-shipped, than they got by the half that is consumed here. For though the woollen manufactures are our own product, yet they stand the merchant that ships them off to foreign countries in as much as they do the shopkeeper here that retails them. So that if the returns for what he sends abroad repay him not what his goods cost him here, with all other charges, until he has the money and a good interest for it in cash, the merchant must run out; and the upshot would be, that the merchants in general finding they lost by the Turkish commodities they sent abroad, would ship no more of our manufactures than what would pay for as much silk, mohair, etc. as would be consumed here. Other nations would soon find ways to supply them with as much as we should send short, and somewhere or other to dispose of the goods we should refuse: So that all we should get by this frugality would be that those in Turkey would take but half the quantity of our manufactures of what they do now, while we encourage and wear their merchandises, without which they are not able to purchase ours. . . . (. . .)

What is laid to the charge of luxury besides is that it increases avarice and rapine, and where they are reigning vices, offices of the greatest trust are bought and sold. The ministers that should serve the public, both great and small, corrupted, and the countries every moment in danger of being betrayed to the highest bidders. And lastly, that it effeminates and enervates the people, by which the nations become an easy prey to the first invaders. These are indeed terrible things, but what is put to the account of luxury belongs to male-administration, and is the fault of bad politics. Every government ought to be thoroughly acquainted with and steadfastly to pursue the interest of the country. Good politicians by dexterous management, laying heavy impositions on some goods, or totally prohibiting them, and lowering the duties on others, may always turn and divert the course of trade which way they please. And as they'll ever prefer, if it be equally considerable, the commerce with such countries as can pay with money as well as goods, to those that can make no returns for what they buy, but in the commodities of their own growth and manufactures, so they will always carefully prevent the traffic with such nations as refuse the goods of others, and will take nothing but money for their own. But above all, they'll keep a watchful eye over the balance of trade in general, and never suffer that all the foreign commodities together, that are imported in one year, shall exceed in value what of their own growth or manufacture is in the same exported to others. Note that I speak now of the interest of those nations that have no gold or silver of their own growth, otherwise this maxim need not to be so much insisted on.

If what I urged last be but diligently looked after, and the imports are never allowed to be superior to the exports, no nation can ever be impoverished by foreign luxury; and they may improve it as much as they please, if they can but in proportion raise the fund of their own that is to purchase it.

Trade is the principal, but not the only requisite to aggrandize a nation. There are other things to be taken care of besides. The *Meum* and *Tuum* must be secured, crimes punished, and all other laws concerning

the administration of justice wisely contrived, and strictly executed. Foreign affairs must be likewise prudently managed, and the ministry of every nation ought to have a good intelligence abroad, and be well acquainted with the public transactions of all those countries, that either by their neighborhood, strength or interest, may be hurtful or beneficial to them, to take the necessary measures accordingly, of crossing some and assisting others, as policy and the balance of power direct. The multitude must be awed, no man's conscience forced, and the clergy allowed no greater share in state affairs than our Savior has bequeathed them in his testament. These are the arts that lead to worldly greatness. What sovereign power soever makes a good use of them, that has any considerable nation to govern, whether it be a monarchy, a commonwealth, or a mixture of both, can never fail of making it flourish in spite of all the other powers upon Earth, and no luxury or other vice is ever able to shake their constitution. But here I expect a full-mouthed cry against me. What! Has God never punished and destroyed great nations for their sins? Yes, but not without means, by infatuating their governors, and suffering them to depart from either all or some of those general maxims I have mentioned. And of all the famous states and empires the world has had to boast of hitherto, none ever came to ruin whose destruction was not principally owing to the bad politics, neglects, or mismanagements of the rulers.

There is no doubt but more health and vigor is to be expected among a people, and their offspring, from temperance and sobriety, than there is from gluttony and drunkenness. Yet I confess, that as to luxury's effeminating and enervating a nation, I have not such frightful notions now as I have had formerly. When we hear or read of things which we are altogether strangers to, they commonly bring to our imagination such ideas of what we have seen, as (according to our apprehension) must come the nearest to them. And I remember that when I have read of the luxury of Persia, Egypt, and other countries where it has been a reigning vice, and that were effeminated and enervated by it, it has sometimes put me in mind of the cramming and swilling of ordinary tradesmen at a city feast, and the beastliness their over-gorging themselves is often attended with. At other times it has made me think on the distraction of dissolute sailors, as I had seen them in company of half a dozen lewd women roaring along with fiddles before them. And was I to have been carried into any of their great cities, I would have expected to have found one third of the people sick a-bed with surfeits; another laid up with the gout, or crippled by a more ignominious distemper; and the rest, that could go without leading, walk along the streets in petticoats.

It is happy for us to have fear for a keeper as long as our reason is not strong enough to govern our appetites. And I believe that the great dread I had more particularly against the word, to enervate, and some consequent thoughts on the etymology of it, did me abundance of good when I was a school boy. But since I have seen something of the world the consequences of luxury to a nation seem not so dreadful to me as they did. As long as men have the same appetites, the same vices will remain. In all large societies, some will love whoring and others drinking. The lustful that can get no handsome clean women will content themselves with dirty drabs; and those that cannot purchase true Hermitage or Pontack, will be glad of more ordinary French claret. Those that can't reach wine, take up with worse liquors, and a foot soldier or a beggar may make himself as drunk with stale beer or malt-spirits, as a lord with Burgundy, Champagne or Tokay. The cheapest and most slovenly way of indulging our passions does as much mischief to a man's constitution as the most elegant and expensive.

The greatest excesses of luxury are shown in buildings, furniture, equipages and clothes. Clean linen weakens a man no more than flannel; tapestry, fine painting or good wainscot are no more unwholesome than bare walls; and a rich couch, or a gilt chariot are no more enervating than the cold floor or a country cart. The refined pleasures of men of sense are seldom injurious to their constitution, and there are many great epicures that will refuse to eat or drink more than their heads or stomachs can bear. Sensual people may take as great care of themselves as any. And the errors of the most viciously luxurious don't so much consist in the frequent repetitions of their lewdness, and their eating and drinking too much (which are the things which would most enervate them), as they do in the operose contrivances, the profuseness and nicety they are served with, and the vast expense they are at in their tables and amours.

But let us once suppose that the ease and pleasures the grandees and the rich people of every great nation live in render them unfit to endure hardships and undergo the toils of war. I'll allow that most of the common council of the city would make but very indifferent foot-soldiers; and I believe heartily that if your horse [troops] were to be composed of aldermen, and such as most of them are, a small artillery of squibs would be sufficient to rout them. But what have the aldermen, the common-council, or indeed all people of any substance to do with the war, but to pay taxes? The hardships and fatigues of war that are personally suffered fall upon them that bear the brunt of everything, the meanest indigent part of the nation, the working slaving people. For how excessive soever the plenty and luxury of a nation may be, somebody must do the work, houses

and ships must be built, merchandise must be removed, and the ground tilled. Such a variety of labors in every great nation require a vast multitude, in which there are always loose, idle, extravagant fellows enough to spare for an army. And those that are robust enough to hedge and ditch, plow and thrash, or else not too much enervated to be smiths, carpenters, sawyers, cloth-workers, porters or carmen, will always be strong and hardy enough in a campaign or two to make good soldiers, who, where good orders are kept, have seldom so much plenty and superfluity come to their share as to do them any hurt.

The mischief then to be feared from luxury among the people of war cannot extend itself beyond the officers. The greatest of them are either men of a very high birth and princely education, or else extraordinary parts, and no less experience. And whoever is made choice of by a wise government to command an army *en chef,* should have a consummate knowledge in martial affairs, intrepidity to keep him calm in the midst of danger, and many other qualifications that must be the work of time and application, on men of a quick penetration, a distinguished genius and a world of honor. Strong sinews and supple joints are trifling advantages not regarded in persons of their reach and grandeur that can destroy cities a-bed, and ruin whole countries while they are at dinner. As they are most commonly men of great age, it would be ridiculous to expect a hale constitution and agility of limbs from them. So their heads be but active and well furnished, it is no great matter what the rest of their bodies are. If they cannot bear the fatigue of being on horseback, they may ride in coaches, or be carried in litters. Men's conduct and sagacity are never the less for their being cripples, and the best general the king of France has now can hardly crawl along. Those that are immediately under the chief commanders must be very nigh of the same abilities, and are generally men that have raised themselves to those posts by their merit. The other officers are all of them in their several stations obliged to lay out so large a share of their pay in fine clothes, accoutrements, and other things by the luxury of the times called necessary, that they can spare but little money for debauches. For as they are advanced and their salaries raised, so they are likewise forced to increase their expenses and their equipages, which as well as everything else, must still be proportionable to their quality. By which means the greatest part of them are in a manner hindered from those excesses that might be destructive to health, while their luxury thus turned another way serves moreover to heighten their pride and vanity, the greatest motives to make them behave themselves like what they would be thought to be. . . .

There is nothing refines mankind more than love and honor. Those two passions are equivalent to many virtues, and therefore the greatest schools of breeding and good manners are courts and armies; the first to accomplish the women, the other to polish the men. What the generality of officers among civilized nations affect is a perfect knowledge of the world and the rules of honor. An air of frankness and humanity peculiar to military men of experience, and such a mixture of modesty and undauntedness as may bespeak them both courteous and valiant. Where good sense is fashionable, and a genteel behavior is in esteem, gluttony and drunkenness can be no reigning vices. What officers of distinction chiefly aim at is not a beastly, but a splendid way of living, and the wishes of the most luxurious in their several degrees of quality are to appear handsomely, and excel each other in finery of equipage, politeness of entertainments, and the reputation of a judicious fancy in everything about them.

But if there should be more dissolute reprobates among officers than there are among men of other professions, which is not true, yet the most debauched of them may be very serviceable if they have but a great share of honor. It is this that covers and makes up for a multitude of defects in them, and it is this that none (how abandoned soever they are to pleasure) dare pretend to be without. But as there is no argument so convincing as matter of a fact, let us look back on what so lately happened in our two last wars with France. How many puny young striplings have we had in our armies, tenderly educated, nice in their dress, and curious in their diet, that underwent all manner of duties with gallantry and cheerfulness?

Those that have such dismal apprehensions of luxury's enervating and effeminating people might in Flanders and Spain have seen embroidered beaux with fine laced shirts and powdered wigs stand as much fire, and lead up to the mouth of a cannon, with as little concern as it was possible for the most stinking slovens to have done in their own hair, though it had not been combed in a month; and met with abundance of wild rakes, who had actually impaired their healths, and broken their constitutions with excesses of wine and women, that yet behaved themselves with conduct and bravery against their enemies. Robustness is the least thing required in an officer, and if sometimes strength is of use, a firm resolution of mind, which the hopes of preferment, emulation, and the love of glory inspire them with, will at a push supply the place of bodily force.

Those that understand their business, and have a sufficient sense of honor, as soon as they are used to danger will always be capable officers. Their luxury, as long as they spend nobody's money but their own, will never be prejudicial to a nation.

By all which I think I have proved what I designed in this remark on luxury. First, that in one sense everything may be called so, and in another there is no such thing. Secondly, that with a wise administration all people may swim in as much foreign luxury as their product can purchase, without being impoverished by it. And lastly, that where military affairs are taken care of as they ought, and the soldiers well paid and kept in good discipline, a wealthy nation may live in all the ease and plenty imaginable; and in many parts of it, show as much pomp and delicacy as human wit can invent, and at the same time be formidable to their neighbors, and come up to the character of the bees in the fable, of which I said, that

> *Flatter'd in Peace, and fear'd in Wars,*
> *They were th' Esteem of Foreigners,*
> *And lavish of their Wealth and Lives,*
> *The balance of all other Hives.*

Remark M

And odious Pride a Million more.

Pride is that natural faculty by which every mortal that has any understanding overvalues and imagines better things of himself than any impartial judge, thoroughly acquainted with all his qualities and circumstances, could allow him. We are possessed of no other quality so beneficial to society, and so necessary to render it wealthy and flourishing as this, yet it is that which is most generally detested. What is very peculiar to this faculty of ours is that those who are the fullest of it are the least willing to connive at it in others; whereas the heinousness of other vices is the most extenuated by those who are guilty of them themselves. The chaste man hates fornication, and drunkenness is most abhorred by the temperate; but none are so much offended at their neighbor's pride, as the proudest of all; and if any one can pardon it, it is the most humble: From which I think we may justly infer that it being odious to all the world is a certain sign that all the world is troubled with it. This all men of sense are ready to confess, and nobody denies but that he has pride in general. But, if you come to particulars, you'll meet with few that will own any action you can name of theirs to have proceeded from that principle. There are likewise many who will allow that among the sinful nations of the times, pride and luxury are the great promoters of trade. But they refuse to own the necessity there is that in a more virtuous age (such a one as should be free from pride) trade would in a great measure decay.

The Almighty, they say, has endowed us with the dominion over all things which the Earth and sea produce or contain. There is nothing to be found in either, but what was made for the use of man; and his skill and industry above other animals were given him that he might render both them and everything else within the reach of his senses more serviceable to him. Upon this consideration they think it impious to imagine that humility, temperance, and other virtues, should debar people from the enjoyment of those comforts of life, which are not denied to the most wicked nations. And so [they] conclude, that without pride or luxury, the same things might be eaten, worn, and consumed, the same number of handicrafts and artificers employed, and a nation be every way as flourishing as where those vices are the most predominant.

As to wearing apparel in particular, they'll tell you that pride, which sticks much nearer to us than our clothes, is only lodged in the heart, and that rags often conceal a greater portion of it than the most pompous attire. And that as it cannot be denied but that there have always been virtuous princes, who with humble hearts have worn their splendid diadems, and swayed their envied scepters, void of ambition, for the good of others, so it is very probable that silver and gold brocades, and the richest embroideries may, without a thought of pride, be worn by many whose quality and fortune are suitable to them. May not (say they) a good man of extraordinary revenues make every year a greater variety of suits than it is possible he should wear out, and yet have no other ends than to set the poor at work, to encourage trade, and by employing many, to promote the welfare of his country? And considering food and raiment to be necessities, and the two chief articles to which all our worldly cares are extended, why may not all mankind set aside a considerable part of their income for the one as well as the other, without the least tincture of pride? Nay, is not every member of the society in a manner obliged, according to his ability, to contribute toward the maintenance of that branch of trade on which the whole has so great a dependence? Besides that, to appear decently is a civility, and often a duty, which, without any regard to ourselves, we owe to those we converse with.

These are the objections generally made use of by haughty moralists, who cannot endure to hear the dignity of their species arraigned. But if we look narrowly into them they may soon be answered.

If we had no vices, I cannot see why any man should ever make more suits than he has occasion for, though he was never so desirous of promoting the good of the nation. For though in the wearing of a well-wrought silk, rather than a slight stuff, and the preferring curious fine cloth to coarse, he had no other view but the setting of more people to work, and consequently the public welfare, yet he could consider clothes no otherwise than lovers of their country do taxes now: they may pay them with alacrity, but nobody gives more than his due, especially where all are justly rated according to their abilities, as it could not otherwise be expected in a very virtuous age. Besides, . . . in such golden times nobody would dress above his condition, nobody pinch his family, cheat or overreach his neighbor to purchase finery, and consequently there would not be half the consumption nor a third part of the people employed as now there are. But to make this more plain and demonstrate that for the support of trade there can be nothing equivalent to pride, I shall examine the several views men have in outward apparel, and set forth what daily experience may teach everybody as to dress.

Clothes were originally made for two ends, to hide our nakedness, and to fence our bodies against the weather, and other outward injuries. To these our boundless pride has added a third, which is ornament. For what else but an excess of stupid vanity could have prevailed upon our reason to fancy that ornamental, which must continually put us in mind of our wants and misery, beyond all other animals that are ready clothed by nature herself? It is indeed to be admired how so sensible a creature as man, that pretends to so many fine qualities of his own, should condescend to value himself upon what is robbed from so innocent and defenseless an animal as a sheep, or what he is beholden for to the most insignificant thing upon earth, a dying [silk] worm. Yet while he is proud of such trifling depredations, he has the folly to laugh at the Hottentots on the furthest promontory of Africa, who adorn themselves with the guts of their dead enemies, without considering that they are the ensigns of their valor those barbarians are fine with, the true *Spolia optima* [greatest spoils], and that if their pride be more savage than ours, it is certainly less ridiculous, because they wear the spoils of the more noble animal.

But whatever reflections may be made on this head, the world has long since decided the matter. Handsome apparel is a main point, fine feathers make fine birds, and people, where they are not known, are generally honored according to their clothes and other accoutrements they have about them. From the richness of them we judge of their wealth, and by their ordering of them we guess at their understanding. It is this which encourages everybody who is conscious of his little merit, if he is anyways able, to wear clothes above his rank, especially in large and populous cities, where obscure men may hourly meet with fifty strangers to one acquaintance, and consequently have the pleasure of being esteemed by a vast majority, not as what they are, but what they appear to be: which is a greater temptation than most people want to be vain.

Whoever takes delight in viewing the various scenes of low life may on Easter, Whitsun, and other great holidays, meet with scores of people, especially women, of almost the lowest rank, that wear good and fashionable clothes. If coming to talk with them you treat them more courteously and with greater respect than what they are conscious they deserve, they'll commonly be ashamed of owning what they are. And often you may, if you are a little inquisitive, discover in them a most anxious care to conceal the business they follow, and the places they live in. The reason is plain: while they receive those civilities that are not usually paid them, and which they think only due to their betters, they have the satisfaction to imagine that they appear what they would be, which to weak minds is a pleasure almost as substantial as they could reap from the very accomplishments of their wishes. This golden dream they are unwilling to be disturbed in, and being sure that the meanness of their condition, if it is known, must sink them very low in your opinion, they hug themselves in their disguise, and take all imaginable precaution not to forfeit by a useless discovery the esteem which they flatter themselves that their good clothes have drawn from you.

Though everybody allows that as to apparel and manner of living we ought to behave ourselves suitable to our conditions, and follow the examples of the most sensible and prudent among our equals in rank and fortune, yet how few, that are not either miserably covetous, or else proud of singularity, have this discretion to boast of? We all look above ourselves, and, as fast as we can, strive to imitate those, that some way or other are superior to us.

The poorest laborer's wife in the parish, who scorns to wear a strong wholesome frize [a tightly curled hairdress], as she might, will half-starve herself and her husband to purchase a second-hand gown and petticoat, that cannot do her half the service, because, forsooth, it is more genteel. The weaver, the shoemaker, the tailor, the barber, and every mean working fellow that can set up with little has the impudence with the first money he gets to dress himself like a tradesman of substance. The ordinary retailer in the clothing of his wife takes pattern from his neighbor that deals in the same commodity by wholesale, and the reason he gives for it is, that twelve years ago the other had not a bigger shop than himself. The druggist, mercer, draper, and other creditable shopkeepers can find no difference between themselves and merchants, and therefore dress and live like them. The merchant's lady, who cannot bear the assurance of those mechanics, flies for refuge to the other end of the town, and scorns to follow any fashion but what she takes from thence. This haughtiness alarms the court, the women of quality are frightened to see merchants' wives and daughters dressed like themselves. This impudence of the city, they cry, is intolerable. Mantua-makers are sent for, and the contrivance of fashions becomes all their study, that they may have always new modes ready to take up as soon as those saucy cits [urban citizens] shall begin to imitate those in being. The same emulation is continued through the several degrees of quality to an incredible expense, until at last the prince's great favorites and those of the first rank of all, having nothing else left to outstrip some of their inferiors, are forced to lay out vast estates in pompous equipages, magnificent furniture, sumptuous gardens and princely palaces.

To this emulation and continual striving to outdo one another it is owing, that after so many various shiftings and changings of modes, in trumping up new ones and renewing of old ones, there is still a *plus ultra* left for the ingenious. It is this, or at least the consequence of it, that sets the poor to work, adds spurs to industry, and encourages the skillful artificer to search after further improvements.

It may be objected that many people of good fashion, who have been used to be well dressed, out of custom wear rich clothes with all the indifference imaginable, and that the benefit to trade accruing from them cannot be ascribed to emulation or pride. To this I answer that it is impossible that those who trouble their heads so little with their dress, could ever have worn those rich clothes if both the stuffs and fashions had not been first invented to gratify the vanity of others who took greater delight in fine apparel than they. Besides that, everybody is not without pride that appears to be so. All the symptoms of that vice are not easily discovered. They are manifold, and vary according to the age, humor, circumstances, and often constitution, of the people.

The choleric city captain seems impatient to come to action, and expressing his warlike genius by the firmness of his steps, makes his pike, for want of enemies, tremble at the valor of his arm. His martial finery, as he marches along, inspires him with an unusual elevation of mind, by which endeavoring to forget his shop as well as himself, he looks up at the balconies with the fierceness of a Saracen conqueror; while the phlegmatic alderman, now become venerable both for his age and his authority, contents himself with being thought a considerable man. And knowing no easier way to express his vanity, [he] looks big in his coach, where being known by his paltry livery, he receives, in sullen state, the homage that is paid him by the meaner sort of people.

The beardless ensign counterfeits a gravity above his years, and with ridiculous assurance strives to imitate the stern countenance of his colonel, flattering himself all the while that by his daring mien you'll judge of his prowess. The youthful fair, in a vast concern of being overlooked, by the continual changing of her posture betrays a violent desire of being observed, and catching, as it were, at everybody's eyes, courts with obliging looks the admiration of her beholders. The conceited coxcomb [simpleton], on the contrary, displaying an air of sufficiency, is wholly taken up with the contemplation of his own perfections, and in public places discovers such a disregard to others, that the ignorant must imagine he thinks himself to be alone.

These and such like are all manifest though different tokens of pride that are obvious to all the world. But man's vanity is not always so soon found out. When we perceive an air of humanity, and men seem not to be employed in admiring themselves, nor altogether unmindful of others, we are apt to pronounce them void of pride, when perhaps they are only fatigued with gratifying their vanity, and become languid from a satiety of enjoyments. That outward show of peace within, and drowsy composure of careless negligence, with which a great man is often seen in his plain chariot to loll at ease, are not always so free from art, as they may seem to be. *Nothing is more ravishing to the proud than to be thought happy.*

The well-bred gentleman places his greatest pride in the skill he has of covering it with dexterity, and some are so expert in concealing this frailty that when they are the most guilty of it the vulgar think them the most exempt. . . . Thus the dissembling courtier, when he appears in state, assumes an air of modesty and good humor. And while he is ready to burst with vanity seems to be wholly ignorant of his greatness, well knowing, that those lovely qualities must heighten him in the esteem of others, and be an addition to that grandeur, which the coronets about his coach and harnesses, with the rest of his equipage, cannot fail to proclaim without his assistance.

And as in these, pride is overlooked because industriously concealed, so in others again it is denied that they have any, when they show (or at least seem to show) it in the most public manner. The wealthy parson being, as well as the rest of his profession, debarred from the gaiety of laymen, makes it his business to look out for an admirable black and the finest cloth that money can purchase, and distinguishes himself by the fullness of his noble and spotless garment. His wigs are as fashionable as that form he is forced to comply with will admit of. But as he is only stinted in their shape, so he takes care that for goodness of hair, and color, few noblemen shall be able to match them. His body is ever clean, as well as his clothes, his sleek face is kept constantly shaved, and his handsome nails are diligently pared. His smooth white hand and a brilliant [diamond] of the first water, mutually becoming, honor each other with double graces. What linen he discovers is transparently curious, and he scorns ever to be seen abroad with a worse beaver [hat] than what a rich banker would be proud of on his wedding-day. To all these niceties in dress he adds a majestic gait, and expresses a commanding loftiness in his carriage. Yet common civility, notwithstanding the evidence of so many concurring symptoms, won't allow us to suspect any of his actions to be the result of pride. Considering the dignity of his office, it is only decency in him what would be vanity in others. And in good manners to his calling we ought to believe that the worthy gentleman, without any regard to his reverend person, puts himself to all this trouble and expense merely out of a respect which is due to the divine order he belongs to, and a religious zeal to preserve his holy function from the contempt of scoffers. With all my heart; nothing of all this shall be called pride. Let me only be allowed to say, that to our human capacities it looks very like it.

But if at last I should grant that there are men who enjoy all the fineries of equipage and furniture as well as clothes, and yet have no pride in them, it is certain, that if all should be such, that emulation I spoke of before must cease, and consequently trade, which has so great a dependence upon it, suffer in every branch. For to say that if all men were truly virtuous they might, without any regard to themselves, consume as much out of zeal to serve their neighbors and promote the public good, as they do now out of self-love and emulation, is a miserable shift and an unreasonable supposition. As there have been good people in all ages, so, without doubt, we are not destitute of them in this. But let us enquire of the periwig-makers and tailors, in what gentlemen, even of the greatest wealth and highest quality, they ever could discover such public-spirited views. Ask the lacemen, the mercers, and the linen-drapers whether the richest, and if you will, the most virtuous ladies, if they buy with ready money, or intend to pay in any reasonable time, will not drive from shop to shop to try the market, make as many words, and stand as hard with them to save a groat or sixpence in a yard as the most necessitous jilts in town. If it be urged that if there are not it is possible there might be such people; I answer that it is as possible that cats, instead of killing rats and mice, should feed them, and go about the house to suckle and nurse their young ones; or that a kite should call the hens to their meat, as the cock does, and sit brooding over their chickens instead of devouring them. But if they should all do so, they would cease to be cats and kites. It is inconsistent with their natures, and the species of creatures which now we mean, when we name cats and kites, would be extinct as soon as that could come to pass.

Remark N

Envy it self, and Vanity,
Were Ministers of Industry.

Envy is that baseness in our nature which makes us grieve and pine at what we conceive to be a happiness in others. I don't believe there is a human creature in his senses arrived to maturity that at one time or other has not been carried away by this passion in good earnest. And yet I never met with anyone that dared own he was guilty of it, but in jest. That we are so generally ashamed of this vice is owing to that strong habit of hypocrisy, by the help of which we have learned from our cradle to hide even from ourselves the vast extent of self-love, and all its different branches. It is impossible man should wish better for another than he does for himself, unless where he supposes an impossibility that himself should attain to those wishes. And from hence we may easily learn after what manner this passion is raised in us. In order to [do] it, we are to consider first that as well as we think of ourselves, so ill we often think of our neighbor with equal injustice. And when we apprehend that others do or will enjoy what we think they don't deserve, it afflicts and makes us angry with the cause of that disturbance. Secondly, that we are ever employed in wishing well for ourselves, everyone according to his judgment and inclinations, and when we observe something we like, and yet are destitute of, in the possession of others, it occasions first sorrow in us for not having the thing we like. This sorrow is incurable while we continue our esteem for the thing we want. But as self-defense is restless, and never suffers us to leave any means untried how to remove evil from us, as far and as well as we are able, experience teaches us that nothing in nature more alleviates this sorrow than our anger against those who are possessed of what we esteem and want. This latter passion, therefore, we cherish and cultivate to save or relieve ourselves, at least in part, from the uneasiness we felt from the first.

Envy then is a compound of grief and anger. The degrees of this passion depend chiefly on the nearness or remoteness of the objects as to circumstances. If one who is forced to walk on foot envies a great man for keeping a coach and six, it will never be with that violence or give him that disturbance which it may to a man who keeps a coach himself, but can only afford to drive with four horses. The symptoms of envy are as various, and as hard to describe, as those of the plague. At some time it appears in one shape, at others in another quite different. Among the fair the disease is very common, and the signs of it very conspicuous in their opinions and censures of one another. In beautiful young women you may often discover this faculty to a high degree. They frequently will hate one another mortally at first sight from no other principle than envy. And you may read this scorn, and unreasonable aversion in their very countenances, if they have not a great deal of art, and well learned to dissemble.

In the rude and unpolished multitude this passion is very barefaced; especially when they envy others for the goods of fortune. They rail at their betters, rip up their faults, and take pains to misconstrue their most commendable actions. They murmur at Providence, and loudly complain that the good things of this world are chiefly enjoyed by those who do not deserve them. The grosser sort of them it often affects so violently, that if they were not withheld by the fear of the laws, they would go directly and beat those their envy is leveled at, from no other provocation than what that passion suggests to them.

The men of letters laboring under this distemper discover quite different symptoms. When they envy a person for his parts and erudition, their chief care is industriously to conceal their frailty, which generally is attempted by denying and depreciating the good qualities they envy. They carefully peruse his works, and are displeased with every fine passage they meet with. They look for nothing but his errors, and wish for no greater feast than a gross mistake. In their censures they are captious as well as severe, make mountains of molehills, and will not pardon the least shadow of a fault, but exaggerate the most trifling omission into a capital blunder.

Envy is visible in brute beasts. Horses show it in their endeavors of outstripping one another; and the best spirited will run themselves to death before they'll suffer another before them. In dogs this passion is likewise plainly to be seen. Those who are used to be caressed will never tamely bear that felicity in others. I have seen a lap-dog that would choke himself with victuals rather than leave anything for a competitor of his own kind; and we may often observe the same behavior in those creatures which we daily see in infants that are froward, and by being overfondled made humorsome. If out of caprice they at any time refuse to eat what they have asked for, and we can but make them believe that somebody else, nay, even the cat or the dog is going to take it from them, they will make an end of their oughts with pleasure, and feed even against their appetite.

If envy was not riveted in human nature, it would not be so common in children, and youth would not be so generally spurred on by emulation. Those who would derive everything that is beneficial to the society from a good principle ascribe the effects of emulation in schoolboys to a virtue of the mind. As it requires labor and pains, so it is evident that they commit a self-denial who act from that disposition. But if we look narrowly into it, we shall find that this sacrifice of ease and pleasure is only made to envy, and the love of glory. If there was not something very like this passion mixed with that pretended virtue, it would be impossible to raise and increase it by the same means that create envy. The boy, who receives a reward for the superiority of his performance, is conscious of the vexation it would have been to him, if he should have fallen short of it. This reflection makes him exert himself, not to be outdone by those whom now he looks upon as his inferiors, and the greater his pride is, the more self-denial he'll practice to maintain his conquest. The other, who, in spite of the pains he took to do well, has missed of the prize, is sorry, and consequently angry with him whom he must look upon as the cause of his grief. But to show this anger would be ridiculous, and of no service to him, so that he must either be contented to be less esteemed than the other boy; or by renewing his endeavors become a greater proficient. And it is ten to one, but the disinterested, good-humored, and peaceable lad will choose the first, and so become indolent and inactive, while the covetous, peevish, and quarrelsome rascal shall take incredible pains, and make himself a conqueror in his turn. . . . (. . .)

Married women, who are guilty of this vice, which few are not, are always endeavoring to raise the same passion in their spouses. And where they have prevailed, envy and emulation have kept more men in bounds, and reformed more ill husbands from sloth, from drinking and other evil courses, than all the sermons that have been preached since the time of the Apostles.

As everybody would be happy, enjoy pleasure and avoid pain if he could, so self-love bids us look on every creature that seems satisfied as a rival in happiness. And the satisfaction we have in seeing that felicity disturbed, without any advantage to ourselves but what springs from the pleasure we have in beholding it, is called loving mischief for mischief's sake; and the motive of which that frailty is the result, malice, another off-spring derived from the same original. For if there was no envy there could be no malice. When the passions lie dormant we have no apprehension of them, and often people think they have not such a frailty in their nature because that moment they are not affected with it.

A gentleman well-dressed, who happens to be dirtied all over by a coach or a cart, is laughed at, and by his inferiors much more than his equals because they envy him more. They know he is vexed at it, and imagining him to be happier than themselves, they are glad to see him meet with displeasures in his turn. But a young lady, if she be in a serious mood, instead of laughing at, pities him, because a clean man is a sight she takes delight in, and there is no room for envy. At disasters, we either laugh, or pity those that befall them, according to the stock we are possessed of either of malice or compassion. If a man falls or hurts himself so slightly that it moves not the latter, we laugh, and here our pity and malice shake us alternately: "Indeed, sir, I am very sorry for it, I beg your pardon for laughing, I am the silliest creature in the world," then laugh again; and again, "I am indeed very sorry," and so on. Some are so malicious they would laugh if a man broke his leg, and others are so compassionate that they can heartily pity a man for the least spot in his clothes. But nobody is so savage that no compassion can touch him, nor any man so good-natured as never to be affected with any malicious pleasure. How strangely our passions govern us! We envy a man for being rich, and then perfectly hate him. But if we come to be his equals, we are calm, and the least condescension in him makes us friends; but if we become visibly superior to him we can pity his misfortunes. The reason why men of true good sense envy less than others is because they admire themselves with less hesitation than fools and silly people. For though they do not show this to others, yet the solidity of their thinking gives them an assurance of their real worth, which men of weak understanding can never feel within, though they often counterfeit it. . . . (. . .)

Love in the first place signifies affection, such as parents and nurses bear to children, and friends to one another. It consists in a liking and well-wishing to the person beloved. We give an easy construction to his words and actions, and feel a proneness to excuse and forgive his faults, if we see any. His interest we make on all accounts our own, even to our prejudice, and receive an inward satisfaction for sympathizing with him in his sorrows, as well as joys. What I said last is not impossible, whatever it may seem to be: for when we are sincere in sharing with another in his misfortunes, self-love makes us believe that the sufferings we feel must alleviate and lessen those of our friend, and while this fond reflection is soothing our pain, a secret pleasure arises from our grieving for the person we love.

Secondly, by love we understand a strong inclination, in its nature distinct from all other affections of friendship, gratitude, and consanguinity, that persons of different sexes, after liking, bear to one another. It is in this signification that love enters into the compound of jealousy, and is the effect as well as happy disguise of that passion that prompts us to labor for the preservation of our species. This latter appetite is innate both in men and women, who are not defective in their formation, as much as hunger or thirst, though they are seldom affected with it before the years of puberty. Could we undress nature, and pry into her deepest recesses, we should discover the seeds of this passion before it exerts itself as plainly as we see the teeth in an embryo before the gums are formed. There are few healthy people of either sex, whom it has made no impression upon before twenty. Yet, as the peace and happiness of the civil society require that this should be kept a secret never to be talked of in public, so among well-bred people it is counted highly criminal to mention before company anything in plain words that is relating to this mystery of succession. By which means the very name of the appetite, though the most necessary for the continuance of mankind, is become odious, and the proper epithets commonly joined to lust are filthy and abominable.

This impulse of nature in people of strict morals and rigid modesty often disturbs the body for a considerable time before it is understood or known to be what it is, and it is remarkable that the most polished and best instructed are generally the most ignorant as to this affair. And here I can but observe the difference between man in the wild state of nature and the same creature in the civil society. In the first, men and women, if left rude and untaught in the sciences of modes and manners, would quickly find out the cause of that disturbance, and be at a loss no more than other animals for a present remedy: Besides that, it is not probable they would want either precept or example from the more experienced. But in the second, where the rules of religion, law and decency are to be followed, and obeyed before any dictates of nature, the youth of both sexes are to be armed and fortified against this impulse, and from their infancy artfully frightened from the most remote approaches of it. The appetite itself, and all the symptoms of it, though they are plainly felt and understood, are to be stifled with care and severity, and in women flatly disowned, and if there be occasion, with obstinacy denied, even when themselves are visibly affected by them. If it throws them into distempers, they must be cured by physic, or else patiently bear them in silence. And it is the interest of the society to preserve decency and politeness; that women should linger, waste, and die, rather than relieve themselves in an unlawful manner. And among the fashionable part of mankind, the people of birth and fortune, it is expected that matrimony should never be entered upon without a curious regard to family, estate, and reputation, and in the making of matches the call of nature be the very last consideration.

Those then who would make love and lust synonymous confound the effect with the cause of it. Yet such is the force of education, and a habit of thinking as we are taught, that sometimes persons of either sex are actually in love without feeling any carnal desires, or penetrating into the intentions of nature, the end proposed by her without which they could never have been affected with that sort of passion. That there are such [persons] is certain, but many more whose pretenses to those refined notions are only upheld by art and dissimulation. Those who are really such Platonic lovers are commonly the pale-faced weakly people of cold and phlegmatic constitutions in either sex. The hale and robust of bilious temperament and a sanguine complexion never entertain any love so spiritual as to exclude all thoughts and wishes that relate to the body. But if the most seraphic lovers would know the original of their inclination, let them but suppose that another should have the corporal enjoyment of the person beloved, and by the tortures they'll suffer from that reflection they will soon discover the nature of their passions. Whereas, on the contrary, parents and friends receive a satisfaction in reflecting on the joys and comforts of a happy marriage, to be tasted by those they wish well to.

The curious that are skilled in anatomizing the invisible part of man will observe that the more sublime and exempt this love is from all thoughts of sensuality, the more spurious it is, and the more it degenerates from its honest original and primitive simplicity. The power and sagacity as well as labor and care of the politician in civilizing the society has been nowhere more conspicuous than in the happy contrivance of playing our passions against one another. By flattering our pride and still increasing the good opinion we have of ourselves on the one hand, and inspiring us on the other with a superlative dread and mortal aversion against shame, the artful moralists have taught us cheerfully to encounter ourselves, and if not subdue, at least so to conceal and disguise our darling passion, lust, that we scarce know it when we meet with it in our own breasts. Oh! the mighty prize we have in view for all our self-denial! Can any man be so serious as to abstain from laughter when he considers that for so much deceit and insincerity practiced upon ourselves as well as others, we have no other recompense than the vain satisfaction of making our species appear more exalted and remote from that of other animals than it really is, and we in our consciences know it to be? Yet this is fact, and in it we plainly perceive the reason why it was necessary to render odious every word or action by which we might discover the innate desire we feel to perpetuate our kind, and why tamely to submit to the violence of a furious appetite (which it is painful to resist) and innocently to obey the most pressing demand of nature without guile or hypocrisy, like other creatures, should be branded with the ignominious name of brutality.

What we call love, then, is not a genuine, but an adulterated appetite, or rather a compound, a heap of several contradictory passions blended in one. As it is a product of nature warped by custom and education, so the true origin and first motive of it, as I have hinted already, is stifled in well-bred people, and almost concealed from themselves. All which is the reason that as those affected with it vary in age, strength, resolution, temper, circumstances, and manners, the effects of it are so different, whimsical, surprising and unaccountable.

It is this passion that makes jealousy so troublesome, and the envy of it often so fatal. Those who imagine that there may be jealousy without love do not understand that passion. Men may not have the least affection for their wives, and yet be angry with them for their conduct, and suspicious of them either with or without a cause. But what in such cases affects them is their pride, the concern for their reputation. They feel a hatred against them without remorse. When they are outrageous, they can beat them and go to sleep contentedly. Such husbands may watch their dames themselves, and have them observed by others. But their vigilance is not so intense; they are not so inquisitive or industrious in their searches, neither do they feel that anxiety of heart at the fear of a discovery, as when love is mixed with the passions.

What confirms me in this opinion is that we never observe this behavior between a man and his mistress. For when his love is gone and he suspects her to be false, he leaves her, and troubles his head no more about her. Whereas it is the greatest difficulty imaginable, even to a man of sense, to part with a mistress as long as he loves her, whatever faults she may be guilty of. If in his anger he strikes her he is uneasy after it. His love makes him reflect on the hurt he has done her, and he wants to be reconciled to her again. He may talk of hating her, and many times from his heart wish her hanged, but if he cannot get entirely rid of his frailty, he can never disentangle himself from her. Though she is represented in the most monstrous guilt to his imagination, and he has resolved and swore a thousand times never to come near her again, there is no trusting him. Even when he is fully convinced of her infidelity, if his love continues, his despair is never so lasting, but between the blackest fits of it he relents, and finds lucid intervals of hope. He forms excuses for her, thinks of pardoning, and in order to [do] it racks his invention for possibilities that may make her appear less criminal.

Remark O

Real Pleasures, Comforts, Ease.

That the highest good consisted in pleasure was the doctrine of Epicurus, who yet led a life exemplary for continence, sobriety, and other virtues, which made people of the succeeding ages quarrel about the significance of pleasure. Those who argued from the temperance of the philosopher said that the delight Epicurus meant was being virtuous. So Erasmus in his *Colloquies* tells us that there are no greater Epicures than pious Christians. Others that reflected on the dissolute manners of the greatest part of his followers would have it, that by pleasures he could have understood nothing but sensual ones, and the gratification of our passions. I shall not decide their quarrel, but am of opinion, that whether men be good or bad, what they take delight in is their pleasure, and not to look out for any further etymology from the learned languages, I believe an Englishman may justly call everything a pleasure that pleases him, and according to this definition we ought to dispute no more about men's pleasures than their tastes: *Trahit sua quemque voluptas.* [Each is drawn to his own pleasure. (Virgil)].

The worldly-minded, voluptuous and ambitious man, notwithstanding he is void of merit, covets precedence everywhere, and desires to be dignified above his betters. He aims at spacious palaces and delicious gardens. His chief delight is in excelling others in stately horses, magnificent coaches, a numerous attendance, and dear-bought furniture. To gratify his lust, he wishes for genteel, young, beautiful women of different charms and complexions that shall adore his greatness, and be really in love with his person. His cellars he would have stored with the flower of every country that produces excellent wines. His table he desires may be served with many courses, and each of them contain a choice variety of dainties not easily purchased, and ample evidences of elaborate and judicious cookery, while harmonious music and well-couched flattery entertain his hearing by turns. He employs, even in the meanest trifles, none but the ablest and most ingenious workmen, that his judgment and fancy may as evidently appear in the least things that belong to him, as his wealth and quality are manifested in those of greater value. He desires to have several sets of witty, facetious, and polite people to converse with, and among them he would have some famous for learning and universal knowledge. For his serious affairs, he wishes to find men of parts and experience, that should be diligent and faithful. Those that are to wait on him he would have handy, mannerly and discreet, of comely aspect, and a graceful mien. What he requires in them besides is a respectful care of everything that is his, nimbleness without hurry, dispatch without noise, and an unlimited obedience to his orders. Nothing he thinks more troublesome than speaking to servants; wherefore he will only be attended by such, as by observing his looks have learned to interpret his will from his slightest motions. He loves to see an elegant nicety in everything that approaches him, and in what is to be employed about his person he desires a superlative cleanliness to be religiously observed. The chief officers of his household he would have to be men of birth, honor and distinction, as well as order, contrivance and economy. For though he loves to be honored by everybody, and receives the respects of the common people with joy, yet the homage that is paid him by persons of quality is ravishing to him in a more transcendent manner.

While thus wallowing in a sea of lust and vanity, he is wholly employed in provoking and indulging his appetites. He desires the world should think him altogether free from pride and sensuality, and put a favorable construction upon his most glaring vices. Nay, if his authority can purchase it, he covets to be thought wise, brave, generous, good-natured, and endued with all the virtues he thinks worth having. He would have us believe that the pomp and luxury he is served with are as many tiresome plagues to him, and [that] all the grandeur he appears in is an ungrateful burden, which, to his sorrow, is inseparable from the high sphere he moves in; that his noble mind, so much exalted above vulgar capacities, aims at higher ends, and cannot relish such worthless enjoyments; that the highest of his ambition is to promote the public welfare, and his greatest pleasure to see his country flourish, and everybody in it made happy. These are called real pleasures by the vicious and earthly-minded, and whoever is able, either by his skill or fortune, after this refined manner at once to enjoy the world, and the good opinion of it, is counted extremely happy by all the most fashionable part of the people.

But on the other side, most of the ancient philosophers and grave moralists, especially the Stoics, would not allow anything to be a real good that was liable to be taken from them by others. They wisely considered the instability of fortune and the favor of princes, the vanity of honor, and popular applause; the precariousness of riches and all earthly possessions. Therefore, [they] placed true happiness in the calm serenity of a contented mind free from guilt and ambition; a mind, that, having subdued every sensual appetite, despises the smiles as well as frowns of fortune, and taking no delight but in contemplation, desires nothing but what everybody is able to give to himself: a mind, that armed with fortitude and resolution has learned to sustain the greatest losses without concern, to endure pain without affliction, and to bear injuries without resentment. Many have owned themselves arrived to this height of self-denial, and then, if we may believe them, they were raised above common mortals, and their strength extended vastly beyond the pitch of their first nature. They could behold the anger of threatening tyrants and the most imminent dangers without terror, and preserved their tranquillity in the midst of torments. Death itself they could meet with intrepidity, and left the world with no greater reluctance than they had showed fondness at their entrance into it.

These among the ancients have always borne the greatest sway. Yet others that were no fools neither have exploded those precepts as impracticable, called their notions romantic, and endeavored to prove that what these Stoics asserted of themselves exceeded all human force and possibility, and that therefore the virtues they boasted of could be nothing but haughty pretense, full of arrogance and hypocrisy. Yet notwithstanding these censures, the serious part of the world, and the generality of wise men that have lived ever since to this day, agree with the Stoics in the most material points. As that there can be no true felicity in what depends on things perishable, that peace within is the greatest blessing, and no conquest like that of our passions; that knowledge, temperance, fortitude, humility, and other embellishments of the mind are the most valuable acquisitions; that no man can be happy but he that is good; and that the virtuous are only capable of enjoying real pleasures.

I expect to be asked why in the fable I have called those pleasures real that are directly opposite to those which I own the wise men of all ages have extolled as the most valuable. My answer is, because I don't call things pleasures which men say are best, but such as they seem to be most pleased with. How can I believe that a man's chief delight is in the embellishments of the mind when I see him ever employed about and daily pursue the pleasures that are contrary to them? John never cuts any pudding, but just enough that you can't say he took none. This little bit, after much chomping and chewing, you see goes down with him like chopped hay. After that he falls upon the beef with a voracious appetite, and crams himself up to his throat. Is it not provoking to hear John cry every day that pudding is all his delight, and that he doesn't value the beef of a farthing?

I could swagger about fortitude and the contempt of riches as much as Seneca himself, and would undertake to write twice as much in behalf of poverty as ever he did, for the tenth part of his estate. I could teach the way to his *Summum bonum* as exactly as I know my way home. I could tell people that to extricate themselves from all worldly engagements, and to purify the mind, they must divest themselves of their passions, as men take out the furniture when they would clean a room thoroughly. And I am clearly of the opinion that the malice and most severe strokes of fortune can do no more injury to a mind thus stripped of all fears, wishes and inclinations, than a blind horse can do in an empty barn. In the theory of all this I am very perfect, but the practice is very difficult; and if you went about picking my pocket, offered to take the victuals from before me when I am hungry, or made but the least motion of spitting in my face, I dare not promise how philosophically I should behave myself. But that I am forced to submit to every caprice of my unruly nature, you'll say, is no argument that others are as little masters of theirs, and therefore I am willing to pay adoration to virtue wherever I can meet with it, with a proviso that I shall not be obliged to admit any as such, where I can see no self-denial, or to judge of men's sentiments from their words, where I have their lives before me. . . . (. . .)

[But consider:] when we see so many of the clergy, to indulge their lust, a brutish appetite, run themselves after this manner upon an inevitable poverty, which unless they could bear it with greater fortitude than they discover in all their actions, must of necessity make them contemptible to all the world, what credit must we give them, when they pretend that they conform themselves to the world, not because they take delight in the several decencies, conveniences, and ornaments of it, but only to preserve their function from contempt, in order to be more useful to others? Have we not reason to believe, that what they say is full of hypocrisy and falsehood, and that concupiscence is not the only appetite they want to gratify; that the haughty airs and quick sense of injuries, the curious elegance in dress, and niceness of palate, to be observed in most of them that are able to show them, are the results of pride and luxury in them as they are in other people, and that the clergy are not possessed of more intrinsic virtue than any other profession?

I am afraid that by this time I have given many of my readers a real displeasure, by dwelling so long upon the reality of pleasure. But I can't help it, there is one thing comes into my head to corroborate what I have urged already, which I can't forbear mentioning. It is this: those who govern others throughout the world are at least as wise as the people that are governed by them, generally speaking. If for this reason we would take pattern from our superiors, we have but to cast our eyes on all the courts and governments in the universe, and we shall soon perceive from the actions of the great ones, which opinion they side with, and what pleasures those in the highest stations of all seem to be most fond of. For if it be allowable at all to judge of people's inclinations from their manner of living, none can be less injured by it than those who are the most at liberty to do as they please.

If the great ones of the clergy as well as the laity of any country whatever had no value for earthly pleasures, and did not endeavor to gratify their appetites, why are envy and revenge so raging among them, and all the other passions improved and refined upon in courts of princes more than anywhere else; and why are their repasts, their recreations, and whole manner of living always such as are approved of, coveted, and imitated by the most sensual people of that same country? If despising all visible decorations they were only in love with the embellishments of the mind, why should they borrow so many of the implements, and make use of the most darling toys of the luxurious? Why should a lord-treasurer, or a bishop, or even the Grand Seignior, or the Pope of Rome, to be good and virtuous, and endeavor the conquest of his passions, have occasion for greater revenues, richer furniture, or a more numerous attendance, as to personal service, than a private man? What virtue is it the exercise of which requires so much pomp and superfluity, as are to be seen by all men in power? A man has as much opportunity to practice temperance, that has but one dish at a meal, as he that is constantly served with three courses and a dozen dishes in each. One may exercise as much patience, and be as full of self-denial on a few flocks, without curtains or tester, as in a velvet bed that is sixteen foot high. The virtuous possessions of the mind are neither [a] charge nor [a] burden. A man may bear misfortunes with fortitude in a garret, forgive injuries afoot, and be chaste, though he has not a shirt to his back. And therefore I shall never believe but that an indifferent skuller [thinker], if he was entrusted with it, might carry all the learning and religion that one man can contain, as well as a barge with six oars, especially if it was but to cross from Lambeth to Westminster; or that humility is so ponderous a virtue, that it requires six horses to draw it. . . . (. . .)

But let us grant that the eyes of the nobility are to be dazzled with a gaudy outside. If virtue was the chief delight of great men, why should their extravagance be extended to things not understood by the mob, and wholly removed from public view: I mean their private diversions, the pomp and luxury of the dining room and the bed-chamber, and the curiosities of the closet? Few of the vulgar know that there is wine of a guinea the bottle, that birds no bigger than larks are often sold for half a guinea apiece, or that a single picture may be worth several thousand pounds. Besides, is it to be imagined that unless it was to please their own appetites men should put themselves to such vast expenses for a political show, and be so solicitous to gain the esteem of those whom they so much despise in everything else? If we allow that the splendor and all the elegance of a court are insipid, and only tiresome to the prince himself, and are altogether made use of to preserve royal majesty from contempt, can we say the same of half a dozen illegitimate children, most of them the offspring of adultery by the same majesty, got, educated, and made princes at the expense of the nation? Therefore it is evident that this awing of the multitude by a distinguished manner of living is only a cloak and pretense, under which great men would shelter their vanity, and indulge every appetite about them without reproach.

A burgomeister of Amsterdam in his plain black suit, followed perhaps by one footman, is fully as much respected and better obeyed than a Lord Mayor of London with all his splendid equipage and great train of attendance. Where there is a real power it is ridiculous to think that any temperance or austerity of life should ever render the person in whom that power is lodged contemptible in his office, from an emperor to the beadle of a parish. Cato in his government of Spain, in which he acquitted himself with so much glory, had only three servants to attend him. Do we hear that any of his orders were ever slighted for this, notwithstanding that he loved his bottle? And when that great man marched on foot through the scorching sands of Libya, and parched up with thirst, refused to touch the water that was brought him before all his soldiers had drunk, do we ever read that this heroic forbearance weakened his authority, or lessened him in the esteem of his army? But what need we go so far off? There has not these many ages been a prince less inclined to pomp and luxury than the present King of Sweden [Charles XII], who enamoured with the title of hero, has not only sacrificed the lives of his subjects, and welfare of his dominions, but (what is more uncommon in sovereigns) his own ease, and all the comforts of life, to an implacable spirit of revenge. Yet he is obeyed to the ruin of his people in obstinately maintaining a war that has almost utterly destroyed his kingdom.

Thus I have proved that the real pleasures of all men in nature are worldly and sensual, if we judge from their practice. I say all men in nature, because devout Christians, who alone are to be excepted here, being regenerated, and preternaturally assisted by the Divine Grace, cannot be said to be in nature. How strange it is that they should all so unanimously deny it! Ask not only the divines and moralists of every nation, but likewise all that are rich and powerful, about real pleasure, and they'll tell you, with the Stoic, that there can be no true felicity in things mundane and corruptible. But then look upon their lives, and you will find they take delight in no other.

What must we do in this dilemma? Shall we be so uncharitable as judging from men's actions to say that all the world prevaricates, and that this is not their opinion, let them talk what they will? Or shall we be so silly, as relying on what they say, to think them sincere in their sentiments, and so not believe our own eyes? Or shall we rather endeavor to believe ourselves and them too, and say with Montaigne, that they imagine, and are fully persuaded, that they believe what yet they do not believe? These are his words: "*Some impose on the world, and would be thought to believe what they really don't: but much the greater number impose upon themselves, not considering nor thoroughly apprehending what it is to believe.*" But this is making all mankind either fools or impostors, which to avoid, there is nothing left us, but to say what Mr. Bayle has endeavored to prove at large in his reflections on comets: that man is so unaccountable a creature as to act most commonly against his principle; and this is so far from being injurious, that it is a compliment to human nature, for we must say either this or worse.

This contradiction in the frame of man is the reason that the theory of virtue is so well understood, and the practice of it so rarely to be met with. If you ask me where to look for those beautiful shining qualities of prime ministers, and the great favorites of princes that are so finely painted in dedications, addresses, epitaphs, funeral sermons and inscriptions, I answer there, and nowhere else. Where would you look for the excellency of a statue, but in that part which you see of it? It is the polished outside only that has the skill and labor of the sculptor to boast of. What's out of sight is untouched. Would you break the head or cut open the breast to look for the brains or the heart, you'd only show your ignorance, and destroy the workmanship. This has often made me compare the virtues of great men to your large china jars. They make a fine show, and are ornamental even to a chimney. One would by the bulk they appear in, and the value that is set upon them, think they might be very useful; but look into a thousand of them, and you'll find nothing in them but dust and cobwebs.

Remark Q

————*for frugally*
They now liv'd on their Salary:

When people have small comings in, and are honest withal, it is then that the generality of them begin to be frugal, and not before. Frugality in ethics is called that virtue from the principle of which men abstain from superfluities, and despising the operose contrivances of art to procure either ease or pleasure, content themselves with the natural simplicity of things, and are carefully temperate in the enjoyment of them without any tincture of covetousness. Frugality thus limited is perhaps scarcer than many may imagine; but what is generally understood by it is a quality more often to be met with, and consists in a medium between profuseness and avarice, rather leaning to the latter. As this prudent economy, which some people call saving, is in private families the most certain method to increase an estate, so some imagine that whether a country be barren or fruitful, the same method, if generally pursued (which they think practicable) will have the same effect upon a whole nation, and that, for example, the English might be much richer than they are, if they would be as frugal as some of their neighbors. This, I think, is an error, which to prove I shall first refer the reader to what has been said upon this head in Remark L and then go on thus.

Experience teaches us, first, that as people differ in their views and perceptions of things, so they vary in their inclinations. One man is given to covetousness, another to prodigality, and a third is only saving. Secondly, that men are never, or at least very seldom, reclaimed from their darling passions, either by reason or precept, and that if anything ever draws them from what they [have a] natural propensity to [do], it must be a change in their circumstances or their fortunes. If we reflect upon these observations, we shall find that to render the generality of a nation lavish, the product of the country must be considerable in proportion to the inhabitants, and what they are profuse of cheap. On the contrary, to make a nation generally frugal, the necessities of life must be scarce, and consequently dear. Therefore, let the best politician do what he can, the profuseness or frugality of a people in general must always depend upon, and will in spite of his teeth, be ever proportional to the fruitfulness and product of the country, the number of inhabitants, and the taxes they are to bear. If anybody would refute what I have said, let him only prove from history that there ever was in any country a national frugality without a national necessity.

Let us examine then what things are requisite to aggrandize and enrich a nation. The first desirable blessings for any society of men are a fertile soil and a happy climate, a mild government, and more land than people. These things will render man easy, loving, honest and sincere. In this condition they may be as virtuous as they can without the least injury to the public, and consequently as happy as they please themselves. But they shall have no arts or sciences, or be quiet longer than their neighbors will let them. They must be poor, ignorant, and almost wholly destitute of what we call the comforts of life, and all the cardinal virtues together won't so much as procure a tolerable coat or a porridge-pot among them. For in this state of slothful ease and stupid innocence, as you need not fear great vices, so you must not expect any considerable virtues. Man never exerts himself but when he is roused by his desires. While they lie dormant, and there is nothing to raise them, his excellence and abilities will be forever undiscovered, and the lumpish machine, without the influence of his passions, may be justly compared to a huge windmill without a breath of air.

Would you render a society of men strong and powerful, you must touch their passions. Divide the land, though there be never so much to spare, and their possessions will make them covetous. Rouse them, though but in jest, from their idleness with praises, and pride will set them to work in earnest. Teach them trades and handicrafts, and you'll bring envy and emulation among them. To increase their numbers, set up a variety of manufactures, and leave no ground uncultivated; let property be inviolably secured, and privileges equal to all men; suffer nobody to act but what is lawful, and everybody to think what he pleases. For a country where everybody may be maintained that will be employed, and the other maxims are observed, must always be thronged and can never want people, as long as there is any in the world. Would you have them bold and warlike, turn to military discipline, make good use of their fear, and flatter their vanity with art and assiduity. But would you moreover render them an opulent, knowing and polite nation, teach them commerce with foreign countries, and if possible get into the sea, which to compass spare no labor nor industry, and let no difficulty deter you from it. Then promote navigation, cherish the merchant, and encourage trade in every branch of it. This will bring riches, and where they are, arts and sciences will soon follow, and by the help of what I have named and good management, it is that politicians can make a people potent, renowned and flourishing.

But would you have a frugal and honest society, the best policy is to preserve men in their native simplicity, strive not to increase their numbers. Let them never be acquainted with strangers or superfluities, but remove and keep from them everything that might raise their desires, or improve their understanding.

Great wealth and foreign treasure will ever scorn to come among men, unless you'll admit their inseparable companions, avarice and luxury. Where trade is considerable fraud will intrude. To be at once well-bred and sincere is no less than a contradiction; and therefore while man advances in knowledge, and his manners are polished, we must expect to see at the same time his desires enlarged, his appetites refined, and his vices increased. . . . (. . .)

The Dutch generally endeavor to promote as much frugality among their subjects as it is possible, not because it is a virtue, but because it is, generally speaking, their interest. . . . For as this latter changes, so they alter their maxims, as will be plain in the following instance.

As soon as their East India ships come home, the company pays off the men, and many of them receive the greatest part of what they have been earning in seven or eight, and some fifteen or sixteen years' time. These poor fellows are encouraged to spend their money with all profuseness imaginable. And considering that most of them, when they set out at first, were reprobates, that under the tuition of a strict discipline, and a miserable diet, have been so long kept at hard labor without money, in the midst of danger, it cannot be difficult to make them lavish as soon as they have plenty.

They squander away in wine, women and music, as much as people of their taste and education are well capable of, and are suffered (so they but abstain from doing of mischief) to revel and riot with greater licentiousness than is customary to be allowed to others. You may in some cities see them accompanied with three or four lewd women, few of them sober, run roaring through the streets by broad daylight with a fiddler before them. And if the money, to their thinking, goes not fast enough these ways, they'll find out others, and sometimes fling it among the mob by handfuls. This madness continues in most of them while they have anything left, which never lasts long, and for this reason, by a nickname, they are called Lords of Six Weeks, that being generally the time by which the company has other ships ready to depart, when these infatuated wretches (their money being gone) are forced to enter themselves again, and may have leisure to repent their folly.

In this stratagem there is a double policy. First, if these sailors that have been inured to the hot climates and unwholesome air and diet, should be frugal, and stay in their own country, the company would be continually obliged to employ fresh men, of which (besides that they are not so fit for their business) hardly one in two ever lives in some places of the East-Indies, which would often prove a great charge as well as disappointment to them. The second is that the large sums so often distributed among those sailors are by this means made immediately to circulate throughout the country, from whence, by heavy excises and other impositions, the greatest part of it is soon drawn back into the public treasure.

To convince the champions for national frugality by another argument, that what they urge is impracticable, we'll suppose that I am mistaken in everything which in Remark L I have said in behalf of luxury, and the necessity of it to maintain trade. After that let us examine what a general frugality, if it was by art and management to be forced upon people whether they have occasion for it or not, would produce in such a nation as ours. We'll grant then that all the people in Great Britain shall consume but four-fifths of what they do now, and so lay by one-fifth part of their income. I shall not speak of what influence this would have upon almost every trade, as well as the farmer, the grazier and the landlord, but favorably suppose (what is yet impossible) that the same work shall be done, and consequently the same handicrafts be employed as there are now. The consequence would be that unless money should all at once fall prodigiously in value, and everything else, contrary to reason, grow very dear, at the five years' end all the working people, and the poorest of laborers (for I won't meddle with any of the rest) would be worth in ready cash as much as they now spend in a whole year; which, by the by, would be more money than ever the nation had at once.

Let us now, overjoyed with this increase of wealth, take a view of the condition the working people would be in, and reasoning from experience, and what we daily observe of them, judge what their behavior would be in such a case. Everybody knows that there is a vast number of journeymen weavers, tailors, clothworkers, and twenty other handicrafts who, if by four days' labor in a week they can maintain themselves, will hardly be persuaded to work the fifth. [Also,] there are thousands of laboring men of all sorts, who will, though they can hardly subsist, put themselves to fifty inconveniences, disoblige their masters, pinch their bellies, and run in debt, to make holidays. When men show such an extraordinary proclivity to idleness and pleasure what reason have we to think that they would ever work, unless they were obliged to it by immediate necessity? When we see an artificer that cannot be driven to his work before Tuesday, because the Monday morning he has two shillings left of his last week's pay; why should we imagine he would go to it at all, if he had fifteen or twenty pounds in his pocket? (. . .)

The great art then to make a nation happy and what we call flourishing consists in giving everybody an opportunity of being employed, which to compass, let a government's first care be to promote as great a variety of manufactures, arts, and handicrafts as human wit can invent. And the second to encourage agriculture and fishery in all their branches, that the whole Earth may be forced to exert itself as well as man. For as the one is an infallible maxim to draw vast multitudes of people into a nation, so the other is the only method to maintain them.

It is from this policy, and not the trifling regulations of lavishness and frugality, (which will ever take their own course, according to the circumstances of the people) that the greatness and felicity of nations must be expected. For let the value of gold and silver either rise or fall, the enjoyment of all societies will ever depend upon the fruits of the Earth, and the labor of the people, both which joined together are a more certain, a more inexhaustible, and a more real treasure, than the gold of Brazil, or the silver of [the] Potosi [silver mines in Peru].

Remark T

————*To live great,*
Had made her Husband rob the State.

What our common rogues when they are going to be hanged chiefly complain of as the cause of their untimely end is, next to the neglect of the Sabbath, their having kept company with ill women, meaning whores. And I don't question but that among the lesser villains many venture their necks to indulge and satisfy their low amours. But the words that have given occasion to this remark may serve to hint to us that among the great ones men are often put upon such dangerous projects, and forced into such pernicious measures by their wives, as the most subtle mistress never could have persuaded them to. I have shown already that the worst of women and most profligate of the sex did contribute to the consumption of superfluities, as well as the necessities of life, and consequently were beneficial to many peaceable drudges, that work hard to maintain their families, and have no worse design than an honest livelihood. "Let them be banished notwithstanding," says a good man. "When every strumpet is gone, and the land wholly freed from lewdness, God Almighty will pour such blessings upon it as will vastly exceed the profits that are now got by harlots." This perhaps would be true, but I can make it evident, that with or without prostitutes nothing could make amends for the detriment trade would sustain, if all those of that sex, who enjoy the happy state of matrimony, should act and behave themselves as a sober wise man could wish them.

The variety of work that is performed, and the number of hands employed to gratify the fickleness and luxury of women is prodigious. And if only the married ones should hearken to reason and just remonstrances, think themselves sufficiently answered with the first refusal, and never ask a second time what had been once denied them; if, I say, married women would do this, and then lay out no money but what their husbands knew and freely allowed of, the consumption of a thousand things they now make use of would be lessened by at least a fourth part. Let us go from house to house and observe the way of the world only among the middling people, creditable shopkeepers, that spend two or three hundred [pounds] a year, and we shall find the women when they have half a score suits of clothes, two or three of them not the worse for wearing, will think it a sufficient plea for new ones, if they can say that they have never a gown or petticoat, but what they have been often seen in, and are known by, especially at church. I don't speak now of profuse extravagant women, but such as are counted prudent and moderate in their desires.

If by this pattern we should in proportion judge of the highest ranks, where the richest clothes are but a trifle to their other expenses, and not forget the furniture of all sorts, equipages, jewels, and buildings of persons of quality, we should find the fourth part I speak of a vast article in trade, and that the loss of it would be a greater calamity to such a nation as ours, than it is possible to conceive any other, a raging pestilence not excepted. For the death of half a million of people could not cause a tenth part of the disturbance to the kingdom, that the same number of poor unemployed would certainly create, if at once they were to be added to those, that already one way or other are a burden to the society.

Some few men have a real passion for their wives, and are fond of them without reserve. Others that don't care, and have little occasion for women, are yet seemingly uxorious, and love out of vanity. They take delight in a handsome wife, as a coxcomb does in a fine horse, not for the use he makes of it, but because it is his. The pleasure lies in the conscious-ness of an uncontrollable possession, and what follows from it, the reflec-tion on the mighty thoughts he imagines others to have of his happiness. The men of either sort may be very lavish to their wives, and often pre-venting their wishes crowd new clothes and other finery upon them faster than they can ask it. But the greatest part are wiser than to indulge the extravagances of their wives so far as to give them immediately everything they are pleased to fancy.

It is incredible what vast quantity of trinkets as well as apparel are pur-chased and used by women, which they could never have come at by any other means, than pinching their families, marketing, and other ways of cheating and pilfering from their husbands. Others, by ever teasing their spouses, tire them into compliance, and conquer even obstinate churls by perseverance and their assiduity of asking. A third sort are outrageous at a denial, and by downright noise and scolding bully their tame fools out of anything they have a mind to, while thousands by the force of wheedling know how to overcome the best weighed reasons and the most positive reiterated refusals. The young and beautiful especially laugh at all remon-strances and denials, and few of them scruple to employ the most tender minutes of wedlock to promote a sordid interest. Here had I time I could inveigh with warmth against those base, those wicked women, who calmly play their arts and false deluding charms against our strength and pru-dence, and act the harlots with their husbands! Nay, she is worse than whore, who impiously profanes and prostitutes the sacred rites of love to vile ignoble ends, that first excites to passion and invites to joys with seeming ardour, then racks our fondness for no other purpose than to extort a gift, while full of guile in counterfeited transports she watches for the moment when men can least deny.

I beg pardon for this start out of my way, and desire the experienced reader duly to weigh what has been said as to the main purpose, and after that call to mind the temporal blessings which men daily hear not only toasted and wished for, when people are merry and doing of nothing, but likewise gravely and solemnly prayed for in churches, and other religious assemblies, by clergymen of all sorts and sizes. And as soon as he shall have laid these things together, and, from what he has observed in the common affairs of life, reasoned upon them consequentially without prej-udice, I dare flatter myself, that he will be obliged to own that a consider-able portion of what the prosperity of London and trade in general, and consequently the honor, strength, safety, and all the worldly interest of the nation consist in, depends entirely on the deceit and vile stratagems of women; and that humility, content, meekness, obedience to reasonable husbands, frugality, and all the virtues together, if they were possessed of them in the most eminent degree, could not possibly be a thousandth part so serviceable, to make an opulent, powerful, and what we call a flourishing kingdom, than their most hateful qualities.

I don't question but many of my readers will be startled at this assertion, when they look on the consequences that may be drawn from it. And I shall be asked whether people may not as well be virtuous in a populous, rich, wide, extended kingdom, as in a small, indigent state or principality, that is poorly inhabited? And if that be impossible, whether it is not the duty of all sovereigns to reduce their subjects as to wealth and numbers, as much as they can? If I allow they may, I own myself in the wrong; and if I affirm the other, my tenets will justly be called impious, or at least dangerous to all large societies. As it is not in this place of the book only, but a great many others, that such queries might be made even by a well-meaning reader, I shall here explain myself, and endeavor to solve those difficulties, which several passages might have raised in him, in order to demonstrate the consistency of my opinion to reason, and the strictest morality.

I lay down as a first principle, that in all societies, great or small, it is the duty of every member of it to be good, that virtue ought to be encouraged, vice discountenanced, the laws obeyed, and the transgressors punished. After this I affirm, that if we consult history both ancient and modern, and take a view of what has passed in the world, we shall find that human nature since the fall of Adam has always been the same, and that the strength and frailties of it have ever been conspicuous in one part of the globe or other, without any regard to ages, climates, or religion. I never said, nor imagined, that man could not be virtuous as well in a rich and mighty kingdom, as in the most pitiful commonwealth. But I own it is my sense that no society can be raised into such a rich and mighty kingdom, or so raised, subsist in their wealth and power for any considerable time, without the vices of man.

This I imagine is sufficiently proved throughout the book. And as human nature still continues the same, as it has always been for so many thousand years, we have no great reason to suspect a future change in it, while the world endures. Now I cannot see what immorality there is in showing a man the origin and power of those passions, which so often, even unknowingly to himself, hurry him away from his reason, or that there is any impiety in putting him upon his guard against himself, and the secret stratagems of self-love, and teaching him the difference between such actions as proceed from a victory over the passions, and those that are only the result of a conquest which one passion obtains over another: that is, between real, and counterfeited virtue. . . . What hurt do I do to man if I make him more known to himself than he was before? But we are all so desperately in love with flattery that we can never relish a truth that is mortifying, and I don't believe that the immortality of the soul, a truth broached long before Christianity, would have ever found such a general reception in human capacities as it has, had it not been a pleasing one, that extolled and was a compliment to the whole species, the meanest and most miserable not excepted.

Everyone lives to hear the thing well spoken of, that he has a share in. Even bailiffs, gaol-keepers, and the hangman himself would have you think well of their functions; nay, thieves and house-breakers have a greater regard to those of their fraternity than they have for honest people. And I sincerely believe that it is chiefly self-love that has gained this little treatise (as it was before the last impression) so many enemies. Everyone looks upon it as an affront done to himself, because it detracts from the dignity, and lessens the fine notions he had conceived of mankind, the most worshipful company he belongs to. When I say that societies cannot be raised to wealth and power, and the top of earthly glory without vices, I don't think that by so saying I bid men be vicious, any more than I bid them be quarrelsome or covetous, when I affirm that the profession of the law could not be maintained in such numbers and splendor if there was not abundance of too selfish and litigious people.

But as nothing would more clearly demonstrate the falsity of my notions than that the generality of the people should fall in with them, so I don't expect the approbation of the multitude. I write not to many nor seek for any well-wishers, but among the few that can think abstractly, and have their minds elevated above the vulgar. If I have shown the way to worldly greatness, I have always without hesitation preferred the road that leads to virtue.

Would you banish fraud and luxury, and prevent profanity and irreligion, and make the generality of the people charitable, good and virtuous, break down the printing-presses, melt the founds, and burn all the books in the island, except those at the universities, where they remain unmolested and suffer no volume in private hands but a Bible; knock down foreign trade, prohibit all commerce with strangers, and permit no ships to go to sea, that ever will return, beyond fishing boats. Restore to the clergy,

the King and the barons their ancient privileges, prerogatives and possessions. Build new churches, and convert all the coin you can come at into
sacred utensils. Erect monasteries and alms houses in abundance, and let
no parish be without a charity school. Enact sumptuary laws and let your
youth be inured to hardship. Inspire them with all the nice and most
refined notions of honor and shame, of friendship and of heroism, and
introduce among them a great variety of imaginary rewards. Then let the
clergy preach abstinence and self-denial to others, and take what liberty
they please for themselves. Let them bear the greatest sway in the management of state affairs, and no man be made lord-treasurer but a bishop.

By such pious endeavors and wholesome regulations the scene would
be soon altered. The greatest part of the covetous, the discontented, the
restless and ambitious villains would leave the land, vast swarms of cheating knaves would abandon the city, and be dispersed throughout the
country. Artificers would learn to hold the plough, merchants turn farm
ers, and the sinful overgrown Jerusalem, without famine, war, pestilence,
or compulsion, be emptied in the most easy manner, and ever after cease
to be dreadful to her sovereigns. The happy reformed kingdom would by
this means be crowded in no part of it, and everything necessary for the
sustenance of man be cheap and abundant. On the contrary, the root of so
many thousand evils, money, would be very scarce, and as little wanted,
where every man should enjoy the fruits of his own labor, and our own
dear manufacture unmixed be promiscuously worn by the lord and the
peasant. It is impossible that such a change of circumstances should not
influence the manners of a nation, and render them temperate, honest,
and sincere, and from the next generation we might reasonably expect a
more healthy and robust offspring than the present; a harmless, innocent
and well-meaning people, that would never dispute the doctrine of pas-
sive obedience, nor any other orthodox principles, but be submissive to
superiors, and unanimous in religious worship.

Here I fancy myself interrupted by an epicure . . . , and I am told that
goodness and probity are to be had at a cheaper rate than the ruin of a
nation, and the destruction of all the comforts of life; that liberty and
property may be maintained without wickedness or fraud, and men be
good subjects without being slaves, and religious though they refused to
be priest-rid; that to be frugal and saving is a duty incumbent only on
those whose circumstances require it, but that a man of a good estate does
his country a service by living up to the income of it; that as to himself, he
is so much master of his appetites that he can abstain from anything upon
occasion; that where true Hermitage was not to be had he could content

himself with plain Bordeaux, if it had a good body; that many a morning instead of St. Lawrence he has made a shift with Fronteniac, and after dinner given Cyprus wine, and even Madeira, when he has had a large company, and thought it extravagant to treat with Tokay; but that all voluntary mortifications are superstitious, only belonging to blind zealots and enthusiasts. He'll quote my Lord Shaftesbury against me, and tell me that people may be virtuous and sociable without self-denial, that it is an affront to virtue to make it inaccessible, that I make a bugbear of it to frighten men from it as a thing impracticable. But that for his part he can praise God, and at the same time enjoy his creatures with a good conscience; neither will he forget anything to his purpose of what I have said. He'll ask me at last, whether the legislature, the wisdom of the nation itself, while they endeavor as much as possible to discourage profanity and immorality, and promote the glory of God, do not openly profess at the same time to have nothing more at heart than the ease and welfare of the subject, the wealth, strength, honor, and what else is called the true interest of the country. And moreover, whether the most devout and most learned of our prelates in their greatest concern for our conversion, when they beseech the deity to turn their own as well as our hearts from the world and all carnal desires, do not in the same prayer as loudly solicit him to pour all earthly blessings and temporal felicity on the kingdom they belong to.

These are the apologies, the excuses and common pleas, not only of those who are notoriously vicious, but the generality of mankind, when you touch the copyhold of their inclinations. And trying the real value they have for spirituals would actually strip them of what their minds are wholly bent upon. Ashamed of the many frailties they feel within, all men endeavor to hide themselves, their ugly nakedness, from each other, and wrapping up the true motives of their hearts in the specious cloak of sociableness, and their concern for the public good, they are in hopes of concealing their filthy appetites and the deformity of their desires, while they are conscious within of the fondness for their darling lusts, and their incapacity, barefaced, to tread the arduous, rugged path of virtue.

As to the two last questions, I own they are very puzzling. To what the epicure asks I am obliged to answer in the affirmative. And unless I would (which God forbid!) arraign the sincerity of kings, bishops, and the whole legislative power, the objection stands good against me. All I can say for myself is that in the connection of the facts there is a mystery past human understanding. And to convince the reader that this is no evasion, I shall illustrate the incomprehensibility of it in the following parable.

In old heathen times there was, they say, a whimsical country, where the people talked much of religion, and the greatest part as to outward appearance seemed really devout. The chief moral evil among them was thirst, and to quench it a damnable sin. Yet they unanimously agreed that everyone was born thirsty more or less. Small beer in moderation was allowed to all, and he was counted an hypocrite, a cynic, or a madman, who pretended that one could live altogether without it. Yet those who owned they loved it, and drank it to excess, were counted wicked. All this while the beer itself was reckoned a blessing from Heaven, and there was no harm in the use of it. All the enormity lay in the abuse, the motive of the heart, that made them drink it. He that took the least drop of it to quench his thirst committed a heinous crime, while others drank large quantities without any guilt, so they did it indifferently, and for no other reason than to mend their complexion.

They brewed for other countries as well as their own, and for the small beer they sent abroad they received large returns of Westphalia hams, neats tongues, hung-beef, and bologna sausages, red herrings, pickled sturgeon, caviar, anchovies, and everything that was proper to make their liquor go down with pleasure. Those who kept great stores of small beer by them without making use of it were generally envied, and at the same time very odious to the public, and nobody was easy that had not enough of it come to his own share. The greatest calamity they thought could befall them was to keep their hops and barley upon their hands, and the more they yearly consumed of them, the more they reckoned the country to flourish.

The government had many very wise regulations concerning the returns that were made for their exports, encouraged very much the importation of salt and pepper, and laid heavy duties on everything that was not well-seasoned, and might any ways obstruct the sale of their own hops and barley. Those at [the] helm, when they acted in public, showed themselves on all accounts exempt and wholly divested from thirst, made several laws to prevent the growth of it, and punish the wicked who openly dared to quench it. If you examined them in their private persons, and pried narrowly into their lives and conversations, they seemed to be more fond, or at least drank larger draughts of small beer, than others, but always under pretense that the mending of complexions required greater quantities of liquor in them, than it did in those they ruled over; and that, what they had chiefly at heart, without any regard to themselves, was to procure great plenty of small beer among the subjects in general, and a great demand for their hops and barley.

As nobody was debarred from small beer, the clergy made use of it as well as the laity, and some of them very plentifully. Yet all of them desired to be thought less thirsty by their function than others, and never would own that they drank any but to mend their complexions. In their religious assemblies they were more sincere, for as soon as they came there, they all openly confessed, the clergy as well as the laity, from the highest to the lowest, that they were thirsty, that mending their complexions was what they minded the least, and that all their hearts were set upon small beer and quenching their thirst, whatever they might pretend to the contrary. What was remarkable is that to have laid hold of those truths to anyone's prejudice, and made use of those confessions afterwards out of their temples would have been counted very impertinent. And everybody thought it an heinous affront to be called thirsty, though you had seen him drink small beer by whole gallons. The chief topics of their preachers was the great evil of thirst, and the folly there was in quenching it. They exhorted their hearers to resist the temptations of it, inveighed against small beer, and often told them it was poison, if they drank it with pleasure, or any other design than to mend their complexions.

In their acknowledgments to the gods they thanked them for the plenty of comfortable small beer they had received from them, notwithstanding they had so little deserved it, and continually quenched their thirst with it. Whereas they were so thoroughly satisfied that it was given them for a better use. Having begged pardon for those offenses, they desired the gods to lessen their thirst, and give them strength to resist the importunities of it. Yet, in the midst of their sorest repentance, and most humble supplications, they never forgot small beer, and prayed that they might continue to have it in great plenty, with a solemn promise that how neglectful soever they might hitherto have been in this point, they would for the future not drink a drop of it with any other design than to mend their complexions.

These were [the] standing petitions put together to last. And having continued to be made use of without any alterations for several hundred years together, it was thought by some that the gods, who understood futurity, and knew that the same promise they heard in June would be made to them the January following, did not rely much more on those vows than we do on those waggish inscriptions by which men offer us their goods, today for money, and tomorrow for nothing. They often began their prayers very mystically, and spoke many things in a spiritual sense. Yet, they never were so abstract from the world in them as to end one without beseeching the gods to bless and prosper the brewing trade in all its branches, and for the good of the whole, more and more to increase the consumption of hops and barley.

Remark Y

T' enjoy the World's Conveniencies.

That the words decency and convenience were very ambiguous, and not to be understood, unless we were acquainted with the quality and circumstances of the persons that made use of them, has been hinted already in Remark L. The goldsmith, mercer, or any other of the most creditable shopkeepers that has three or four thousand pounds to set up with, must have two dishes of meat every day, and something extraordinary for Sundays. His wife must have a damask bed against her lying-in, and two or three rooms very well furnished. The following summer she must have a house, or at least very good lodgings in the country. A man that has a being out of town, must have a horse; his footman must have another. If he has a tolerable trade, he expects in eight or ten years' time to keep his coach, which notwithstanding he hopes that after he has slaved (as he calls it) for two or three and twenty years, he shall be worth at least a thousand a year for his eldest son to inherit, and two or three thousand pounds for each of his other children to begin the world with. And when men of such circumstances pray for their daily bread, and mean nothing more extravagant by it, they are counted pretty modest people. Call this pride, luxury, superfluity, or what you please, it is nothing but what ought to be in the capital of a flourishing nation. Those of inferior condition must content themselves with less costly conveniences, as others of higher rank will be sure to make theirs more expensive. Some people call it but decency to be served in plate, and reckon a coach and six among the necessary comforts of life. And if a peer has not above three or four thousand a year, his Lordship is counted poor.

Since the first edition of this book, several have attacked me with demonstrations of the certain ruin which excessive luxury must bring upon all nations, who yet were soon answered, when I showed them the limits within which I had confined it. And therefore that no reader for the future may misconstrue me on this head, I shall point at the cautions I have given, and the provisos I have made in the former as well as this present impression, and which if not overlooked, must prevent all rational censure, and obviate several objections that otherwise might be made against me. I have laid down as maxims never to be departed from that the poor should be kept strictly to work, and that it was prudence to relieve their wants, but folly to cure them; that agriculture and fishery should be promoted in all their branches in order to render provisions, and consequently labor cheap. I have named ignorance as a necessary ingredient in the mixture of society. From all which it is manifest that I could never have imagined that luxury was to be made general through every part of a kingdom. I have likewise required that property should be well-secured, justice impartially administered, and in everything the interest of the nation taken care of. But what I have insisted on the most, and repeated more than once, is the great regard that is to be had to the balance of trade, and the care the legislature ought to take that the yearly imports never exceed the exports. Where this is observed, and the other things I spoke of are not neglected, I still continue to assert that no foreign luxury can undo a country. The height of it is never seen but in nations that are vastly populous, and there only in the upper part of it, and the greater that is the larger still in proportion must be the lowest, the basis that supports all, the multitude of working poor.

Those who would too nearly imitate others of superior fortune must thank themselves if they are ruined. This is nothing against luxury, for whoever can subsist and lives above his income is a fool. Some persons of quality may keep three or four coaches and six, and at the same time lay up money for their children, while a young shopkeeper is undone for keeping one sorry horse. It is impossible there should be a rich nation without prodigals, yet I never knew a city so full of spendthrifts, but there were covetous people enough to answer their number. As an old merchant breaks for having been extravagant or careless a great while, so a young beginner falling into the same business gets an estate by being saving or more industrious before he is forty years old. Besides, the frailties of men often work by contraries: some narrow souls can never thrive because they are too stingy, while longer heads amass great wealth by spending their money freely, and seeming to despise it. But the vicissitudes of fortune are necessary, and the most lamentable are no more detrimental to society than the death of the individual members of it. Christenings are a proper balance to burials. Those who immediately lose by the misfortunes of others are very sorry, complain and make a noise. But the others who get by them, as there always are such, hold their tongues, because it is odious to be thought the better for the losses and calamities of our neighbor. The various ups and downs compose a wheel that always turning round gives motion to the whole machine. Philosophers that dare extend their thoughts beyond the narrow compass of what is immediately before them look on the alternate changes in the civil society no otherwise than they do on the risings and fallings of the lungs, the latter of which are as much a part of respiration in the more perfect animals as the first. So that the fickle breath of never-stable fortune is to the body politic the same as floating air is to a living creature.

Avarice then and prodigality are equally necessary to the society. That in some countries men are more generally lavish than in others proceeds from the difference in circumstances that dispose to either vice, and arise from the condition of the social body as well as the temperament of the natural. I beg pardon of the attentive reader if here in behalf of short memories I repeat some things, the substance of which they have already seen in Remark Q. More money than land, heavy taxes and scarcity of provisions, industry, laboriousness, an active and stirring spirit, ill-nature and saturnine temper; old age, wisdom, trade, riches, acquired by our own labor, and liberty and property well secured, are all things that dispose to avarice. On the contrary, indolence, content, good-nature, a jovial temper, youth, folly, arbitrary power, money easily got, plenty of provisions and the uncertainty of possessions, are circumstances that render men prone to prodigality: where there is the most of the first the prevailing vice will be avarice, and prodigality. Where the other turns the scale; but a national frugality there never was nor never will be without a national necessity.

Sumptuary laws may be of use to an indigent country, after great calamities of war, pestilence, or famine, when work has stood still, and the labor of the poor been interrupted. But to introduce them into an opulent kingdom is the wrong way to consult the interest of it. I shall end my remarks on the Grumbling Hive with assuring the champions of national frugality that it would be impossible for the Persians and other Eastern people to purchase the vast quantities of fine English cloth they consume should we load our women with less cargoes of Asiatic silks.

An Essay on Charity and Charity-Schools

Charity is that virtue by which part of that sincere love we have for ourselves is transferred pure and unmixed to others not tied to us by the bonds of friendship or consanguinity, and even [to] mere strangers, whom we have no obligation to, nor hope or expect anything from. If we lessen any ways the rigor of this definition, part of the virtue must be lost. What we do for our friends and kindred, we do partly for ourselves. When a man acts in behalf of nephews or nieces, and says, "they are my brother's children, I do it out of charity," he deceives you. For if he is capable, it is expected from him, and he does it partly for his own sake: If he values the esteem of the world, and is nice as to honor and reputation, he is obliged to have a greater regard to them than for strangers, or else he must suffer in his character.

The exercise of this virtue relates either to opinion or to action, and is manifested in what we think of others, or what we do for them. To be charitable, then, in the first place, we ought to put the best construction on all that others do or say that the things are capable of. If a man builds a fine house, though he has not one symptom of humility, furnishes it richly, and lays out a good estate in plate and pictures, we ought not to think that he does it out of vanity, but to encourage artists, employ hands, and set the poor to work for the good of his country. And if a man sleeps at church and does not snore, we ought to think he shuts his eyes to increase his attention. The reason is, because in our turn we desire that our utmost avarice should pass for frugality; and that for religion, which we know to be hypocrisy. Secondly, that virtue is conspicuous in us when we bestow our time and labor for nothing, or employ our credit with others in behalf of those who stand in need of it, and yet could not expect such an assistance from our friendship or nearness of blood. The last branch of charity consists in giving away (while we are alive) what we value ourselves, to such as I have already named; being contented rather to have and enjoy less, than not relieve those who want, and shall be the objects of our choice.

This virtue is often counterfeited by a passion of ours called pity or compassion, which consists in a fellow-feeling and condolence for the misfortunes and calamities of others. All mankind are more or less affected with it, but the weakest minds generally the most. It is raised in us when the sufferings and misery of other creatures make so forcible an impression upon us as to make us uneasy. It comes in either at the eye or ear, or both; and the nearer and more violently the object of compassion strikes those senses, the greater disturbance it causes in us, often to such a degree as to occasion great pain and anxiety.

Should any of us be locked up in a ground-room, where in a yard joining to it there was a thriving good-humored child at play of two or three years old, so near us that through the grates of the window we could almost touch it with our hand; and if while we took delight in the harmless diversion, and imperfect prittle-prattle of the innocent babe, a nasty overgrown sow should come in upon the child, set it a-screaming, and frighten it out of its wits; it is natural to think that this would make us uneasy, and that with crying out, and making all the menacing noise we could, we should endeavor to drive the sow away. But if this should happen to be a half-starved creature, that mad with hunger went roaming about in quest of food, and we should behold the ravenous brute, in spite of our cries and all the threatening gestures we could think of, actually lay hold of the helpless infant, destroy and devour it; to see her widely open her destructive jaws and the poor lamb beat down with greedy haste; to look on the defenseless posture of tender limbs first trampled on, then torn asunder; to see the filthy snout digging in the yet living entrails suck up the smoking blood, and now and then to hear the crackling of the bones, and the cruel animal with savage pleasure grunt over the horrid banquet; to hear and see all this, what tortures would it give the soul beyond expression! Let me see the most shining virtue the moralists have to boast of so manifest either to the person possessed of it, or those who behold his actions. Let me see courage, or the love of one's country so apparent without any mixture, cleared and distinct, the first from pride and anger, the other from the love of glory, and every shadow of self-interest, as this pity would be cleared and distinct from all other passions. There would be no need of virtue or self-denial to be moved at such a scene; and not only a man of humanity, of good morals and commiseration, but likewise an highwayman, an house breaker, or a murderer could feel anxieties on such an occasion. How calamitous soever a man's circumstances might be, he would forget his misfortunes for the time, and the most troublesome passion would give way to pity, and not one of the species has a heart so obdurate or engaged that it would not ache at such a sight, as no language has an epithet to fit it.

Many will wonder at what I have said of pity, that it comes in at the eye or ear, but the truth of this will be known when we consider that the nearer the object is the more we suffer, and the more remote it is the less we are troubled with it. To see people executed for crimes, if [they are] a great way off, moves us but little, in comparison to what it does when we are near enough to see the motion of the soul in their eyes, observe their fears and agonies, and are able to read the pangs in every feature of the face. When the object is quite removed from our senses, the relation of the calamities or the reading of them can never raise in us the passion called pity. We may be concerned at bad news, the loss and misfortunes of friends and those whose cause we espouse, but this is not pity, but grief or sorrow; the same as we feel for the death of those we love, or the destruction of what we value.

When we hear that three or four thousand men, all strangers to us, are killed with the sword, or forced into some river where they are drowned, we say and perhaps believe that we pity them. It is humanity bids us have compassion with the sufferings of others, and reason tells us, that whether a thing be far off or done in our sight, our sentiments concerning it ought to be the same, and we should be ashamed to own that we felt no commiseration in us when anything requires it. He is a cruel man, he has no bowels of compassion: all these things are the effects of reason and humanity, but nature makes no compliments. When the object does not strike, the body does not feel it; and when men talk of pitying people out of sight, they are to be believed in the same manner as when they say that they are our humble servants. In paying the usual civilities at first meeting, those who do not see one another every day are often very glad and very sorry alternately for five or six times together in less than two minutes, and yet at parting carry away not a jot more of grief or joy than they met with. The same it is with pity, and it is a thing of choice no more than fear or anger. Those who have a strong and lively imagination, and can make representations of things in their minds, as they would be if they were actually before them, may work themselves up into something that resembles compassion; but this is done by art, and often the help of a little enthusiasm, and is only an imitation of pity. The heart feels little of it, and it is as faint as what we suffer at the acting of a tragedy. Where our judgment leaves part of the mind uninformed, and to indulge a lazy wantonness suffers it to be led into an error, which is necessary to have a passion raised, the slight strokes of which are not unpleasant to us when the soul is in an idle inactive humor.

As pity is often by ourselves and in our own cases mistaken for charity, so it assumes the shape, and borrows the very name of it. A beggar asks you to exert that virtue for Jesus Christ's sake, but all the while his great design is to raise your pity. He represents to your view the worst side of his ailments and bodily infirmities; in chosen words he gives you an epitome of his calamities real or fictitious. And while he seems to pray God that he will open your heart, he is actually at work upon your ears. The greatest profligate of them flies to religion for aid, and assists his cant with a doleful tone and a studied dismality of gestures; but he trusts not to one passion only, he flatters your pride with titles and names of honor and distinction. Your avarice he soothes with often repeating to you the smallness of the gift he sues for, and conditional promises of future returns with an interest extravagant beyond the statute of usury though out of the reach of it. People not used to great cities, being thus attacked on all sides, are commonly forced to yield, and can't help giving something though they can hardly spare it themselves. How oddly are we managed by self-love! It is ever watching in our defense, and yet, to soothe a predominant passion, obliges us to act against our interest. For when pity seizes us, if we can but imagine that we contribute to the relief of him we have compassion with, and are instrumental to the lessening of his sorrows, it eases us, and therefore pitiful people often give an alms when they really feel that they would rather not.

When sores are very bare or seem otherwise afflicting in an extraordinary manner, and the beggar can bear to have them exposed to the cold air, it is very shocking to some people. It is a shame, they cry, such sights should be suffered. The main reason is [that] it touches their pity feelingly, and at the same time they are resolved, either because they are covetous, or count it an idle expense, to give nothing, which makes them more uneasy. They turn their eyes, and where the cries are dismal, some would willingly stop their ears if they were not ashamed. What they can do is to mend their pace, and be very angry in their hearts that beggars should be about the streets. But it is with pity as it is with fear: the more we are conversant with objects that excite either passion, the less we are disturbed by them; and those to whom all these scenes and tones are by custom made familiar, they make little impression upon. The only thing the industrious beggar has left to conquer those fortified hearts, if he can walk either with or without crutches, is to follow close, and with uninterrupted noise tease and importune them, to try if he can make them buy their peace. Thus thousands give money to beggars from the same motive as they pay their corn-cutter, to walk easy. And many a half-penny is given to impudent and designedly persecuting rascals, whom, if it could be done handsomely, a man would cane with much greater satisfaction. Yet all this by the courtesy of the country is called charity.

The reverse of pity is malice. I have spoken of it where I treat of envy. Those who know what it is to examine themselves will soon own that it is very difficult to trace the root and origin of this passion. It is one of those we are most ashamed of, and therefore the hurtful part of it is easily subdued and corrected by a judicious education. When anybody near us stumbles, it is natural even before reflection to stretch out our hands to hinder or at least break the fall, which shows that while we are calm we are rather bent to pity. But though malice by itself is little to be feared, yet assisted with pride, it is often mischievous, and becomes most terrible when egged on and heightened by anger. There is nothing that more readily or more effectually extinguishes pity than this mixture, which is called cruelty. From whence we may learn that to perform a meritorious action, it is not sufficient barely to conquer a passion, unless it likewise be done from a laudable principle; and consequently how necessary that clause was in the definition of virtue, that our endeavors were to proceed from a rational ambition of being good.

Pity, as I have said somewhere else, is the most amiable of all our passions, and there are not many occasions on which we ought to conquer or curb it. A surgeon may be as compassionate as he pleases, so it does not make him omit or forbear to perform what he ought to do. Judges likewise and juries may be influenced with pity, if they take care that plain laws and justice itself are not infringed and do not suffer by it. No pity does more mischief in the world than what is excited by the tenderness of parents, and hinders them from managing their children as their rational love to them would require, and themselves could wish it. The sway likewise which this passion bears in the affections of women is more considerable than is commonly imagined, and they daily commit faults that are altogether ascribed to lust, and yet are in a great measure owing to pity.

What I named last is not the only passion that mocks and resembles charity; pride and vanity have built more hospitals than all the virtues together. Men are so tenacious of their possessions, and selfishness is so riveted in our nature, that whoever can but any ways conquer it shall have the applause of the public, and all the encouragement imaginable to conceal his frailty and soothe any other appetite he shall have a mind to indulge. The man that supplies with his private fortune what the whole must otherwise have provided for, obliges every member of the society, and therefore all the world are ready to pay him their acknowledgment, and think themselves in duty bound to pronounce all such actions virtuous, without examining or so much as looking into the motives from which they were performed. Nothing is more destructive to virtue or religion itself than to make men believe that giving money to the poor, though they should not part with it until after death, will make a full atonement in the next world for the sins they have committed in this. A villain who has been guilty of a barbarous murder may, by the help of false witnesses, escape the punishment he deserved: he prospers, we'll say, heaps up great wealth and by the advice of his father confessor leaves all his estate to a monastery, and his children beggars. What fine amends has this good Christian made for his crime, and what an honest man was the priest who directed his conscience. He who parts with all he has in his lifetime, whatever principle he acts from, only gives away what was his own; but the rich miser who refuses to assist his nearest relations while he is alive, though they never designedly disobliged him, and disposes of his money for what we call charitable uses after his death, may imagine of his goodness what he pleases, but he robs his posterity. . . . (. . .)

Should it be said that to . . . look into matters, and men's consciences . . . will discourage people from laying out their money this way . . . I would not disown the charge, but am of opinion, that this is no injury to the public, should one prevent men from crowding too much treasure into the dead stock of the kingdom. There ought to be a vast disproportion between the active and inactive part of the society to make it happy, and where this is not regarded, the multitude of gifts and endowments may soon be excessive and detrimental to a nation. Charity, where it is too extensive, seldom fails of promoting sloth and idleness, and is good for little in the commonwealth but to breed drones and destroy industry. The more colleges and alms-houses you build the more you may. The first founders and benefactors may have just and good intentions, and would perhaps for their own reputations seem to labor for the most laudable purposes. But the executors of those wills, the governors that come after them, have quite other views, and we seldom see charities long applied as it was first intended they should be. I have no design that is cruel, nor the least aim that savors of inhumanity. To have sufficient hospitals for sick and wounded I look upon as an indispensable duty both in peace and war. Young children without parents, old age without support, and all that are disabled from working, ought to be taken care of with tenderness and alacrity. But as on the one hand I would have none neglected that are helpless, and really necessitous without being wanting to themselves, so on the other I would not encourage beggary or laziness in the poor. All should be set to work that are any ways able, and scrutinies should be made even among the infirm. Employments might be found out for most of our lame, and many that are unfit for hard labor, as well as the blind, as long as their health and strength would allow of it. What I have now under consideration leads me naturally to that kind of distraction the nation has labored under for some time: the enthusiastic passion for charity-schools.

The generality are so bewitched with the usefulness and excellency of them, that whoever dares openly oppose them is in danger of being stoned by the rabble. Children that are taught the principles of religion and can read the word of God have a greater opportunity to improve in virtue and good morality, and must certainly be more civilized than others that are suffered to run at random and have nobody to look after them. How perverse must be the judgment of those who would not rather see children decently dressed, with clean linen at least once a week, that in an orderly manner follow their master to church, than in every open place meet with a company of blackguards without shirts or anything whole about them, that, insensible of their misery, are continually increasing it with oaths and imprecations! Can anyone doubt but these are the great nursery of thieves and pick-pockets? What numbers of felons and other criminals have we tried and convicted every [court] sessions! This will be prevented by charity-schools, and when the children of the poor receive a better education, the society will in a few years reap the benefit of it, and the nation be cleared of so many miscreants as now this great city and all the country about it are filled with.

This is the general cry, and he that speaks the least word against it [is] an uncharitable, hard-hearted and inhuman, if not a wicked, profane, and atheistic wretch. As to the comeliness of the sight, nobody disputes it; but I would not have a nation pay too dear for so transient a pleasure, and if we might set aside the finery of the show, everything that is material in this popular oration might soon be answered.

As to religion, the most knowing and polite part of a nation have everywhere the least of it. Craft has a greater hand in making rogues than stupidity, and vice in general is nowhere more predominant than where arts and sciences flourish. Ignorance is, to a proverb, counted to be the mother of devotion, and it is certain that we shall find innocence and honesty nowhere more general than among the most illiterate, the poor silly country people. The next to be considered are the manners and civility that by charity-schools are to be grafted into the poor of the nation. I confess that in my opinion to be in any degree possessed of what I named is a frivolous if not a hurtful quality, at least nothing is less requisite in the laborious poor. It is not compliments we want of them, but their work and assiduity. But I give up this article with all my heart. Good manners we'll say are necessary to all people, but which way will they be furnished with them in a charity-school? Boys there may be taught to pull off their caps promiscuously to all they meet, unless it be a beggar; but that they should acquire in it any civility beyond that I can't conceive.

The master is not greatly qualified, as may be guessed by his salary, and if he could teach them manners he has not time for it. While they are at school they are either learning or saying their lesson to him, or employed in writing or arithmetic, and as soon as school is done, they are as much at liberty as other poor people's children. It is precept and the example of parents, and those they eat, drink and converse with, that have an influence upon the minds of children: reprobate parents that take ill courses and are regardless of their children, won't have a mannerly civilized offspring, though they went to a charity-school until they were married. The honest painstaking people, be they never so poor, if they have any notion of goodness and decency themselves, will keep their children in awe, and never suffer them to rake about the streets, and lie out a-nights. Those who will work themselves, and have any command over their children, will make them do something or other that turns to profit as soon as they are able, be it never so little; and such as are so ungovernable, that neither words nor blows can work upon them, no charity school will mend. . . . (. . .)

In a populous city it is not difficult for a young rascal that has pushed himself into a crowd, with a small hand and nimble fingers to whip away a handkerchief or snuff-box from a man who is thinking on business, and [is] regardless of his pocket. Success in small crimes seldom fails of ushering in greater, and he that picks pockets with impunity at twelve is likely to be a house-breaker at sixteen, and a thorough-paced villain long before he is twenty. Those who are cautious as well as bold, and no drunkards, may do a world of mischief before they are discovered; and this is one of the greatest inconveniences of such vast overgrown cities as London or Paris, that they harbor rogues and villains as granaries do vermin. They afford a perpetual shelter to the worst of people, and are places of safety to thousands of criminals, who daily commit thefts and burglaries, and yet by often changing their places of abode, may conceal themselves for many years, and will perhaps forever escape the hands of justice unless by chance they are apprehended in a fact. And when they are taken, the evidences perhaps want clearness or are otherwise insufficient, the depositions are not strong enough, juries and often judges are touched with compassion; prosecutors though vigorous at first often relent before the time of trial comes on. Few men prefer the public safety to their own ease. A man of good nature is not easily reconciled with taking away of another man's life, though he has deserved the gallows. To be the cause of anyone's death, though justice requires it, is what most people are startled at, especially men of conscience and probity, when they want judgment or resolution. As this is the reason that thousands escape that deserve to be capitally punished, so it is likewise the cause that there are so many offenders who boldly venture in hopes that if they are taken they shall have the same good fortune of getting off.

But if men did imagine and were fully persuaded that as surely as they committed a fact that deserved hanging, so surely they would be hanged, executions would be very rare, and the most desperate felon would almost as soon hang himself as he would break open a house. To be stupid and ignorant is seldom the character of a thief. Robberies on the highway and other bold crimes are generally perpetrated by rogues of spirit and a genius, and villains of any fame are commonly subtle cunning fellows that are well-versed in the method of trials, and acquainted with every quirk in the law that can be of use to them, that overlook not the smallest flaw in an indictment, and know how to make an advantage of the least slip of an evidence and everything else, that can serve their turn to bring them off.

It is a mighty saying, that it is better that five hundred guilty people should escape, than that one innocent person should suffer. This maxim is only true as to futurity, and in relation to another world; but it is very false in regard to the temporal welfare of the society. It is a terrible thing a man should be put to death for a crime he is not guilty of, yet so oddly circumstances may meet in the infinite variety of accidents, that it is possible it should come to pass, all the wisdom that judges, and conscientiousness that juries may be possessed of, notwithstanding. But where men endeavor to avoid this with all the care and precaution human prudence is able to take, should such a misfortune happen perhaps once or twice in half a score years, on condition that all that time justice should be administered with all the strictness and severity, and not one guilty person suffered to escape with impunity, it would be a vast advantage to a nation, not only as to the securing of everyone's property and the peace of the society in general, but it would likewise save the lives of hundreds, if not thousands, of necessitous wretches, that are daily hanged for trifles, and who would never have attempted anything against the law, or at least not have ventured on capital crimes, if the hopes of getting off, should they be taken, had not been one of the motives that animated their resolution. Therefore, where the laws are plain and severe, all the remissness in the execution of them, leniency of juries and frequency of pardons are in the main a much greater cruelty to a populous state or kingdom, than the use of racks and the most exquisite torments. . . . (. . .)

Human nature is everywhere the same. Genius, wit and natural parts are always sharpened by application, and may be as much improved in the practice of the meanest villainy as they can in the exercise of industry or the most heroic virtue. There is no station of life where pride, emulation, and the love of glory may not be displayed. A young pickpocket, that makes a jest of his angry prosecutor, and dexterously wheedles the old justice into an opinion of his innocence, is envied by his equals and admired by all the fraternity. Rogues have the same passions to gratify as other men, and value themselves on their honor and faithfulness to one another, their courage, intrepidity, and other manly virtues, as well as people of better professions; and in daring enterprises, the resolution of a robber may be as much supported by his pride, as that of an honest soldier, who fights for his country.

The evils then we complain of are owing to quite other causes than what we assign for them. Men must be very wavering in their sentiments, if not inconsistent with themselves, that at one time will uphold knowledge and learning to be the most proper means to promote religion, and defend at another that ignorance is the mother of devotion.

But if the reasons alleged for this general education are not the true ones, whence comes it that the whole kingdom both great and small are so unanimously fond of it? There is no miraculous conversion to be perceived among us, no universal bent to goodness and morality that has on a sudden overspread the island. There is as much wickedness as ever, charity is as cold, and real virtue as scarce. The year 1720 [when the South Sea Company's shares collapsed on the London exchange] has been as prolific in deep villainy, and remarkable for selfish crimes and premeditated mischief, as can be picked out of any century whatever; not committed by poor ignorant rogues that could neither read nor write, but the better sort of people as to wealth and education, that most of them were great masters in arithmetic, and lived in reputation and splendor. To say that when a thing is once in vogue, the multitude follows the common cry, that charity schools are in fashion in the same manner as hooped petticoats, by caprice, and that no more reason can be given for the one than the other, I am afraid will not be satisfactory to the curious, and at the same time I doubt much, whether it will be thought of great weight by many of my readers, what I can advance besides. (. . .)

These [men are] diminutive patriots [who,] increasing, form themselves into a society and appoint stated meetings, where everyone concealing his vices has liberty to display his talents. Religion is the theme, or else the misery of the times occasioned by atheism and profanity. Men of worth, who live in splendor, and thriving people that have a great deal of business of their own, are seldom seen among them. Men of sense and education likewise, if they have nothing to do, generally look out for better diversion. All those who have a higher aim shall have their attendance easily excused, but contribute they must or else lead a weary life in the parish. Two sorts of people come in voluntarily, staunch church men, who have good reasons for it in petto [in their own hearts], and your sly sinners that look upon it as meritorious, and hope that it will expiate their guilt, and Satan be non-suited by it at a small expense. Some come into it to save their credit, others to retrieve it, according as they have either lost or are afraid of losing it. Others again do it prudentially to increase their trade and get acquaintance, and many would own to you, if they dared to be sincere and speak the truth, that they would never have been concerned in it, but to be better known in the parish. Men of sense that see the folly of it, and have nobody to fear, are persuaded into it not to be thought singular or to run counter to all the world. Even those who are resolute at first in denying it, it is ten to one but at last they are teased and importuned into a compliance. The charge being calculated for most of the inhabitants, the insignificance of it is another argument that prevails much, and many are drawn in to be contributors, who without that would have stood out and strenuously opposed the whole scheme.

The governors are made of the middling people, and many inferior to that class are made use of, if the forwardness of their zeal can but overbalance the meanness of their condition. If you should ask these worthy rulers why they take upon them so much trouble to the detriment of their own affairs and loss of time, either singly or the whole body of them, they would all unanimously answer that it is the regard they have for religion and the Church, and the pleasure they take in contributing to the good and eternal welfare of so many poor innocents that in all probability would run into perdition in these wicked times of scoffers and freethinkers. They have no thought of interest. Even those who deal in and provide these children with what they want have not the least design of getting by what they sell for their use, and though in everything else their avarice and greediness after lucre be glaringly conspicuous, in this affair they are wholly divested from selfishness, and have no worldly ends. One motive above all, which is none of the least with the most of them, is to be carefully concealed: I mean the satisfaction there is in ordering and directing. There is a melodious sound in the word governor that is charming to mean people: everybody admires sway and superiority . . . ; there is a pleasure in ruling over anything, and it is this chiefly that supports human nature in the tedious slavery of schoolmasters. But if there be the least satisfaction in governing the children, it must be ravishing to govern the schoolmaster himself. What fine things are said and perhaps written to a governor, when a schoolmaster is to be chosen! How the praises tickle, and how pleasant it is not to find out the fulsomeness of the flattery, the stiffness of the expressions, or the pedantry of the style! (. . .)

The whole earth being cursed, and no bread to be had but what we eat in the sweat of our brows, vast toil must be undergone before man can provide himself with necessities for his sustenance and the bare support of his corrupt and defective nature as he is a single creature; but infinitely more to make life comfortable in a civil society, where men are become taught animals, and great numbers of them have by mutual compact framed themselves into a body politic. And the more man's knowledge increases in this state, the greater will be the variety of labor required to make him easy. It is impossible that a society can long subsist, and suffer many of its members to live in idleness, and enjoy all the ease and pleasure they can invent, without having at the same time great multitudes of people that to make good this defect will condescend to be quite the reverse, and by use and patience inure their bodies to work for others and themselves besides.

The plenty and cheapness of provisions depends in a great measure on the price and value that is set upon this labor, and consequently the welfare of all societies, even before they are tainted with foreign luxury, requires that it should be performed by such of their members as in the first place are sturdy and robust and never used to ease or idleness; and in the second, soon contented as to the necessities of life such as are glad to take up with the coarsest manufacture in everything they wear, and in their diet have no other aim than to feed their bodies when their stomachs prompt them to eat, and with little regard to taste or relish, refuse no wholesome nourishment that can be swallowed when men are hungry, or ask anything for their thirst but to quench it.

As the greatest part of the drudgery is to be done by daylight, so it is by this only that they actually measure the time of their labor without any thought of the hours they are employed, or the weariness they feel. The hireling in the country must get up in the morning, not because he has rested enough, but because the sun is going to rise. This last article alone would be an intolerable hardship to grown people under thirty, who during nonage had been used to lie abed as long as they could sleep. But all three together make up such a condition of life as a man more mildly educated would hardly choose; though it should deliver him from a jail or a shrew.

If such people there must be, as no great nation can be happy without vast numbers of them, would not a wise legislature cultivate the breed of them with all imaginable care, and provide against their scarcity as he would prevent the scarcity of provision itself? No man would be poor and fatigue himself for a livelihood if he could help it. The absolute necessity all stand in for victuals and drink, and in cold climates for clothes and lodging, makes them submit to anything that can be borne with. If nobody did want nobody would work; but the greatest hardships are looked upon as solid pleasures when they keep a man from starving.

From what has been said, it is manifest that in a free nation where slaves are not allowed of the surest wealth consists in a multitude of laborious poor. For besides that they are the never-failing nursery of fleets and armies, without them there could be no enjoyment, and no product of any country could be valuable. To make the society happy and people easy under the meanest circumstances, it is requisite that great numbers of them should be ignorant as well as poor. Knowledge both enlarges and multiplies our desires, and the fewer things a man wishes for, the more easily his necessities may be supplied.

The welfare and felicity, therefore, of every state and kingdom require that the knowledge of the working poor should be confined within the verge of their occupations, and never extended (as to things visible) beyond what relates to their calling. The more a shepherd, a plowman or any other peasant knows of the world, and the things that are foreign to his labor or employment, the less fit he'll be to go through the fatigues and hardships of it with cheerfulness and content.

Reading, writing and arithmetic are very necessary to those whose business require such qualifications, but where people's livelihood has no dependence on these arts, they are very pernicious to the poor, who are forced to get their daily bread by their daily labor. Few children make any progress at school, but at the same time they are capable of being employed in some business or other, so that every hour those of poor people spend at their book is so much time lost to the society. Going to school in comparison to working is idleness, and the longer boys continue in this easy sort of life, the more unfit they'll be when grown up for downright labor, both as to strength and inclination. Men who are to remain and end their days in a laborious, tiresome and painful station of life, the sooner they are put upon it at first, the more patiently they'll submit to it forever after. Hard labor and the coarsest diet are a proper punishment to several kinds of malefactors, but to impose either on those that have not been used and brought up to both is the greatest cruelty, when there is no crime you can charge them with.

(. . .)

When obsequiousness and mean services are required, we shall always observe that they are never so cheerfully nor so heartily performed as from inferiors to superiors. I mean inferiors not only in riches and quality, but likewise in knowledge and understanding. A servant can have no unfeigned respect for his master as soon as he has sense enough to find out that he serves a fool. When we are to learn or to obey, we shall experience in ourselves that the greater opinion we have of the wisdom and capacity of those that are either to teach or command us, the greater deference we pay to their laws and instructions. No creatures submit contentedly to their equals, and should a horse know as much as a man, I should not desire to be his rider. (. . .)

I have sufficiently shown already why going to school was idleness if compared to working, and exploded this sort of education in the children of the poor, because it incapacitates them ever after for downright labor, which is their proper province, and in every civil society a portion they ought not to repine or grumble at, if exacted from them with discretion and humanity. What remains is that I should speak as to their putting them out to trades, which I shall endeavor to demonstrate to be destructive to the harmony of a nation, and an impertinent intermeddling with what few of these governors know anything of.

In order to this, let us examine into the nature of societies, and what the compound ought to consist of if we would raise it to as high a degree of strength, beauty and perfection as the ground we are to do it upon will let us. The variety of services that are required to supply the luxurious and wanton desires as well as real necessities of man, with all their subordinate callings, is in such a nation as ours prodigious. Yet it is certain that, though the number of those several occupations be excessively great, it is far from being infinite. If you add one more than is required it must be superfluous. . . . As it is folly to set up trades that are not wanted, so what is next to it is to increase in any one trade the numbers beyond what are required. As things are managed with us, it would be preposterous to have as many brewers as there are bakers, or as many woollen-drapers as there are shoemakers. This proportion as to numbers in every trade finds itself, and is never better kept, than when nobody meddles or interferes with it.

People that have children to educate that must get their livelihood are always consulting and deliberating what trade or calling they are to bring them up to, until they are fixed; and thousands think on this that hardly think at all on anything else. First they confine themselves to their circumstances, and he that can give but ten pounds with his son must not look out for a trade where they ask an hundred with an apprentice. But the next they think on is always which will be the most advantageous; if there be a calling where at that time people are more generally employed than they are in any other in the same reach, there are presently half a score fathers ready to supply it with their sons. Therefore the greatest care most companies have is about the regulation of the number of apprentices. Now, when all trades complain, and perhaps justly, that they are overstocked, you manifestly injure that trade to which you add one member more than would flow from the nature of society. Besides that, the governors of charity schools don't deliberate so much what trade is the best, but what tradesmen they can get that will take the boys, with such a sum. Few men of substance and experience will have anything to do with these children; they are afraid of a hundred inconveniences from the necessitous parents of them. So that they are bound, at least most commonly, either to sots and neglectful masters, or else such as are very needy and don't care what becomes of their apprentices, after they have received the money. By which it seems as if we studied nothing more than to have a perpetual nursery for charity schools.

When all trades and handicrafts are overstocked it is a certain sign there is a fault in the management of the whole. For it is impossible there should be too many people if the country is able to feed them. Are provisions dear? Whose fault is that, as long as you have ground untilled and hands unemployed? But I shall be answered, that to increase plenty, must at long run undo the farmer or lessen the rents all over England. To which I reply, that what the husbandman complains of most is what I would redress. The greatest grievance of farmers, gardeners and others, where hard labor is required, and dirty work to be done, is that they can't get servants for the same wages they used to have them at. The day-laborer grumbles at sixteen pence to do no other drudgery than what thirty years ago his grandfather did cheerfully for half the money. As to the rents, it is impossible they should fall while you increase your numbers, but the price of provisions and all labor in general must fall with them if not before. And a man of a hundred and fifty pounds a year has no reason to complain that his income is reduced to one hundred, if he can buy as much for that one hundred as before he could have done for two.

There is no intrinsic worth in money but what is alterable with the times, and whether a guinea goes for twenty pounds or for a shilling, it is (as I have already hinted before) the labor of the poor, and not the high and low value that is set on gold or silver, which all the comforts of life must arise from. It is in our power to have a much greater plenty than we enjoy, if agriculture and fishery were taken care of, as they might be; but we are so little capable of increasing our labor that we have hardly poor enough to do what is necessary to make us subsist. The proportion of the society is spoiled, and the bulk of the nation, which should everywhere consist of laboring poor that are unacquainted with everything but their work, is too little for the other parts. In all business where downright labor is shunned or overpaid there is plenty of people. To one merchant you have ten bookkeepers, or at least pretenders; and everywhere in the country the farmer wants hands. Ask for a footman that for some time has been in gentlemen's families, and you'll get a dozen that are all butlers. You may have chambermaids by the score, but you can't get a cook under extravagant wages.

Nobody will do the dirty slavish work that can help it. I don't discommend them; but all these things show that the people of the meanest rank know too much to be serviceable to us. Servants require more than masters and mistresses can afford, and what madness is it to encourage them in this by industriously increasing at our cost that knowledge which they will be sure to make us pay for over again! And it is not only that those who are educated at our own expense encroach upon us, but the raw ignorant country wenches and boobily fellows that can do, and are good for, nothing, impose upon us likewise. The scarcity of servants occasioned by the education of the first gives a handle to the latter of advancing their price, and demanding what ought only to be given to servants that understand their business, and have most of the good qualities that can be required in them. (. . .)

Some perhaps will lay the things I complain of to the charge of luxury, of which I said that it could do no hurt to a rich nation if the imports never did exceed the exports. But I don't think this imputation just, and nothing ought to be scored on the account of luxury that is downright the effect of folly. A man may be very extravagant in indulging his ease and his pleasure, and render the enjoyment of the world as operose and expensive as they can be made, if he can afford it, and at the same time show his good sense in everything about him. This he cannot be said to do if he industriously renders his people incapable of doing him that service he expects from them. It is too much money, excessive wages, and unreasonable vails that spoil servants in England. A man may have five and twenty horses in his stables without being guilty of folly if it suits with the rest of his circumstances. But if he keeps but one, and overfeeds it to show his wealth, he is a fool for his pains. Is it not madness to suffer that servants should take three and others five per cent of what they pay to tradesmen for their masters, as is so well known to watchmakers and others that sell toys, superfluous knickknacks, and other curiosities, if they deal with people of quality and fashionable gentlemen that are above telling their own money? If they should accept of a present when offered, it might be connived at, but it is an unpardonable impudence that they should claim it as their due, and contend for it if refused. Those who have all the necessities of life provided for can have no occasion for money but what does them hurt as servants, unless they were to hoard it up for age or sickness which among our skip kennels [footmen] is not very common and even then it makes them saucy and insupportable.

(. . .)

The only thing of weight then that can be said in behalf [of the charity schools] is that so many thousand children are educated . . . in the Christian faith and the principles of the Church of England. To demonstrate that this is not a sufficient plea for them, I must desire the reader, as I hate repetitions, to look back on what I have said before, to which I shall add, that whatever is necessary to salvation and requisite for poor laboring people to know concerning religion, that children learn at school, may fully as well either by preaching or catechizing be taught at church, from which or some other place of worship I would not have the meanest of a parish that is able to walk to it be absent on Sundays. It is the Sabbath, the most useful day in seven, that is set apart for divine service and religious exercise as well as resting from bodily labor, and it is a duty incumbent on all magistrates to take particular care of that day. The poor more especially and their children should be made to go to church on it both in the fore and afternoon, because they have no time on any other. By precept and example they ought to be encouraged and used to it from their very infancy. The willful neglect of it ought to be counted scandalous, and if downright compulsion to what I urge might seem too harsh and perhaps impracticable, all diversions at least ought strictly to be prohibited, and the poor hindered from every amusement abroad that might allure or draw them from it.

Where this care is taken by the magistrates, as far as it lies in their power, Ministers of the Gospel may instill into the smallest capacities more piety and devotion, and better principles of virtue and religion than charity schools ever did or ever will produce, and those who complain, when they have such opportunities, that they cannot imbue their parishioners with sufficient knowledge of what they stand in need of as Christians, without the assistance of reading and writing, are either very lazy or very ignorant and undeserving themselves.

That the most knowing are not the most religious will be evident if we make a trial between people of different abilities even in this juncture, where going to church is not made such an obligation on the poor and illiterate as it might be. Let us pitch upon a hundred poor men, the first we can light on, that are above forty, and were brought up to hard labor from their infancy, such as never went to school at all, and always lived remote from knowledge and great towns. Let us compare to these an equal number of very good scholars, that shall all have had university education; and be, if you will, half of them divines, well versed in philology and polemic learning. Then let us impartially examine into the lives and conversations of both, and I dare engage that among the first who can neither read nor write, we shall meet with more union and neighborly love, less wickedness and attachment to the world, more content of mind, more innocence, sincerity, and other good qualities that conduce to the public peace and real felicity, than we shall find among the latter, where, on the contrary, we may be assured of the height of pride and insolence, eternal quarrels and dissensions, irreconcilable hatreds, strife, envy, calumny and other vices destructive to mutual concord, which the illiterate laboring poor are hardly ever tainted with to any considerable degree.

(. . .)

Abundance of hard and dirty labor is to be done, and coarse living is to be complied with. Where shall we find a better nursery for these necessities than the children of the poor? None certainly are nearer to it or fitter for it. Besides that the things I called hardships, neither seem nor are such to those who have been brought up to them, and know no better. There is not a more contented people among us than those who work the hardest and are the least acquainted with the pomp and delicacies of the world.

These are truths that are undeniable, yet I know few people will be pleased to have them divulged. What makes them odious is an unreasonable vein of petty reverence for the poor, that runs through most multitudes, and more particularly in this nation, and arises from a mixture of pity, folly and superstition. It is from a lively sense of this compound that men cannot endure to hear or see anything said or acted against the poor without considering how just the one, or insolent the other. So a beggar must not be beat though he strikes you first. Journeymen tailors go to law with their masters and are obstinate in a wrong cause, yet they must be pitied; and murmuring weavers must be relieved, and have fifty silly things done to humor them, though in the midst of their poverty they insult their betters, and on all occasions appear to be more prone to make holy days and riots than they are to working or sobriety.

This puts me in mind of our wool, which considering the posture of our affairs, and the behavior of the poor, I sincerely believe ought not upon any account to be carried abroad. But if we look into the reason why suffering it to be fetched away is so pernicious, our heavy complaint and lamentations that it is exported can be no great credit to us. Considering the mighty and manifold hazards that must be run before it can be got off the coast, and safely landed beyond sea, it is manifest that the foreigners, before they can work our wool, must pay more for it very considerably, than what we can have it for at home. Yet notwithstanding this great difference in the prime cost, they can afford to sell the manufactures made of it cheaper at foreign markets than ourselves. This is the disaster we groan under, the intolerable mischief, without which the exportation of that commodity could be no greater prejudice to us than that of tin or lead, as long as our hands were fully employed, and we had still wool to spare.

There is no people yet come to higher perfection in the woollen manufacture, either as to dispatch or goodness of work, at least in the most considerable branches, than ourselves; and therefore what we complain of can only depend on the difference in the management of the poor, between other nations and ours. If the laboring people in one country will work twelve hours in a day, and six days in a week, and in another they are employed but eight hours in a day, and not above four days in a week, the one is obliged to have nine hands for what the other does with four. But if, moreover, the living, the food and raiment, and what is consumed by the workmen of the industrious costs but half the money of what is expended among an equal number of the other, the consequence must be that the first will have the work of eighteen men for the same price as the other gives for the work of four. I would not insinuate, neither do I think, that the difference either in diligence or necessaries of life between us and any neighboring nation is near so great as what I speak of, yet I would have it considered that half of that difference and much less is sufficient to overbalance the disadvantage they labor under as to the price of wool.

Nothing to me is more evident than that no nation in any manufacture whatever can undersell their neighbors with whom they are at best but equals as to skill and dispatch, and the convenience for working; more especially when the prime cost of the thing to be manufactured is not in their favor, unless they have provisions, and whatever is relating to their sustenance cheaper, or else workmen that are either more assiduous, and will remain longer at their work, or be content with a meaner and coarser way of living than those of their neighbors. This is certain, that where numbers are equal, the more laborious people are, and the fewer hands the same quantity of work is performed by, the greater plenty there is in a country of the necessities for life, the more considerable and the cheaper that country may render its exports.

It being granted, then, that abundance of work is to be done, the next thing which I think to be likewise undeniable is that the more cheerfully it is done the better, as well for those that perform it as for the rest of the society. To be happy is to be pleased, and the less notion a man has of a better way of living, the more content he'll be with his own. And on the other hand, the greater a man's knowledge and experience is in the world, the more exquisite the delicacy of his taste, and the more consummate judge he is of things in general, certainly the more difficult it will be to please him. I would not advance anything that is barbarous or inhuman: but when a man enjoys himself, laughs and sings, and in his gesture and behavior shows me all the tokens of content and satisfaction, I pronounce him happy, and have nothing to do with his wit or capacity. I never enter into the reasonableness of his mirth, at least I ought not to judge of it by my own standard and argue from the effect which the thing that makes him merry would have upon me. At that rate a man that hates cheese must call me fool for loving blue mold. *De gustibus non est disputandum* [one's taste is indisputable] is as true in a metaphorical as it is in the literal sense, and the greater the distance is between people as to their condition, their circumstances and manner of living, the less capable they are of judging of one another's troubles or pleasures.

(. . .)

Was impartial reason to be judge between real good and real evil, and a catalogue made accordingly of the several delights and vexations differently to be met with in both stations, I question whether the condition of kings would be at all preferable to that of peasants, even as ignorant and laborious as I seem to require the latter to be. The reason why the generality of people would rather be kings than peasants is first owing to pride and ambition, that is deeply riveted in human nature, and which to gratify we daily see men undergo and despise the greatest hazards and difficulties. Secondly, to the difference there is in the force with which our affection is wrought upon as the objects are either material or spiritual. Things that immediately strike our outward senses act more violently upon our passions than what is the result of thought and the dictates of the most demonstrative reason, and there is a much stronger bias to gain our liking or aversion in the first than there is in the latter.

Having thus demonstrated that what I urge could be no injury or the least diminution of happiness to the poor, I leave it to the judicious reader whether it is not more probable we should increase our exports by the methods I hint at than by sitting still and damning and sinking our neighbors for beating us at our own weapons; some of them outselling us in manufactures made of our own product which they dearly purchased, others growing rich in spite of distance and trouble, by the same fish which we neglect, though it is ready to jump into our mouths.

As by discouraging idleness with art and steadiness you may compel the poor to labor without force, so by bringing them up in ignorance you may inure them to real hardships without being ever sensible themselves that they are such. By bringing them up in ignorance, I mean no more, as I have hinted long ago, than that as to worldly affairs their knowledge should be confined within the verge of their own occupations, at least that we should not take pains to extend it beyond those limits. When by these two engines we shall have made provisions, and consequently labor cheap, we must infallibly outsell our neighbors, and at the same time increase our numbers. This is the noble and manly way of encountering the rivals of our trade, and by dint of merit outdoing them at foreign markets.

(. . .)

Here I should have concluded this rhapsody of thoughts, but something comes in my head concerning the main scope and design of this essay—which is to prove the necessity there is for a certain portion of ignorance in a well-ordered society—that I must not omit, because by mentioning it I shall make an argument on my side of what, if I had not spoken of it, might easily have appeared as a strong objection against me. It is the opinion of most people, and mine among the rest, that the most commendable quality of the present Czar of Muscovy [Peter the Great] is his unwearied application in raising his subjects from their native stupidity, and civilizing his nation. But then we must consider it is what they stood in need of, and that not long ago the greatest part of them were next to brute beasts. In proportion to the extent of his dominions and the multitudes he commands, he had not that number or variety of tradesmen and artificers which the true improvement of the country required, and therefore was in the right in leaving no stone unturned to procure them. But what is that to us who labor under a contrary disease? Sound politics are to the social body what the art of medicine is to the natural, and no physician would treat a man in a lethargy as if he was sick for want of rest, or prescribe in a dropsy what should be administered in a diabetes. In short, Russia has too few knowing men, and Great Britain too many.

A Search into the Nature of Society

The generality of moralists and philosophers have hitherto agreed that there could be no virtue without self-denial. But a late author, who is now much read by men of sense, is of a contrary opinion, and imagines that men without any trouble or violence upon themselves may be naturally virtuous. He seems to require and expect goodness in his species, as we do a sweet taste in grapes and China oranges, of which, if any of them are sour, we boldly pronounce that they are not come to that perfection their nature is capable of. This noble writer (for it is the Lord Shaftesbury I mean in his *Characteristics*) fancies, that as man is made for society, so he ought to be born with a kind affection to the whole, of which he is a part, and a propensity to seek the welfare of it. In pursuance of this supposition, he calls every action performed with regard to the public good, virtuous; and all selfishness, wholly excluding such a regard, vice. In respect to our species he looks upon virtue and vice as permanent realities that must ever be the same in all countries and all ages, and imagines that a man of sound understanding, by following the rules of good sense, may not only find out that *pulchrum & honestum* [excellence and virtue] both in morality and the works of art and nature, but likewise govern himself by his reason with as much ease and readiness as a good rider manages a well-taught horse by the bridle.

The attentive reader, who perused the foregoing part of this book, will soon perceive that two systems cannot be more opposite than his lordship's and mine. His notions I confess are generous and refined. They are a high compliment to humankind, and capable by the help of a little enthusiasm of inspiring us with the most noble sentiments concerning the dignity of our exalted nature. What pity it is that they are not true: I would not advance this much if I had not already demonstrated in almost every page of this treatise that the solidity of them is inconsistent with our daily experience. But to leave not the least shadow of an objection that might be made unanswered, I design to expatiate on some things which hitherto I have but slightly touched upon, in order to convince the reader, not only that the good and amiable qualities of man are not those that make him beyond other animals a sociable creature; but moreover that it would be utterly impossible, either to raise any multitudes into a populous, rich and flourishing nation, or when so raised, to keep and maintain them in that condition, without the assistance of what we call evil both natural and moral. . . . (. . .)

It is manifest then that the hunting after this *pulchrum & honestum* is not much better than a wild-goose chase that is but little to be depended upon. But this is not the greatest fault I find with it. The imaginary notions that men may be virtuous without self-denial are a vast inlet to hypocrisy, which being once made habitual, we must not only deceive others, but likewise become altogether unknown to ourselves, and in an instance I am going to give, it will appear how for want of duly examining himself this might happen to a person of quality of parts and erudition, one every way resembling the author of the characteristics himself.

A man that has been brought up in ease and affluence, if he is of a quiet indolent nature, learns to shun everything that is troublesome, and chooses to curb his passions, more because of the inconveniences that arise from the eager pursuit after pleasure, and the yielding to all the demands of our inclinations, than any dislike he has to sensual enjoyments. And it is possible that a person educated under a great philosopher [John Locke], who was a mild and good-natured as well as able tutor, may in such happy circumstances have a better opinion of his inward state than it really deserves, and believe himself virtuous, because his passions lie dormant. He may form fine notions of the social virtues and the contempt of death, write well of them in his closet and talk eloquently of them in company, but you shall never catch him fighting for his country, or laboring to retrieve any national losses. A man that deals in metaphysics may easily throw himself into an enthusiasm, and really believe that he does not fear death while it remains out of sight. But should he be asked why, having this intrepidity either from nature or acquired by philosophy, he did not follow arms when his country was involved in war; or when he saw the nation daily robbed by those at the helm, and the affairs of the Exchequer perplexed, why he did not go to court, and make use of all his friends and interest to be a lord treasurer, that by his integrity and wise management he might restore the public credit; it is probable he would answer that he loved retirement, had no other ambition than to be a good man, and never aspired to have any share in the government, or that he hated all flattery and slavish attendance, the insincerity of courts and bustle of the world. I am willing to believe him. But may not a man of an indolent temper and inactive spirit say, and be sincere in all this, and at the same time indulge his appetites without being able to subdue them, though his duty summons him to it? Virtue consists in action, and whoever is possessed of this social love and kind affection to his species, and by his birth or quality can claim any post in the public management ought not to sit still when he can be serviceable, but exert himself to the utmost for the good of his fellow subjects. Had this noble person been of a warlike genius or a boisterous temper, he would have chosen another part in the drama of life, and preached a quite contrary doctrine. For we are ever pushing our reason which way soever we feel passion to draw it, and self-love pleads to all human creatures for their different views, still furnishing every individual with arguments to justify their inclinations.

That boasted middle way, and the calm virtue recommended in the *Characteristics*, are good for nothing but to breed drones, and might qualify a man for the stupid enjoyments of a monastic life, or at best a country justice of peace, but they would never fit him for labor and assiduity, or stir him up to great achievements and perilous undertakings. Man's natural love of ease and idleness, and proneness to indulge his sensual pleasures, are not to be cured by precept. His strong habits and inclinations can only be subdued by passions of greater violence. Preach and demonstrate to a coward the unreasonableness of his fears and you'll not make him valiant, any more than you can make him taller by bidding him to be ten foot high, whereas the secret to raise courage, as I have made it public in Remark R, is almost infallible.

The fear of death is the strongest when we are in our greatest vigor, and our appetite is keen, when we are sharp-sighted, quick of hearing, and every part performs its office. The reason is plain, because then life is most delicious and ourselves most capable of enjoying it. How comes it then that a man of honor should so easily accept of a challenge, though at thirty and in perfect health? It is his pride that conquers his fear, for when his pride is not concerned this fear will appear most glaringly. If he is not used to the sea let him but be in a storm, or, if he never was ill before, have but a sore throat or a slight fever, and he'll show a thousand anxieties, and in them the inestimable value he sets on life. Had man been naturally humble and proof against flattery, the politician could never have had his ends, or known what to have made of him. Without vices the excellency of the species would have ever remained undiscovered, and every worthy that has made himself famous in the world is a strong evidence against this amiable system.

If the courage of the great Macedonian [Alexander the Great] came up to distraction when he fought alone against a whole garrison, his madness was not less when he fancied himself to be a god, or at least doubted whether he was or not. And as soon as we make this reflection, we discover both the passion, and the extravagance of it, that buoyed up his spirits in the most imminent dangers, and carried him through all the difficulties and fatigues he underwent.

There never was in the world a brighter example of an able and complete magistrate than Cicero. When I think of his care and vigilance, the real hazards he slighted, and the pains he took for the safety of Rome; his wisdom and sagacity in detecting and disappointing the stratagems of the boldest and most subtle conspirators, and at the same time of his love to literature, arts and sciences, his capacity in metaphysics, the justness of his reasoning, the force of his eloquence, the politeness of his style, and the genteel spirit that runs through his writings; when I think, I say, of all these things together, I am struck with amazement, and the least I can say of him is that he was a prodigious man. But when I have set the many good qualities he had in the best light, it is as evident to me on the other side, that had his vanity been inferior to his greatest excellency, the good sense and knowledge of the world he was so eminently possessed of could never have let him be such a fulsome as well as noisy trumpeter as he was of his own praises, or suffered him rather than not proclaim his own merit, to make a verse that a schoolboy would have been laughed at for. . . .

How strict and severe was the morality of rigid Cato, how steady and unaffected the virtue of that grand asserter of Roman liberty! But though the equivalent this Stoic enjoyed, for all the self-denial and austerity he practiced, remained long concealed, and his peculiar modesty hid from the world, and perhaps himself, a vast . . . frailty of his heart that forced him into heroism. Yet it was brought to light in the last scene of his life, and by his suicide it plainly appeared that he was governed by a tyrannical power superior to the love of his country, and that the implacable hatred and superlative envy he bore to the glory, the real greatness and personal merit of Caesar, had for a long time swayed all his actions under the most noble pretenses. Had not this violent motive overruled his consummate prudence he might not only have saved himself, but likewise most of his friends that were ruined by the loss of him, and would in all probability, if he could have stooped to it, been the second man in Rome. But he knew the boundless mind and unlimited generosity of the victor [Julius Caesar]. It was his clemency he feared, and therefore chose death because it was less terrible to his pride than the thought of giving his mortal foe so tempting an opportunity of showing the magnanimity of his soul, as Caesar would have found in forgiving such an inveterate enemy as Cato, and offering him his friendship; and which, it is thought by the judicious, that penetrating as well as ambitious conqueror would not have slipped, if the other had dared to live. . . . (. . .)

What I have endeavored hitherto, has been to prove, that the *pulchrum & honestum*, excellency and real worth of things, are most commonly precarious and alterable as modes and customs vary; that consequently the inferences drawn from their certainty are insignificant, and that the generous notions concerning the natural goodness of man are hurtful as they tend to mislead, and are merely chimerical. The truth of this latter I have illustrated by the most obvious examples in history. I have spoken of our love of company and aversion to solitude, examined thoroughly the various motives of them, and made it appear that they all center in self-love. I intend now to investigate into the nature of society, and diving into the very rise of it, make it evident, that not the good and amiable, but the bad and hateful qualities of man, his imperfections and the want of excellencies which other creatures are endued with, are the first causes that made man sociable beyond other animals the moment after he lost Paradise. And that if he had remained in his primitive innocence, and continued to enjoy the blessings that attended it, there is no shadow of probability that he ever would have become that sociable creature he is now.

How necessary our appetites and passions are for the welfare of all trades and handicrafts has been sufficiently proven throughout the book, and that they are our bad qualities, or at least produce them, nobody denies. It remains then that I should set forth the variety of obstacles that hinder and perplex man in the labor he is constantly employed in, the procuring of what he wants, and which in other words is called the business of self-preservation. While at the same time I demonstrate that the sociableness of man arises only from these two things . . . , the multiplicity of his desires, and the continual opposition he meets with in his endeavors to gratify them.

The obstacles I speak of relate either to our own frame, or the globe we inhabit, I mean the condition of it, since it has been cursed. I have often endeavored to contemplate separately on the two things I named last, but could never keep them asunder. They always interfere and mix with one another, and at last make up together a frightful chaos of evil. All the elements are our enemies, water drowns and fire consumes those who unskillfully approach them. The Earth in a thousand places produces plants and other vegetables that are hurtful to man, while she feeds and cherishes a variety of creatures that are noxious to him and suffers a legion of poisons to dwell within her. But the most unkind of all the elements is that which we cannot live one moment without. It is impossible to repeat all the injuries we receive from the wind and weather; and though the greatest part of mankind have ever been employed in defending their species from the inclemency of the air, yet no art or labor have hitherto been able to find a security against the wild rage of some meteors. . . . (. . .)

There is nothing good in all the universe to the best-designing man, if either through mistake or ignorance he commits the least failing in the use of it. There is no innocence or integrity that can protect a man from a thousand mischiefs that surround him. On the contrary, everything is evil which art and experience have not taught us to turn into a blessing. Therefore, how diligent in harvest time is the husbandman in getting in his crop and sheltering it from rain, without which he could never have enjoyed it! As seasons differ with the climates, experience has taught us differently to make use of them, and in one part of the globe we may see the farmer sow while he is reaping in the other. From all [of] which we may learn how vastly this Earth must have been altered since the fall of our first parents. For should we trace man from his beautiful, his divine original, not proud of wisdom acquired by haughty precept or tedious experience, but endued with consummate knowledge the moment he was formed; I mean the state of innocence, in which no animal nor vegetable upon Earth, nor mineral underground, was noxious to him, and himself secure from the injuries of the air as well as all other harms, was contented with the necessities of life, which the globe he inhabited furnished him with, without his assistance. When yet not conscious of guilt, he found himself in every place to be the well-obeyed unrivaled lord of all, and unaffected with his greatness was wholly rapt up in sublime meditations on the infinity of his Creator, who daily did vouchsafe intelligibly to speak to him, and visit without mischief.

In such a golden age no reason or probability can be alleged why mankind ever should have raised themselves into such large societies as there have been in the world, as long as we can give any tolerable account of it. Where a man has everything he desires, and nothing to vex or disturb him, there is nothing [that] can be added to his happiness. And it is impossible to name a trade, art, science, dignity or employment that would not be superfluous in such a blessed state. If we pursue this thought we shall easily perceive that no societies could have sprung from the amiable virtues and loving qualities of man, but on the contrary that all of them must have had their origin from his wants, his imperfections, and the variety of his appetites. We shall find likewise that the more their pride and vanity are displayed and all their desires enlarged, the more capable they must be of being raised into large and vastly numerous societies.

[If the] air [was] always as inoffensive to our naked bodies, and as pleasant as to our thinking it is to the generality of birds in fair weather, and man had not been affected with pride, luxury and hypocrisy, as well as lust, I cannot see what could have put us upon the invention of clothes and houses. I shall say nothing of jewels, of plate, painting, sculpture, fine furniture, and all that rigid moralists have called unnecessary and superfluous. But if we were not soon tired with walking afoot, and were as nimble as some other animals; if men were naturally laborious, and none unreasonable in seeking and indulging their ease, and likewise free from other vices, and the ground was everywhere even, solid and clean, who would have thought of coaches or ventured on a horse's back? What occasion has the dolphin for a ship, or what carriage would an eagle ask to travel in?

I hope the reader knows that by society I understand a body politic, in which man either subdued by superior force, or by persuasion drawn from his savage state, is become a disciplined creature, that can find his own ends in laboring for others, and where under one head or other form of government each member is rendered subservient to the whole, and all of them by cunning management are made to act as one. For if by society we only mean a number of people, that without rule or government should keep together out of a natural affection to their species or love of company, as a herd of cows or a flock of sheep, then there is not in the world a more unfit creature for society than man. A hundred of them that should be all equals, under no subjection, or fear of any superior upon Earth, could never live together awake two hours without quarreling, and the more knowledge, strength, wit, courage and resolution there was among them, the worse it would be.

It is probable that in the wild state of nature parents would keep a superiority over their children, at least while they were in strength, and that even afterwards the remembrance of what the others had experienced might produce in them something between love and fear, which we call reverence. It is probable likewise that the second generation following the example of the first, a man with a little cunning would always be able, as long as he lived and had his senses, to maintain a superior sway over all his own offspring and descendants, how numerous soever they might grow. But the old stock once dead, the sons would quarrel, and there could be no peace long, before there had been war. Eldership in brothers is of no great force, and the preeminence that is given to it only invented as a shift to live in peace. Man as he is a fearful animal, naturally not rapacious, loves peace and quiet, and he would never fight, if nobody offended him, and he could have what he fights for without it. To this fearful disposition and the aversion he has to his being disturbed, are owing all the various projects and forms of government. Monarchy without doubt was the first. Aristocracy and democracy were two different methods of mending the inconveniences of the first, and a mixture of these three an improvement on all the rest.

But be we savages or politicians, it is impossible that man, mere fallen man, should act with any other view but to please himself while he has the use of his organs, and the greatest extravagance either of love or despair can have no other center. There is no difference between will and pleasure in one sense, and every motion made in spite of them must be unnatural and convulsive. Since then action is so confined, and we are always forced to do what we please, and at the same time our thoughts are free and uncontrolled, it is impossible we could be sociable creatures without hypocrisy. The proof of this is plain, since we cannot prevent the ideas that are continually arising within us, all civil commerce would be lost, if by art and prudent dissimulation we had not learned to hide and stifle them. And if all we think was to be laid open to others in the same manner as it is to ourselves, it is impossible that endowed with speech we could be sufferable to one another. I am persuaded that every reader feels the truth of what I say; and I tell my antagonist that his conscience flies in his face, while his tongue is preparing to refute me. In all civil societies men are taught insensibly to be hypocrites from their cradle, nobody dares to own that [which] he gets by public calamities, or even by the loss of private persons. The sexton would be stoned should he wish openly for the death of the parishioners, though everybody knew that he had nothing else to live upon.

To me it is a great pleasure, when I look on the affairs of human life, to behold into what various and often strangely opposite forms the hope of gain and thoughts of lucre shape men, according to the different employments they are of, and stations they are in. How gay and merry does every face appear at a well-ordered ball, and what a solemn sadness is observed at the masquerade of a funeral! But the undertaker is as much pleased with his gains as the dancing master. Both are equally tired in their occupations, and the mirth of the one is as much forced as the gravity of the other is affected. Those who have never minded the conversation of a spruce mercer, and a young lady his customer that comes to his shop, have neglected a scene of life that is very entertaining. . . . (. . .)

It is certain that the fewer desires a man has and the less he covets, the more easy he is to himself. The more active he is to supply his own wants, and the less he requires to be waited upon, the more he will be beloved and the less trouble he is in a family. The more he loves peace and concord, the more charity he has for his neighbor, and the more he shines in real virtue, there is no doubt but that in proportion he is acceptable to God and man. But let us be just, what benefit can these things be of, or what earthly good can they do, to promote the wealth, the glory and worldly greatness of nations? It is the sensual courtier that sets no limits to his luxury; the fickle strumpet that invents new fashions every week;

the haughty duchess that in equipage, entertainments, and all her behavior would imitate a princess; the profuse rake and lavish heir, that scatter about their money without wit or judgment, buy everything they see, and either destroy or give it away the next day; the covetous and perjured villain that squeezed an immense treasure from the tears of widows and orphans, and left the prodigals the money to spend: it is these that are the prey and proper food of a full grown Leviathan. Or in other words, such is the calamitous condition of human affairs that we stand in need of the plagues and monsters I named to have all the variety of labor performed, which the skill of men is capable of inventing in order to procure an honest livelihood to the vast multitudes of working poor, that are required to make a large society. And it is folly to imagine that great and wealthy nations can subsist, and be at once powerful and polite without.

I protest against Popery as much as ever Luther and Calvin did, or Queen Elizabeth herself, but I believe from my heart, that the Reformation has scarce been more instrumental in rendering the kingdoms and states that have embraced it, flourishing beyond other nations, than the silly and capricious invention of hooped and quilted petticoats. But if this should be denied me by the enemies of priestly power, at least I am sure that, bar the great men who have fought for and against that layman's blessing, it has from its first beginning to this day not employed so many hands, honest industrious laboring hands, as the abominable improvement on female luxury I named has done in few years. Religion is one thing and trade is another. He that gives most trouble to thousands of his neighbors, and invents the most operose manufactures is, right or wrong, the greatest friend to the society.

What a bustle is there to be made in several parts of the world, before a fine scarlet or crimson cloth can be produced, what multiplicity of trades and artificers must be employed! Not only such as are obvious, as woolcombers, spinners, the weaver, the clothworker, the scourer, the dyer, the setter, the drawer and the packer; but others that are more remote and might seem foreign to it; [such] as the millwright, the pewterer and the chemist, which yet are all necessary as well as a great number of other handicrafts to have the tools, utensils and other implements belonging to the trades already named. But all these things are done at home, and may be performed without extraordinary fatigue or danger. The most frightful prospect is left behind when we reflect on the toil and hazard that are to be undergone abroad, the vast seas we are to go over, the different climates we are to endure, and the several nations we must be obliged to for their assistance. Spain alone it is true might furnish us with wool to make the finest cloth. But what skill and pains, what experience and ingenuity are required to dye it of those beautiful colors! How widely are the drugs and other ingredients dispersed throughout the universe that are to meet in one kettle! Alum indeed we have of our own; argol we might have from the Rhine, and vitriol from Hungary. All this is in Europe; but then for saltpeter in quantity we are forced to go as far as the East Indies. Cochenille [insect bodies reared on cactus and used to make crimson dye], unknown to the ancients, is not much nearer to us, though in a quite different part of the Earth. We buy it, it is true, from the Spaniards; but not being their product they are forced to fetch it for us from the remotest corner of the new world in the West Indies. While so many sailors are broiling in the sun and sweltered with heat in the east and west of us, another set of them are freezing in the north to fetch potash from Russia.

When we are thoroughly acquainted with all the variety of toil and labor, the hardships and calamities that must be undergone to compass the end I speak of, and we consider the vast risks and perils that are run in those voyages, and that few of them are ever made but at the expense, not only of the health and welfare, but even the lives of many, when we are acquainted with, I say, and duly consider the things I named, it is scarcely possible to conceive a tyrant so inhuman and void of shame, that beholding things in the same view, he should exact such terrible services from his innocent slaves, and at the same time dare to own, that he did it for no other reason, than the satisfaction a man receives from having a garment made of scarlet or crimson cloth. But to what height of luxury must a nation be arrived, where not only the king's officers, but likewise his guards, even the private soldiers should have such impudent desires!

But if we turn the prospect, and look on all those labors as so many voluntary actions, belonging to different callings and occupations that men are brought up to for a livelihood, and in which everyone works for himself, how much soever he may seem to labor for others; if we consider, that even the sailors who undergo the greatest hardships, as soon as one voyage is ended, even after shipwreck, are looking out and soliciting for employment in another; if we consider, I say, and look on these things in another view, we shall find that the labor of the poor is so far from being a burden and an imposition upon them, that to have employment is a blessing, which in their addresses to Heaven they pray for, and to procure it for the generality of them is the greatest care of every legislature.

As children and even infants are the apes of others, so all youth have an ardent desire of being men and women, and become often ridiculous by their impatient endeavors to appear what everybody sees they are not. All large societies are not a little indebted to this folly for the perpetuity or at least long continuance of trades once established. What pains will young people take, and what violence will they not commit upon themselves, to attain to insignificant and often blameable qualifications, which for want of judgment and experience they admire in others, that are superior to them in age! This fondness of imitation makes them accustom themselves by degrees to the use of things that were irksome, if not intolerable to them at first, till they know not how to leave them, and are often very sorry for having inconsiderately increased the necessaries of life without any necessity. What estates have been gotten by tea and coffee! What a vast traffic is driven, what a variety of labor is performed in the world to the maintenance of thousands of families that altogether depend on two silly if not odious customs, the taking of snuff and smoking of tobacco, both which it is certain do infinitely more hurt than good to those that are addicted to them! I shall go further, and demonstrate the usefulness of private losses and misfortunes to the public, and the folly of our wishes, when we pretend to be most wise and serious. The fire of London [of 1666] was a great calamity, but if the carpenters, bricklayers, smiths, and all, not only that are employed in building but likewise those that made and dealt in the same manufactures and other merchandises that were burnt, and other trades again that got by them when they were in full employ, were to vote against those who lost by the fire, the rejoicings would equal if not exceed the complaints. In recruiting what is lost and destroyed by fire, storms, sea fights, sieges, battles, a considerable part of trade consists; the truth of which and whatever I have said of the nature of society will plainly appear from what follows.

It would be a difficult task to enumerate all the advantages and different benefits that accrue to a nation on account of shipping and navigation. But if we only take into consideration the ships themselves, and every vessel great and small that is made use of for water-carriage, from the least wherry to a first-rate man of war—the timber and hands that are employed in the building of them; and consider the pitch, tar, rosin, grease; the masts, yards, sails and riggings; the variety of smiths' work, the cables, oars and everything else belonging to them—we shall find that to furnish only such a nation as ours with all these necessaries makes up a considerable part of the traffic of Europe, without speaking of the stores and ammunition of all sorts that are consumed in them, or the mariners, water men and others with their families, that are maintained by them.

But should we on the other hand take a view of the manifold mischiefs and variety of evils, moral as well as natural, that befall nations on the score of seafaring and their commerce with strangers, the prospect would be very frightful. And could we suppose a large populous island, that should be wholly unacquainted with ships and sea affairs, but otherwise a wise and well-governed people; and that some angel or their genius should lay before them a scheme or draft, where they might see, on the one side, all the riches and real advantages that would be acquired by navigation in a thousand years, and on the other, the wealth and lives that would be lost, and all the other calamities, that would be unavoidably sustained on account of it during the same time, I am confident, they would look upon ships with horror and detestation, and that their prudent rulers would severely forbid the making and inventing all buildings or machines to go to sea with, of what shape or denomination soever, and prohibit all such abominable contrivances on great penalties, if not the pain of death. But to let alone the necessary consequence of foreign trade, the corruption of manners, as well as plagues, poxes, and other diseases, that are brought to us by shipping, should we only cast our eyes on what is either to be imputed to the wind and weather, the treachery of the seas, the ice of the north, the vermin of the south, the darkness of nights, and unwholesomeness of climates, or else occasioned by the want of good provisions and the faults of mariners, the unskillfulness of some, and the neglect and drunkenness of others. And should we consider the losses of men and treasure swallowed up in the deep, the tears and necessities of widows and orphans made by the sea, the ruin of merchants and the consequences, the continual anxieties that parents and wives are in for the safety of their children and husbands, and not forget the many pangs and heartaches that are felt throughout a trading nation by owners and insurers at every blast of wind; should we cast our eyes, I say, on these things, consider with due attention and give them the weight they deserve, would it not be amazing, how a nation of thinking people should talk of their ships and navigation as a peculiar blessing to them, and placing an uncommon felicity in having an infinity of vessels dispersed through the wide world, and always some going to and others coming from every part of the universe?

But let us once in our consideration on these things confine ourselves to what the ships suffer only, the vessels themselves with their rigging and appurtenances, without thinking on the freight they carry, or the hands that work them, and we shall find that the damage sustained that way only is very considerable, and must one year with another amount to vast sums: the ships that are foundered at sea, split against rocks and swallowed up by sands, some by the fierceness of tempests altogether, others by that and the want of pilots' experience and knowledge of the coasts; the masts that are blown down or forced to be cut and thrown overboard, the yards, sails and cordage of different sizes that are destroyed by storms, and the anchors that are lost; add to these the necessary repairs of leaks sprung and other hurts received from the rage of winds, and the violence of the waves. Many ships are set on fire by carelessness, and the effects of strong liquors, which none are more addicted to than sailors. Sometimes unhealthy climates, at others the badness of provision breed fatal distempers that sweep away the greatest part of the crew, and not a few ships are lost for want of hands.

These are all calamities inseparable from navigation, and seem to be great impediments that clog the wheels of foreign commerce. How happy would a merchant think himself if his ships should always have fine weather, and the wind he wished for, and every mariner he employed, from the highest to the lowest, be a knowing experienced sailor, and a careful, sober, good man! Was such a felicity to be had for prayers, what owner of ships is there or dealer in Europe, nay the whole world, who would not be all day long teasing Heaven to obtain such a blessing for himself, without regard what detriment it would do to others? Such a petition would certainly be a very unconscionable one, yet where is the man who imagines not that he has a right to make it? And therefore, as everyone pretends to an equal claim to those favors, let us, without reflecting on the impossibility of its being true, suppose all their prayers effectual and their wishes answered, and afterwards examine into the result of such a happiness.

Ships would last as long as timber houses to the full, because they are as strongly built, and the latter are liable to suffer by high winds and other storms, which the first by our supposition are not to be. So that before there would be any real occasion for new ships, the master builders now in being and everybody under them that is set to work about them would all die a natural death, if they were not starved or come to some untimely end. For in the first place, all ships having prosperous gales, and never waiting for the wind, they would make very quick voyages both out and home. Secondly, no merchandises would be damaged by the sea, or by stress of weather thrown overboard, but the entire lading would always come safe ashore. And hence it would follow, that three parts in four of the merchantmen already made would be superfluous for the present, and the stock of ships that are now in the world serve a vast many years. Masts and yards would last as long as the vessels themselves, and we should not need to trouble Norway on that score a great while yet. The sails and rigging indeed of the few ships made use of would wear out, but not a quarter part so fast as now they do, for they often suffer more in one hour's storm, than in ten days' fair weather.

Anchors and cables there would be seldom any occasion for, and one of each would last a ship time out of mind. This article alone would yield many a tedious holiday to the anchorsmiths and the rope yards. This general want of consumption would have such an influence on the timber merchants, and all that import iron, sail-cloth, hemp, pitch, tar, etc., that four parts in five of what, in the beginning of this reflection on sea-affairs, I said, made a considerable branch of the traffic of Europe, would be entirely lost.

I have only touched hitherto on the consequences of this blessing in relation to shipping, but it would be detrimental to all other branches of trade besides, and destructive to the poor of every country, that exports anything of their own growth or manufacture. The goods and merchandises that every year go to the deep that are spoiled at sea by salt water, by heat, by vermin, destroyed by fire, or lost to the merchant by other accidents, all owing to storms or tedious voyages, or else the neglect or rapacity of sailors. Such goods, I say, and merchandises are a considerable part of what every year is sent abroad throughout the world, and must have employed great multitudes of poor before they could come on board. A hundred bales of cloth that are burnt or sunk in the Mediterranean are as beneficial to the poor in England, as if they had safely arrived at Smyrna or Aleppo, and every yard of them had been retailed in the [Sultan's] dominions.

The merchant may break, and by him the clothier, the dyer, the packer, and other tradesmen, the middling people, may suffer; but the poor that were set to work about them can never lose. Day laborers commonly receive their earnings once a week, and all the working people that were employed either in any of the various branches of the manufacture itself, or the several land and water carriages it requires to be brought to perfection, from the sheep's back, to the vessel it was entered in, were paid, at least much the greatest part of them, before the parcel came on board. Should any of my readers draw conclusions *in infinitum* from my assertions that goods sunk or burnt are as beneficial to the poor as if they had been well sold and put to their proper uses, I would count him a caviller and not worth answering. Should it always rain and the sun never shine, the fruits of the Earth would soon be rotten and destroyed; and yet it is no paradox to affirm, that to have grass or corn, rain is as necessary as the sunshine.

In what manner this blessing of fair winds and fine weather would affect the mariners themselves, and the breed of sailors, may be easily conjectured from what has been said already. As there would hardly one ship in four be made use of, so the vessels themselves being always exempt from storms, fewer hands would be required to work them, and consequently five in six of the seamen we have might be spared, which in this nation, most employments of the poor being overstocked, would be but an untoward article. As soon as those superfluous seamen should be extinct, it would be impossible to man such large fleets as we could at present. But I do not look upon this as a detriment, or the least inconvenience, for the reduction of mariners as to numbers being general throughout the world, all the consequence would be, that in case of war the maritime powers would be obliged to fight with fewer ships, which would be a happiness instead of an evil. And would you carry this felicity to the highest pitch of perfection, it is but to add one desirable blessing more, and no nation shall ever fight at all. The blessing I hint at is, what all good Christians are bound to pray for, [that is], that all princes and states would be true to their oaths and promises, and just to one another, as well as their own subjects; that they might have a greater regard for the dictates of conscience and religion, than those of state politics and worldly wisdom, and prefer the spiritual welfare of others to their own carnal desires, and the honesty, the safety, the peace and tranquillity of the nations they govern, to their own love of glory, spirit of revenge, avarice, and ambition.

The last paragraph will to many seem a digression, that makes little for my purpose. But what I mean by it is to demonstrate that goodness, integrity, and a peaceful disposition in rulers and governors of nations, are not the proper qualifications to aggrandize them, and increase their numbers, any more than the uninterrupted series of success that every private person would be blest with, if he could, and which I have shown would be injurious and destructive to a large society, that should place a felicity in worldly greatness, and being envied by their neighbors, and value themselves upon their honor and their strength.

No man needs to guard himself against blessings, but calamities require hands to avert them. The amiable qualities of man put none of the species upon stirring. His honesty, his love of company, his goodness, content and frugality are so many comforts to an indolent society, and the more real and unaffected they are, the more they keep everything at rest and peace, and the more they will everywhere prevent trouble and motion itself. The same almost may be said of the gifts and munificence of heaven, and all the bounties and benefits of nature. This is certain, that the more extensive they are, and the greater plenty we have of them, the more we save our labor. But the necessities, the vices and imperfections of man, together with the various inclemencies of the air and other elements, contain in them the seeds of all arts, industry and labor. It is the extremities of heat and cold, the inconstancy and badness of seasons, the violence and uncertainty of winds, the vast power and treachery of water, the rage and untractableness of fire, and the stubbornness and sterility of the Earth, that rack our invention, how we shall either avoid the mischiefs they may produce, or correct the malignity of them and turn their several forces to our own advantage a thousand different ways, while we are employed in supplying the infinite variety of our wants, which will ever be multiplied as our knowledge is enlarged, and our desires increase. Hunger, thirst and nakedness are the first tyrants that force us to stir. Afterwards, our pride, sloth, sensuality and fickleness are the great patrons that promote all arts and sciences, trades, handicrafts and callings, while the great task masters, necessity, avarice, envy, and ambition, each in the class that belongs to him, keep the members of the society to their labor, and make them all submit, most of them cheerfully, to the drudgery of their station; kings and princes not excepted.

The greater the variety of trades and manufactures, the more operose they are, and the more they are divided in many branches, the greater numbers may be contained in a society without being in one another's way, and the more easily they may be rendered a rich, potent and flourishing people. Few virtues employ any hands, and therefore they may render a small nation good, but they can never make a great one. To be strong and laborious, patient in difficulties, and assiduous in all business, are commendable qualities. But as they do their own work, so they are their own reward, and neither art nor industry have ever paid their compliments to them; whereas the excellency of human thought and contrivance has been and is yet nowhere more conspicuous than in the variety of tools and instruments of workmen and artificers, and the multiplicity of engines, that were all invented either to assist the weakness of man, to correct his many imperfections, to gratify his laziness, or obviate his impatience.

It is in morality as it is in nature, there is nothing so perfectly good in creatures that it cannot be hurtful to any one of the society, nor anything so entirely evil, but it may prove beneficial to some part or other of the creation. So that things are only good and evil in reference to something else, and according to the light and position they are placed in. What pleases us is good in that regard, and by this rule every man wishes well for himself to the best of his capacity, with little respect to his neighbor. There never was any rain yet, though in a very dry season when public prayers had been made for it, but somebody or other who wanted to go abroad wished it might be fair weather only for that day. When the corn stands thick in the spring, and the generality of the country rejoice at the pleasing object, the rich farmer who kept his last year's crop for a better market, pines at the sight, and inwardly grieves at the prospect of a plentiful harvest. Nay, we shall often hear your idle people openly wish for the possessions of others, and not to be injurious forsooth add this wise proviso, that it should be without detriment to the owners: but I'm afraid they often do it without any such restriction in their hearts.

It is a happiness that the prayers as well as wishes of most people are insignificant and good for nothing, or else the only thing that could keep mankind fit for society, and the world from falling into confusion, would be the impossibility that all the petitions made to Heaven should be granted. A dutiful pretty young gentleman newly come from his travels lies at the Briel waiting with impatience for an easterly wind to waft him over to England, where a dying father, who wants to embrace and give him his blessing before he yields his breath, lies moaning after him, melted with grief and tenderness. In the meanwhile a British minister, who is to take care of the Protestant interest in Germany, is riding post to Harwich, and in violent haste to be at Ratisbon before the Diet breaks up. At the same time a rich fleet lies ready for the Mediterranean, and a fine squadron is bound for the Baltic. All these things may probably happen at once, at least there is no difficulty in supposing they should. If these people are not atheists, or very great reprobates, they will all have some good thoughts before they go to sleep, and consequently about bedtime they must all differently pray for a fair wind and a prosperous voyage. I don't say but it is their duty, and it is possible they may be all heard, but I am sure they can't be all served at the same time.

After this I flatter myself to have demonstrated that neither the friendly qualities and kind affections that are natural to man, nor the real virtues he is capable of acquiring by reason and self-denial, are the foundation of society; but that what we call evil in this world, moral as well as natural, is the grand principle that makes us sociable creatures, the solid basis, the life and support of all trades and employments without exception: that there we must look for the true origin of all arts and sciences, and that the moment evil ceases, the society must be spoiled, if not totally dissolved.

I could add a thousand things to enforce and further illustrate this truth with abundance of pleasure. But for fear of being troublesome I shall make an end, though I confess that I have not been half so solicitous to gain the approbation of others as I have studied to please myself in this amusement.

Yet if ever I hear, that by following this diversion I have given any to the intelligent reader, it will always add to the satisfaction I have received in the performance. In the hope my vanity forms of this I leave him with regret, and conclude with repeating the seeming paradox, the substance of which is advanced in the title page, that private vices by the dexterous management of a skillful politician may be turned into public benefits.

A Vindication of the Book

Whereas in the *Evening Post* of Thursday, July 11, a Presentment was inserted of the Grand Jury of Middlesex, against the publisher of a book entitled *The Fable of the Bees, or, Private Vices, Public Benefits*, and since that, a passionate and abusive letter has been published against the same book and the author of it, in the *London Journal* of Saturday, July 27; I think myself indispensably obliged to vindicate the above-said book against the black aspersions that undeservedly have been cast upon it, being conscious that I have not had the least ill design in composing it. The accusations against it having been made openly in the public papers, it is not equitable the defense of it should appear in a more private manner. What I have to say in my behalf I shall address to all men of sense and sincerity, asking no other favor of them than their patience and attention. Setting aside what in that letter relates to others, and everything that is foreign and immaterial, I shall begin with the passage that is quoted from the book: "After this, I flatter myself to have demonstrated that neither the friendly qualities and kind affections that are natural to man, nor the real virtues he is capable of acquiring by reason and self-denial are the foundations of society; but that what we call evil in this world, moral as well as natural, is the grand principle that makes us sociable creatures; the solid basis, the life and support of all trades and employments without exception: that there we must look for the true origin of all arts and sciences; and that the moment evil ceases, the society must be spoiled, if not totally dissolved." These words I own are in the book, and, being both innocent and true, [are] like[ly] to remain there in all future impressions. But I will likewise own very freely, that, if I had written with a design to be understood by the meanest capacities, I would not have chosen the subject there treated of; or if I had, I would have amplified and explained every period, talked and distinguished magisterially, and never appeared without the fescue [a pointer used as an aid in teaching children to read] in my hand. As for example, to make the passage pointed at intelligible, I would have bestowed a page or two on the meaning of the word "evil";

after that I would have taught them that every defect, every want was an evil; that on the multiplicity of those wants depended all those mutual services which the individual members of a society pay to each other; and that consequently, the greater variety there was of wants, the larger number of individuals might find their private interest in laboring for the good of others, and united together, compose one body. Is there a trade or handicraft but what supplies us with something we wanted? This want certainly, before it was supplied, was an evil, which that trade or handicraft was to remedy, and without which it could never have been thought of. Is there an art or science that was not invented to mend some defect? Had this latter not existed, there could have been no occasion for the former to remove it. I say, "The excellency of human thought and contrivance has been, and is yet nowhere more conspicuous than in the variety of tools and instruments of workmen and artificers, and the multiplicity of engines, that were all invented, either to assist the weakness of man, to correct his many imperfections, to gratify his laziness, or obviate his impatience." Several foregoing pages run in the same strain. But what relation has all this to religion or infidelity, more than it has to navigation of the peace in the North?

The many hands that are employed to supply our natural wants, that are really such, as hunger, thirst, and nakedness, are inconsiderable to the vast numbers that are all innocently gratifying the depravity of our corrupt nature. I mean the industrious, who get a livelihood by their honest labor, to which the vain and voluptuous must be beholden for all their tools and implements of ease and luxury. "The short-sighted vulgar, in the chain of causes, seldom can see farther than one link; but those who can enlarge their view, and will give themselves leisure of gazing on the prospect of concatenated events, may in an hundred places see good spring up and pullulate from evil, as naturally as chickens do from eggs."

The words are to be found in the Remark made on the seeming paradox, that in the grumbling hive

> *The worst of all the Multitude*
> *Did something for the Common Good:*

Where in many instances may be amply discovered, how unsearchable Providence daily orders the comforts of the laborious, and even the deliverances of the oppressed, secretly to come forth not only from the vices of the luxurious, but likewise the crimes of the flagitious [person guilty of or addicted to atrocious crimes] and most abandoned.

Men of candor and capacity perceive at first sight that in the passage censured there is no meaning hidden or expressed that is not altogether contained in the following words: "Man is a necessitous creature on innumerable accounts, and yet from those very necessities, and nothing else, arise all trades and employments." But it is ridiculous for men to meddle with books above their sphere.

The Fable of the Bees was designed for the entertainment of people of knowledge and education, when they have an idle hour which they know not how to spend better. It is a book of severe and exalted morality that contains a strict test of virtue, an infallible touchstone to distinguish the real from the counterfeited, and shows many actions to be faulty that are palmed upon the world for good ones. It describes the nature and symptoms of human passions, detects their force and disguises, and traces self-love in its darkest recesses; I might safely add, beyond any other system of ethics: the whole is a rhapsody void of order or method, but no part of it has anything in it that is sour or pedantic. The style I confess is very unequal, sometimes very high and rhetorical, and sometimes very low and even very trivial. Such as it is, I am satisfied that it has diverted persons of great probity and virtue, and unquestionable good sense; and I am in no fear that it will ever cease to do so while it is read by such. Whoever has seen the violent charge against this book will pardon me for saying more in commendation of it, than a man not laboring under the same necessity would do of his own work on any other occasion.

The encomiums upon stews [brothels] complained of in the Presentment are nowhere in the book. What might give a handle to this charge must be a political dissertation [*A Modest Defense of Public Stews*] concerning the best method to guard and preserve women of honor and virtue from the insults of dissolute men, whose passions are often ungovernable. As in this there is a dilemma between two evils, which it is impracticable to shun both, so I have treated it with the utmost caution, and begin thus: "I am far from encouraging vice, and should think it an unspeakable felicity for a state, if the sin of uncleanness could be utterly banished from it; but I am afraid it is impossible." I give my reasons why I think it so, and speaking occasionally of the music houses at Amsterdam, I give a short account of them, than which nothing can be more harmless; and I appeal to all impartial judges, whether what I have said of them is not ten times more proper to give men (even the voluptuous of any taste) a disgust and aversion against them, than it is to raise any criminal desire. I am sorry the Grand Jury should conceive that I published this with a design to debauch the nation, without considering that in the first place there is not a sentence nor a syllable that can either offend the chastest ear, or sully the imagination of the most vicious, or in the second [place], the matter complained of is manifestly addressed to magistrates and politicians, or at least the more serious and thinking part of mankind; whereas a general corruption of manners as to lewdness, to be produced by reading, can only be apprehended from obscenities easily purchased, and every way adapted to the tastes and capacities of the heedless multitude and inexperienced youth of both sexes: but that the performance, so outrageously exclaimed against, was never calculated for either of these classes of people, is self-evident from every circumstance. The beginning of the prose is altogether philosophical, and hardly intelligible to any that have not been used to matters of speculation. And the running title of it is so far from being specious or inviting, that without having read the book itself nobody knows what to make of it, while at the same time the price is five shillings. From all [of] which it is plain that if the book contains any dangerous tenets, I have not been very solicitous to scatter them among the people. I have not said a word to please or engage them, and the greatest compliment I have made them has been, *apage vulgus* [away with the masses!]. "But as nothing," I say, "would more clearly demonstrate the falsity of my notions than that the generality of the people should fall in with them, so I don't expect the approbation of the multitude. I write not to many, nor seek for any well-wishers, but among the few that think abstractly, and have their minds elevated above the vulgar." Of this I have made no ill use, and ever preserved such a tender regard to the public, that when I have advanced any uncommon sentiments, I have used all the precautions imaginable, that they might not be hurtful to weak minds that might casually dip into the book. When I owned, "That it was my sentiment that no society could be raised into a rich and mighty kingdom, or so raised subsist in their wealth and power for any considerable time, without the vices of man," I had premised what was true, "that I had never said or imagined, that man could not be virtuous as well in a rich and mighty kingdom, as in the most pitiful commonwealth." This caution a man less scrupulous than myself might have thought superfluous, when he had already explained himself on that head in the very same paragraph, which begins thus: "I lay down as a first principle, that in all societies, great or small, it is the duty of every member of it to be good; that virtue ought to be encouraged, vice discountenanced, the laws obeyed, and the transgressors punished." There is not a line in the book that contradicts this doctrine, and I defy my enemies to disprove what I have advanced, that "if I have shown the way to worldly greatness, I have always without hesitation preferred the road that leads to virtue." No man ever took more pains not to be misconstrued than myself. Mind when I say that societies cannot be raised to wealth and power, and the top of earthly glory, without vices. I don't think that by so saying I bid men be vicious, any more than I bid them be quarrelsome or covetous, when I affirm, that "the profession of the law could not be maintained in such numbers and splendor, if there was not abundance of too selfish and litigious people." A caution of the same nature I had already given towards the end of the Preface, on account of a palpable evil inseparable from the felicity of London. To search into the real causes of things imports no ill design, nor has any tendency to do harm. A man may write on poisons and be an excellent physician. I say, "No man needs to guard himself against blessings, but calamities require hands to avert them." And lower, "It is the extremities of heat and cold, the inconstancy and badness of seasons, the violence and uncertainty of winds, the vast power and treachery of water, the rage and untractableness of fire, and the stubbornness and sterility of the Earth, that rack our invention, how we shall either avoid the mischiefs they produce, or correct the malignity of them, and turn their several forces to our own advantage a thousand different ways." While a man is enquiring into the occupation of vast multitudes, I cannot see why he may not say all this and much more, without being accused of depreciating and speaking slightly of the gifts and munificence of Heaven, when at the same time he demonstrates that without rain and sunshine this globe would not be habitable to creatures like ourselves. It is an out-of-the-way subject, and I would never quarrel with the man who should tell me that it might as well have been let alone. Yet I always thought it would please men of any tolerable taste, and not be easily lost.

My vanity I could never conquer, so well as I could wish; and I am too proud to commit crimes. And as to the main scope, the intent of the book, I mean the view it was written with, I protest that it has been with the utmost sincerity, what I have declared of it in the Preface, where . . . you will find these words: "If you ask me, why I have done all this, *cui bono?* and what good these notions will produce? truly, besides the reader's diversion, I believe none at all; but if I was asked, what naturally ought to be expected from them? I would answer, that in the first place the people who continually find fault with others, by reading them would be taught to look at home, and examining their own consciences, be made ashamed of always railing at what they are more or less guilty of themselves; and that in the next, those who are so fond of the ease and comforts of a great and flourishing nation, would learn more patiently to submit to those inconveniences, which no government upon Earth can remedy, when they should see the impossibility of enjoying any great share of the first, without partaking likewise of the latter."

The first impression of *The Fable of the Bees*, which came out in 1714, was never carped at, or publicly taken notice of; and all the reason I can think on why this second edition should be so unmercifully treated, though it has many precautions which the former wanted, is an essay on charity and charity-schools, which is added to what was printed before. I confess that it is my sentiment that all hard and dirty work ought in a well-governed nation to be the lot and portion of the poor, and that to divert their children from useful labor until they are fourteen or fifteen years old is a wrong method to qualify them for it when they are grown up. I have given several reasons for my opinion in that essay, to which I refer all impartial men of understanding, assuring them that they will not meet with such monstrous impiety in it as reported. What an advocate I have been for libertinism and immorality, and what an enemy to "all instructions of youth in the Christian faith," may be collected from the pains I have taken on education for above seven pages together. And afterwards again, where speaking of the instructions the children of the poor might receive at church; "from which," I say, "or some other place of worship, I would not have the meanest of a parish that is able to walk it, be absent on Sundays," I have these words: "It is the Sabbath, the most useful day in seven, that is set apart for divine service and religious exercise, as well as resting from bodily labor; and it is a duty incumbent on all magistrates to take a particular care of that day. The poor more especially, and their children, should be made to go to church on it, both in the fore and the afternoon, because they have no time on any other. By precept and example they ought to be encouraged to it from their very infancy. The willful neglect of it ought to be counted scandalous; and if downright compulsion to what I urge might seem too harsh and perhaps impracticable, all diversions at least ought strictly to be prohibited, and the poor hindered from every amusement abroad, that might allure or draw them from it." If the arguments I have made use of are not convincing, I desire they may be refuted, and I will acknowledge it as a favor in anyone that shall convince me of my error, without ill language, by showing me wherein I have been mistaken. But calumny, it seems, is the shortest way of confuting an adversary, when men are touched in a sensible part. Vast sums are gathered for these charity schools, and I understand human nature too well to imagine that the sharers of the money should hear them spoken against with any patience. I foresaw therefore the usage I was to receive, and having repeated the common cant that is made for charity schools, I told my readers, "This is the general cry, and he that speaks the least word against it is uncharitable, hard-hearted and inhuman, if not a wicked, profane and atheistic wretch." For this reason it cannot be thought that it was a great surprise to me, when . . . I saw myself called "proligfate author"; the publication of my tenets, "an open and avowed proposal to extirpate the Christian faith and all virtue," and what I had done "so stunning, so shocking, so frightful, so flagrant an enormity," that it cried for the vengeance of Heaven. This is no more than what I have always expected from the enemies to truth and fair dealing, and I shall retort nothing on the angry author of that letter, who endeavors to expose me to the public fury. I pity him, and have charity enough to believe that he has been imposed upon himself, by trusting to fame and the hearsay of others, for no man in his wits can imagine that he should have read one quarter part of my book, and write as he does.

I am sorry if the words "Private Vices, Public Benefits" have ever given any offense to a well-meaning man. The mystery of them is soon unfolded when once they are rightly understood. But no man of sincerity will question the innocence of them, that has read the last paragraph, where I take my leave of the reader, "and conclude with repeating the seeming paradox, the substance of which is advanced in the title page; that private vices by the dexterous management of a skillful politician, may be turned into public benefits." These are the last words of the book, printed in the same large character with the rest. But I set aside all what I have said in my Vindication; and if in the whole book called *The Fable of the Bees,* and presented by the Grand Jury of Middlesex to the judges of the King's Bench, there is to be found the least tittle of blasphemy or profanity, or anything tending to immorality or the corruption of manners, I desire it may be published. And if this be done without invective, personal reflections, or setting the mob upon me, things I never design to answer, I will not only recant, but likewise beg pardon of the offended public in the most solemn manner and (if the hangman might be thought too good for the office) burn the book myself at any reasonable time and place my adversaries shall be pleased to appoint.

The Author of *The Fable of the Bees.*

The Fable of the Bees:
or,
Private Vices, Public Benefits
(Volume II)

The Preface

(. . .)

I am far from believing that among the fashionable people there are not in all Christian countries many persons of stricter virtue and greater sincerity in religion than I have here described. But that a considerable part of mankind have a great resemblance to the picture I have been drawing, I appeal to every knowing and candid reader. Horatio, Cleomenes, and Fulvia are the names I have given to my interlocutors. The first represents one of the modish people I have been speaking of, but rather of the better sort of them as to morality; though he seems to have a greater distrust of the sincerity of clergymen, than he has of that of any other profession, and to be of the opinion, which is expressed in that trite and specious as well as false and injurious saying, "priests of all religions are the same." As to his studies, he is supposed to be tolerably well versed in the classics, and to have read more than is usual for people of quality, that are born to great estates. He is a man of strict honor, and of justice as well as humanity; rather profuse than covetous, and altogether disinterested in his principles. He has been abroad, seen the world, and is supposed to be possessed of the greatest part of the accomplishments that usually gain a man the reputation of being very much of a gentleman.

Cleomenes had been just such another, but was much reformed. As he had formerly, for his amusement only, been dipping into anatomy, and several parts of natural philosophy, so, since he was come home from his travels, he had studied human nature and the knowledge of himself with great application. It is supposed, that, while he was thus employing most of his leisure hours he met with *The Fable of the Bees;* and making a right use of what he read, compared what he felt himself, within, as well as what he had seen in the world, with the sentiments set forth in that book, and found the insincerity of men fully as universal as it was there represented.

He had no opinion of the pleas and excuses that are commonly made to cover the real desires of the heart. And he ever suspected the sincerity of men, whom he saw to be fond of the world, and with eagerness grasping at wealth and power, when they pretended that the great end of their labors was to have opportunities of doing good to others upon earth, and becoming themselves more thankful to Heaven; especially, if they conformed with the *beau monde*, and seemed to take delight in a fashionable way of living. He had the same suspicion of all men of sense, who, having read and considered the Gospel, would maintain the possibility that persons might pursue worldly glory with all their strength, and at the same time be good Christians. Cleomenes himself believed the Bible to be the word of God, without reserve, and was entirely convinced of the mysterious as well as historical truths that are contained in it. But as he was fully persuaded, not only of the veracity of the Christian religion, but likewise of the severity of its precepts, so he attacked his passions with vigor, but never scrupled to own his want of power to subdue them, or the violent opposition he felt from within, often complaining that the obstacles he met with from flesh and blood were insurmountable. As he understood perfectly well the difficulty of the task required in the Gospel, so he ever opposed those easy casuists that endeavored to lessen and extenuate it for their own ends. And he loudly maintained that men's gratitude to Heaven was an unacceptable offering, whilst they continued to live in ease and luxury, and were visibly solicitous after their share of the pomp and vanity of this world. In the very politeness of conversation, the complacency, with which fashionable people are continually soothing each other's frailties, and in almost every part of a gentleman's behavior, he thought, there was a disagreement between the outward appearances, and what is felt within, that was clashing with uprightness and sincerity. Cleomenes was of opinion that of all religious virtues nothing was more scarce, or more difficult to acquire, than Christian humility; and that to destroy the possibility of ever attaining to it, nothing was so effectual as what is called a gentleman's education, and that the more dexterous, by this means, men grew in concealing the outward signs, and every symptom of pride, the more entirely they became enslaved by it within. He carefully examined the felicity that accrues from the applause of others, and the invisible wages which men of sense and judicious fancy received for their labors, and what it was at the bottom, that rendered those airy rewards so ravishing to mortals. He had often observed and watched narrowly the countenances and behavior of men when anything of theirs was admired or commended, such as the choice of their furniture, the politeness of their entertainments, the elegance of their equipages, their dress, their diversions, or the fine taste displayed in their buildings.

Cleomenes seemed charitable, and was a man of strict morals. Yet he would often complain that he was not possessed of one Christian virtue, and found fault with his own actions that had all the appearances of goodness because he was conscious, he said, that they were performed from a wrong principle. The effects of his education, and his aversion to infamy, had always been strong enough to keep him from turpitude. But this he ascribed to his vanity, which he complained was in such full possession of his heart, that he knew no gratification of any appetite from which he was able to exclude it. Having always been a man of unblameable behavior, the sincerity of his belief had made no visible alteration in his conduct to outward appearances. But in private he never ceased from examining himself. As no man was less prone to enthusiasm than himself, so his life was very uniform; and as he never pretended to high flights of devotion, so he never was guilty of enormous offenses. He had a strong aversion to rigorists of all sorts. And when he saw men quarreling about forms of creeds, and the interpretation of obscure places, and requiring of others the strictest compliance to their own opinions in disputable matters, it raised his indignation to see the generality of them want charity, and many of them scandalously remiss in the plainest and most necessary duties. He took uncommon pains to search into human nature, and left no stone unturned to detect the pride and hypocrisy of it, and among his intimate friends to expose the stratagems of the one, and the exorbitant power of the other. He was sure that the satisfaction which arose from worldly enjoyments was something distinct from gratitude, and foreign to religion. And he felt plainly, that as it proceeded from within, so it centered in himself: the very relish of life, he said, was accompanied with an elevation of mind, that seemed to be inseparable from his being. Whatever principle was the cause of this, he was convinced within himself, that the sacrifice of the heart, which the Gospel requires, consisted in the utter extirpation of that principle; confessing at the same time, that this satisfaction he found in himself, this elevation of mind, caused his chief pleasure, and that in all the comforts of life, it made the greatest part of the enjoyment.

Cleomenes with grief often owned his fear, that his attachment to the world would never cease whilst he lived. The reasons he gave, were the great regard he continued to have for the opinion of worldly men; the stubbornness of his indocile heart, that could not be brought to change the objects of its pride; and refused to be ashamed of what from his infancy it had been taught to glory in; and lastly, the impossibility, he found in himself, of being ever reconciled to contempt, and enduring, with patience, to be laughed at and despised for any cause, or on any consideration whatever. These were the obstacles, he said, that hindered him from breaking off all commerce with the *beau monde*, and entirely changing his manner of living; without which he thought it mockery to talk of renouncing the world, and bidding adieu to all the pomp and vanity of it. . . .

As to the fable, or what is supposed to have occasioned the first dialogue between Horatio and Cleomenes, it is this: Horatio, who had found great delight in my Lord Shaftesbury's polite manner of writing, his fine raillery, and blending virtue with good manners, was a great stickler for the social system; and wondered how Cleomenes could be an advocate for such a book as *The Fable of the Bees*, of which he had heard a very vile character from several quarters. Cleomenes, who loved and had a great friendship for Horatio, wanted to undeceive him. But [Horatio], who hated satire, was prepossessed, and having been told likewise, that martial courage, and honor itself were ridiculed in that book he was very much exasperated against the author and his whole scheme. He had two or three times heard Cleomenes discourse on this subject with others; but would never enter into the argument himself. And finding his friend often pressing to come to it, he began to look coolly upon him, and at last to avoid all opportunities of being alone with him until Cleomenes drew him in. . . .

I should not wonder to see men of candor, as well as good sense, find fault with the manner, in which I have chosen to publish these thoughts of mine to the world. There certainly is something in it which I confess I don't know how to justify to my own satisfaction. That such a man as Cleomenes, having met with a book agreeable to his own sentiments, should desire to be acquainted with the author of it, has nothing in it that is improbable or unseemly. But then it will be objected that whoever the interlocutors are, it was I myself who wrote the dialogues, and that it is contrary to all decency that a man should proclaim concerning his own work, all that a friend of his, perhaps, might be allowed to say. This is true; and the best answer, which, I think, can be made to it, is, that such an impartial man, and such a lover of truth, as Cleomenes is represented to be, would be as cautious in speaking of his friend's merit as he would be of his own. It might be urged, likewise, that when a man professes himself to be an author's friend, and exactly to entertain the same sentiments with another, it must naturally put every reader upon his guard, and render him as suspicious and distrustful of such a man, as he would be of the author himself. But how good soever the excuses are that might be made for this manner of writing, I would never have ventured upon it if I had not liked it in the famous Gassendi, who by the help of several dialogues and a friend, who is the chief personage in them, has not only explained and illustrated his system, but likewise refuted his adversaries. Him I have followed, and I hope the reader will find that whatever opportunity I have had by this means of speaking well of myself indirectly, I had no design to make that or any other ill use of it.

As it is supposed that Cleomenes is my friend, and speaks my sentiments, so it is but justice that everything which he advances should be looked upon and considered as my own. But no man in his senses would think that I ought to be equally responsible for everything that Horatio says, who is his antagonist. If ever he offers anything that savors of libertinism, or is otherwise exceptionable, which Cleomenes does not reprove him for in the best and most serious manner, or to which he gives not the most satisfactory and convincing answer that can be made, I am to blame, otherwise not. Yet from the fate the first volume has met with, I expect to see in a little time several things transcribed and cited from this, in that manner, by themselves, without the replies that are made to them, and so shown to the world, as my words and my opinion. The opportunity of doing this will be greater in this book than it was in the former, and should I always have fair play, and never be attacked, but by such adversaries as would make their quotations from me without artifice, and use me with common honesty, it would go a great way to the refuting of me; and I should myself begin to suspect the truth of several things I have advanced, and which hitherto I can't help believing. (. . .)

The Third Dialogue
between Horatio and Cleomenes

(. . .)

Horatio: I have twenty questions to ask about pride, and I don't know where to begin. There's another thing I don't understand; which is, that there can be no virtue without self-denial.

Cleomenes: This was the opinion of all the ancients. Lord Shaftesbury was the first that maintained the contrary.

Hor: But are there no persons in the world that are good by choice?

Cleo: Yes, but then they are directed in that choice by reason and experience, and not by nature, I mean, not by untaught nature. But there is an ambiguity in the word good which I would avoid. Let us stick to that of virtuous, and then I affirm, that no action is such, which does not suppose and point at some conquest or other, some victory great or small over untaught nature. Otherwise the epithet is improper.

Hor: But if by the help of a careful education this victory is obtained, when we are young, may we not be virtuous afterwards voluntarily and with pleasure?

Cleo: Yes, if it really was obtained. But how shall we be sure of this, and what reason have we to believe that it ever was? When it is evident that, from our infancy, instead of endeavoring to conquer our appetites, we have always been taught, and have taken pains ourselves to conceal them; and we are conscious within that whatever alterations have been made in our manners and our circumstances, the passions themselves always remained? The system, that virtue requires no self-denial, is, as my friend has justly observed, a vast inlet to hypocrisy. It will on all accounts furnish men with a more obvious handle, and a greater opportunity of counterfeiting the love of society and regard to the I public, than ever they could have received from the contrary doctrine, that there is no merit but in the conquest of the passions, nor any virtue without apparent self-denial. Let us ask those that have had long experience and are well skilled in human affairs whether they have found the generality of men such impartial judges of themselves as never to think better of their own worth than it deserved, or so candid in the acknowledgment of their hidden faults and slips, they could never be convinced of, that there is no fear, they should ever stifle or deny them. Where is the man that has at no time covered his failings, and screened himself with false appearances, or never pretended to act from principles of social virtue and his regard to others, when he knew in his heart that his greatest care had been to oblige himself? The

160

best of us sometimes receive applause without undeceiving those who give it; though at the same time we are conscious that the actions for which we suffer ourselves to be thought well of are the result of a powerful frailty in our nature, that has often been prejudicial to us, and which we have wished a thousand times in vain that we could have conquered. The same motives may produce very different actions, as men differ in temper and circumstances. Persons of an easy fortune may appear virtuous from the same turn of mind that would show their frailty if they were poor. If we would know the world, we must look into it. You take no delight in the occurrences of low life. But if we always remain among persons of quality, and extend our enquiries no farther, the transactions there will not furnish us with a sufficient knowledge of everything that belongs to our nature. There are among the middling people men of low circumstances tolerably well-educated, that set out with the same stock of virtues and vices, and though equally qualified, meet with very different success, visibly owing to the difference in their temper. Let us take a view of two persons bred to the same business that have nothing but their parts and the world before them, launching out with the same helps and disadvantages. Let there be no difference between them, but in their temper; the one active, and the other indolent. The latter will never get an estate by his own industry, though his profession be gainful, and himself master of it. Chance, or some uncommon accident, may be the occasion of great alterations in him, but without that he will hardly ever raise himself to mediocrity. Unless his pride affects him in an extraordinary manner, he must always be poor, and nothing but some share of vanity can hinder him from being despicably so. If he be a man of sense he'll be strictly honest, and a middling stock of covetousness will never divert him from it. In the active stirring man that is easily reconciled to the bustle of the world, we shall discover quite different symptoms under the same circumstances; and a very little avarice will egg him on to pursue his aim with eagerness and assiduity. Small scruples are no opposition to him; where sincerity will not serve he uses artifice, and in compassing his ends the greatest use he will make of his good sense will be to preserve as much as is possible the appearance of honesty when his interest obliges him to deviate from it. To get wealth, or even a livelihood, by arts and sciences. It is not sufficient to understand them: it is a duty incumbent on all men who have their maintenance to seek to make known and forward themselves in the world, as far as decency allows of, without bragging of themselves, or doing prejudice to others. Here the indolent man is very deficient and wanting to himself. But [he] seldom will own his fault, and often blames the public for not making use of him, and encouraging that merit, which they never were acquainted with, and himself perhaps took pleasure to conceal. And though you convince him of his error, and that he has neglected even the most warrantable methods of soliciting employment, he'll endeavor to color over his frailty with the appearance of virtue. What is altogether owing to his too easy temper, and an excessive fondness for the calmness of his mind, he'll ascribe to his modesty and the great aversion he has to impudence and boasting. The man of a contrary temper trusts not to his merit only, or the setting it off to the best advantage; he takes pains to heighten it in the opinion of others, and make his abilities seem greater than he knows them to be. As it is counted folly for a man to proclaim his own excellencies, and speak magnificently of himself, so his chief business is to seek acquaintance, and make friends on purpose to do it for him. All other passions he sacrifices to his ambition; he laughs at disappointments, is inured to refusals, and no repulse dismays him. This renders the whole man always flexible to his interest. He can defraud his body of necessities, and allow no tranquillity to his mind; and counterfeit, if it will serve his turn, temperance, chastity, compassion, and piety itself without one grain of virtue or religion. His endeavors to advance his fortune . . . are always restless and have no bounds, but where he is obliged to act openly, and has reason to fear the censure of the world. It is very diverting to see, how, in the different persons I speak of, natural temper will warp and model the very passions to its own bias. Pride, for example, has not the same, but almost a quite contrary effect on the one to what it has on the other. The stirring active man it makes in love with finery, clothes, furniture, equipages, building, and everything his superiors enjoy. The other it renders sullen, and perhaps morose; and if he has wit prone to satire, though he be otherwise a good-natured man. Self-love in every individual ever bestirs itself in soothing and flattering the darling inclination, always turning from us the dismal side of the prospect. And the indolent man in such circumstances, finding nothing pleasing without, turns his view inward upon himself; there looking on everything with great indulgence, admires and takes delight in his own parts, whether natural or acquired. Hence he is easily induced to despise all others, who have not the same good qualifications, especially the powerful and wealthy, whom yet he never hates or envies with any violence, because that would ruffle his temper. All things that are difficult he looks upon as impossible, which makes him despair of meliorating his condition. And as he has no possessions, and his gettings will but just maintain him in a low station of life, so his good sense, if he would enjoy so much as the appearance of happiness, must necessarily put him upon two things: to be frugal, and pretend to have no value for riches; for by neglecting either, he must be blown up, and his frailty unavoidably discovered.

Hor: I am pleased with your observations, and the knowledge you display of mankind. But pray is not the frugality you now speak of a virtue?

Cleo: I think not.

Hor: Where there is but a small income, frugality is built upon reason, and in this case there is an apparent self-denial, without which an indolent man that has no value for money cannot be frugal. And when we see indolent men, that have no regard for wealth, reduced to beggary, as it often happens, it is most commonly for want of this virtue.

Cleo: I told you before that the indolent man, setting out as he did, would be poor, and that nothing but some share of vanity could hinder him from being despicably so. A strong fear of shame may gain so much upon the indolence of a man of sense that he'll bestir himself sufficiently to escape contempt; but it will hardly make him do any more. Therefore, he embraces frugality as being instrumental and assisting to him in procuring his *summum bonum*, the darling quiet of his easy mind. Whereas the active man with the same share of vanity would do anything rather than submit to the same frugality, unless his avarice forced him to it. Frugality is no virtue when it is imposed upon us by any of the passions, and the contempt of riches is seldom sincere. I have known men of plentiful estates, that on account of posterity, or other warrantable views of employing their money, were saving and more penurious, than they would have been if their wealth had been greater. But I never yet found a frugal man without avarice or necessity. And again, there are innumerable spendthrifts, lavish and extravagant to a high degree, who seem not to have the least regard to money, while they have any to fling away: But these wretches are the least capable of bearing poverty of any, and the money once gone, hourly discover how uneasy, impatient and miserable they are without it. But what several in all ages have made pretense to, the contempt of riches, is more scarce than is commonly imagined. To see a man of a very good estate, in health and strength of body and mind, one that has no reason to complain of the world or fortune, actually despise both, and embrace a voluntary poverty for a laudable purpose, is a great rarity. . . .

Hor: To me it seems to be more difficult to be virtuous without money than with. It is senseless for a man to be poor when he can help it, and if I saw anybody choose it when he might as lawfully be rich, I would think him to be distracted.

Cleo: But you would not think him so if you saw him sell his estate and give the money to the poor. You know where that was required.

Hor: It is not required of us.

Cleo: Perhaps not. But what say you to renouncing the world, and the solemn promise we have made of it?

Hor: In a literal sense that is impossible, unless we go out of it. And therefore I don't think that to renounce the world signifies any more than not to comply with the vicious, wicked part of it.

Cleo: I did not expect a more rigid construction from you, though it is certain that wealth and power are great snares, and strong impediments to all Christian virtue. But the generality of mankind that have anything to lose are of your opinion; and let us bar saints and madmen, we shall find everywhere, that those who pretend to undervalue, and are always haranguing against, wealth, are generally poor and indolent. But who can blame them? They act in their own defense. Nobody that could help it would ever be laughed at; for it must be owned, that of all the hardships of poverty it is that which is the most intolerable.

> *Nil habet infelix paupertas durius in se,*
> *Quam quod ridiculos homines faciat.*

> [Miserable poverty contains no greater hardship
> Than that which makes one laughable. (Juvenal)]

In the very satisfaction that is enjoyed by those who excel in, or are possessed of things valuable, there is interwoven a spice of contempt for others that are destitute of them, which nothing keeps from public view but a mixture of pity and good manners. Whoever denies this let them consult within, and examine whether it is not the same with happiness, as what Seneca says of the reverse, *nemo est miser nisi comparatus* [no one is wretched save by comparison with another]. The contempt and ridicule I speak of is, without doubt, what all men of sense and education endeavor to avoid, or disappoint. Now look upon the behavior of the two contrary tempers before us, and mind how differently they set about this task, everyone suitably to his own inclination. The man of action, you see, leaves no stone unturned to acquire *quod oportet habere* [what is appropriate for him]. But this is impossible for the indolent. He can't stir; his idol ties him down hand and foot; and therefore the easiest, and indeed the only thing he has left, is to quarrel with the world, and find out arguments to depreciate what others value themselves upon.

(. . .)

Hor: I am convinced that in the opinion of virtue's requiring self-denial there is greater certainty, and hypocrites have less latitude than in the contrary system.

Cleo: Whoever follows his own inclinations, be they never so kind, beneficent, or humane, never quarrels with any vice but what is clashing with his temperament and nature. Whereas those who act from a principle of virtue take always reason for their guide, and combat without exception every passion that hinders them from their duty! The indolent man will never deny a just debt. But, if it be large, he will not give himself the trouble which, poor as he is, he might and ought to take to discharge it, or at least satisfy his creditor, unless he is often dunned or threatened to be sued for it. He will not be a litigious neighbor, nor make mischief among his acquaintance. But he will never serve his friend, or his country, at the expense of his quiet. He will not be rapacious, oppress the poor, or commit vile actions for lucre; but then he will never exert himself and be at the pains another would take on all opportunities, to maintain a large family, make provision for children, and promote his kindred and relations. And his darling frailty will incapacitate him from doing a thousand things for the benefit of the society which with the same parts and opportunities he might and would have done, had he been of another temper.

Hor: Your observations are very curious, and, as far as I can judge from what I have seen myself, very just and natural.

Cleo: Everybody knows that there is no virtue so often counterfeited as charity, and yet so little regard have the generality of men to truth that, how gross and barefaced soever the deceit is in pretenses of this nature, the world never fails of being angry with [it], and hates those who detect or take notice of the fraud. It is possible, that, with blind fortune on his side, a mean shopkeeper, by driving a trade prejudicial to his country on the one hand, and grinding on all occasions the face of the poor on the other, may accumulate great wealth, which in process of time, by continual scraping and sordid saving, may be raised into an exorbitant and unheard-of estate for a tradesman. Should such a one, when old and decrepit, lay out the greatest part of his immense riches in the building or largely endowing a hospital, and I was thoroughly acquainted with his temper and manners, I could have no opinion of his virtue, though he parted with the money, while he was yet alive. More especially, if I was assured that in his last will he had been highly unjust, and had not only left unrewarded several, whom he had great obligations to, but likewise defrauded others, to whom in his conscience, he knew that he was and would die actually indebted. I desire you to tell me what name, knowing all I have said to be true, you would give to this extraordinary gift, this mighty donation!

Hor: I am of opinion that when an action of our neighbor may admit of different constructions, it is our duty to side with and embrace the most favorable.

Cleo: The most favorable construction, with all my heart: but what is that to the purpose, when all the straining in the world cannot make it a good one? I don't mean the thing itself, but the principle it came from, the inward motive of the mind that put him upon performing it, for it is that which in a free agent I call the action. And therefore call it what you please, and judge as charitably of it as you can, what can you say of it?

Hor: He might have had several motives, which I don't pretend to determine. But it is an admirable contrivance of being extremely beneficial to all posterity in this land, a noble provision, that will perpetually relieve, and be an unspeakable comfort to a multitude of miserable people. And it is not only a prodigious, but likewise a well-concerted bounty, that was wanting, and for which in after-ages thousands of poor wretches will have reason to bless his memory, when everybody else shall have neglected them.

Cleo: All that I have nothing against; and if you would add more, I shan't dispute it with you, as long as you confine your praises to the endowment itself, and the benefit the public is likely to receive from it. But to ascribe it to, or suggest that it was derived from a public spirit in the man, a generous sense of humanity and benevolence to his kind, a liberal heart, or any other virtue or good quality, which it is manifest the donor was an utter stranger to, is the utmost absurdity in an intelligent creature, and can proceed from no other cause than either a willful wronging of his own understanding, or else ignorance and folly.

Hor: I am persuaded, that many actions are put off for virtuous, that are not so; and that according as men differ in natural temper, and turn of mind, so they are differently influenced by the same passions: I believe likewise that these last are born with us, and belong to our nature, that some of them are in us, or at least the seeds of them, before we perceive them. But since they are in every individual, how comes it that pride is more predominant in some than it is in others? For from what you have demonstrated already it must follow that one person is more affected with the passion within than another; I mean, that one man has actually a greater share of pride than another, as well among the artful that are dexterous in concealing it, as among the ill-bred that openly show it.

Cleo: What belongs to our nature all men may justly be said to have actually or virtually in them at their birth; and whatever is not born with us, either the thing itself, or that which afterwards produces it, cannot be said to belong to our nature. But as we differ in our faces and stature, so we do in other things, that are more remote from sight. All these depend only upon the different frame, the inward formation of either the solids or the fluids; and there are vices of complexion, that are peculiar, some to the pale and phlegmatic, others to the sanguine and choleric. Some are more lustful, others more fearful in their nature, than the generality are. But I believe of man, generally speaking, what my friend has observed of other creatures, that the best of the kind, I mean the best formed within, such as have the finest natural parts, are born with the greatest aptitude to be proud. Yet I am convinced, that the difference there is in men, as to the degrees of their pride, is more owing to circumstances and education, than anything in their formation. Where passions are most gratified and least controlled, the indulgence makes them stronger. Whereas those persons, that have been kept under, and whose thoughts have never been at liberty to rove beyond the first necessities of life, such as have not been suffered or had no opportunity to gratify this passion, have commonly the least share of it. But whatever portion of pride a man may feel in his heart, the quicker his parts are, the better his understanding is, and the more experience he has, the more plainly he'll perceive the aversion which all men have to those that discover their pride: and the sooner persons are imbued with good manners, the sooner they grow perfect in concealing that passion. Men of mean birth and education that have been kept in great subjection, and consequently had no great opportunities to exert their pride, if ever they come to command others, have a sort of revenge mixed with that passion, which makes it often very mischievous, especially in places where they have no superiors or equals, before whom they are obliged to conceal the odious passion.

Hor: Do you think women have more pride from nature than men?

Cleo: I believe not: but they have a great deal more from education.

Hor: I don't see the reason. For among the better sort, the sons, especially the eldest, have as many ornaments and fine things given them from their infancy to stir up their pride, as the daughters.

Cleo: But among people equally well-educated the ladies have more flattery bestowed upon them than the gentlemen, and it begins sooner.

Hor: But why should pride be more encouraged in women than in men?

Cleo: For the same reason that it is encouraged in soldiers, more than it is in other people: to increase their fear of shame, which makes them always mindful of their honor.

Hor: But to keep both to their respective duties, why must a lady have more pride than a gentleman?

Cleo: Because the lady is in the greatest danger of straying from it. She has a passion within that may begin to affect her at twelve or thirteen, and perhaps sooner, and she has all the temptations of the men to withstand besides. She has all the artillery of our sex to fear. A seducer of uncommon address and resistless charms may court her to what nature prompts and solicits her to do; he may add great promises, actual bribes. This may be done in the dark, and when nobody is by to dissuade her. Gentlemen very seldom have occasion to show their courage before they are six or seventeen years of age, and rarely so soon. They are not put to the trial, until by conversing with men of honor, they are confirmed in their pride. In the affair of a quarrel they have their friends to consult, and these are so many witnesses of their behavior that awe them to their duty, and in a manner oblige them to obey the laws of honor. All these things conspire to increase their fear of shame; and if they can but render that superior to the fear of death, their business is done: they have no pleasure to expect from breaking the rules of honor, nor any crafty tempter that solicits them to be cowards. That pride, which is the cause of honor in men, only regards their courage; and if they can but appear to be brave, and will but follow the fashionable rules of manly honor, they may indulge all other appetites, and brag of incontinence without reproach. The pride likewise that produces honor in women has no other object than their chastity. And whilst they keep that jewel entire they can apprehend no shame. Tenderness and delicacy are a compliment to them, and there is no fear of danger so ridiculous, but they may own it with ostentation. But notwithstanding the weakness of their frame, and the softness in which women are generally educated, if overcome by chance they have sinned in private, what real hazards will they not run, what torments will they not stifle, and what crimes will they not commit, to hide from the world that frailty which they were taught to be most ashamed of!

Hor: It is certain, that we seldom hear of public prostitutes, and such as have lost their shame, that they murder their infants, though they are otherwise the most abandoned wretches. I took notice of this in *The Fable of the Bees*, and it is very remarkable.

Cleo: It contains a plain demonstration that the same passion may produce either a palpable good or a palpable evil in the same person, according as self-love and his present circumstances shall direct. The same fear of shame, that makes men sometimes appear so highly virtuous, may at others oblige them to commit the most heinous crimes. Therefore, that honor is not founded upon any principle, either of real virtue or true religion, must be obvious to all that will but mind what sort of people they are, that are the greatest votaries of that idol, and the different duties it requires in the two sexes. In the first place the worshippers of honor are the vain and voluptuous, the strict observers of modes and fashions, that take delight in pomp and luxury, and enjoy as much of the world as they are able. In the second, the word itself, I mean the sense of it, is so whimsical, and there is such a prodigious difference in the significance of it, according as the attribute is differently applied, either to a man or to a woman, that neither of them shall forfeit their honor, though each should be guilty, and openly boast of what would be the other's greatest shame.

Hor: I am sorry that I cannot charge you with injustice. But it is very strange that to encourage and industriously increase pride in a refined education, should be the most proper means to make men solicitous in concealing the outward appearances of it.

Cleo: Yet nothing is more true. But where pride is so much indulged, and yet to be so carefully kept from all human view, as it is in persons of honor of both sexes, it would be impossible for mortal strength to endure the restraint if men could not be taught to play the passion against itself, and were not allowed to change the natural home-bred symptoms of it, for artificial foreign ones.

Hor: By playing the passion against itself, I know you mean placing a secret pride in concealing the barefaced signs of it. But I don't rightly understand what you mean by changing the symptoms of it.

Cleo: When a man exults in his pride and gives a loose to that passion, the marks of it are as visible in his countenance, his mien, his gait, and behavior, as they are in a prancing horse, or a strutting turkey cock. These are all very odious, everyone feeling the same principle within, which is the cause of those symptoms. And, man being endued with speech, all the open expressions, the same passion can suggest to him, must for the same reason be equally displeasing. These therefore have in all societies been strictly prohibited by common consent in the very infancy of good manners; and men have been taught, in the room of them, to substitute other symptoms, equally evident with the first, but less offensive, and more beneficial to others.

Hor: Which are they?

Cleo: Fine clothes and other ornaments about them, the cleanliness observed about their persons, the submission that is required of servants, costly equipages, furniture, buildings, titles of honor, and everything that men can acquire to make themselves esteemed by others, without discovering any of the symptoms that are forbidden. Upon a satiety of enjoying these, they are allowed likewise to have the vapors and be whimsical, though otherwise they are known to be in health and of good sense.

Hor: But since the pride of others is displeasing to us in every shape, and these latter symptoms, you say, are equally evident with the first, what is gotten by the change?

Cleo: A great deal. When pride is designedly expressed in looks and gestures, either in a wild or tame man, it is known by all human creatures that see it. It is the same, when vented in words, by everybody that understands the language they are spoken in. These are marks and tokens that are all the world over the same. Nobody shows them but to have them seen and understood, and few persons ever display them without designing that offense to others, which they never fail to give. Whereas the other symptoms may be denied to be what they are, and many pretences, that they are derived from other motives, may be made for them, which the same good manners teach us never to refute, nor easily to disbelieve. In the very excuses that are made for them there is a condescension that satisfies and pleases us. In those that are altogether destitute of the opportunities to display the symptoms of pride that are allowed of, the least portion of that passion is a troublesome, though often an unknown guest. For in them it is easily turned into envy and malice, and on the least provocation it sallies out in those disguises, and is often the cause of cruelty, and there never was a mischief committed by mobs or multitudes, which this passion had not a hand in. Whereas the more room men have to vent and gratify the passion in the warrantable ways, the more easy it is for them to stifle the odious part of pride, and seem to be wholly free from it.

Hor: I see very well that real virtue requires a conquest over untaught nature, and that the Christian religion demands a still stricter self-denial. It likewise is evident that to make ourselves acceptable to an omniscient power, nothing is more necessary than sincerity, and that the heart should be pure. But setting aside sacred matters and a future state, don't you think that this complaisance and easy construction of one another's actions do a great deal of good upon earth; and don't you believe that good manners and politeness make men more happy, and their lives more comfortable in this world, than anything else could make them without those arts?

Cleo: If you will set aside what ought to employ our first care, and be our greatest concern. Men will have no value for that felicity and peace of mind, which can only arise from a consciousness of being good, it is certain, that in a great nation, and among a flourishing people, whose highest wishes seem to be ease and luxury, the upper part could not, without those arts, enjoy so much of the world as that can afford; and that none stand more in need of them than the voluptuous men of parts, that will join worldly prudence to sensuality, and make it their chief study to refine upon pleasure.

Hor: When I had the honor of your company at my house, you said that nobody knew, when or where, nor in what king's or emperor's reign the laws of honor were enacted. Pray, can you inform me, when or which way, what we call good manners or politeness, came into the world? What moralist or politician was it, that could teach men to be proud of hiding their pride?

Cleo: The restless industry of man to supply his wants, and his constant endeavors to meliorate his condition upon Earth, have produced and brought to perfection many useful arts and sciences, of which the beginnings are of uncertain eras, and to which we can assign no other causes, than human sagacity in general, and the joint labor of many ages, in which men have always employed themselves in studying and contriving ways and means to soothe their various appetites, and make the best of their infirmities. Whence had we the first rudiments of architecture? How came sculpture and painting to be what they have been these many hundred years; and who taught every nation the respective languages they speak now? When I have a mind to dive into the origin of any maxim or political invention, for the use of society in general, I don't trouble my head with enquiring after the time or country, in which it was first heard of, nor what others have written or said about it. But I go directly to the fountainhead, human nature itself, and look for the frailty or defect in man, that is remedied or supplied by that invention: when things are very obscure, I sometimes make use of conjectures to find my way.

Hor: Do you argue, or pretend to prove anything from those conjectures?

Cleo: No. I never reason but from the plain observations which everybody may make on man, the phenomena that appear in the lesser world.

Hor: You have, without doubt, thought on this subject before now; would you communicate to me some of your guesses?

Cleo: With abundance of pleasure. . . . That self-love was given to all animals, at least, the most perfect, for self-preservation, is not disputed. But as no creature can love what it dislikes, it is necessary, moreover, that everyone should have a real liking to its own being, superior to what they have to any other. I am of opinion, begging pardon for the novelty, that if this liking was not always permanent; the love, which all creatures have for themselves, could not be so unalterable as we see it is.

Hor: What reason have you to suppose this liking, which creatures have for themselves, to be distinct from self-love, since the one plainly comprehends the other?

Cleo: I will endeavor to explain myself better. I fancy that to increase the care in creatures to preserve themselves, nature has given them an instinct, by which every individual values itself above its real worth. This in us, I mean, in man, seems to be accompanied with a diffidence, arising from a consciousness, or at least an apprehension, that we do overvalue ourselves. It is this that makes us so fond of the approbation, liking and assent of others, because they strengthen and confirm us in the good opinion we have of ourselves. The reasons why this self-liking, give me leave to call it so, is not plainly to be seen in all animals that are of the same degree of perfection, are many. Some want ornaments, and consequently the means to express it; others are too stupid and listless. It is to be considered, likewise, that creatures, which are always in the same circumstances, and meet with little variation in their way of living, have neither opportunity nor temptation to show it; that the more mettle and liveliness creatures have, the more visible this liking is; and that in those of the same kind, the greater spirit they are of, and the more they excel in the perfections of their species, the fonder they are of showing it. In most birds it is evident, especially in those that have extraordinary finery to display. In a horse it is more conspicuous than in any other irrational creature. It is most apparent in the swiftest, the strongest, the most healthy and vigorous; and may be increased in that animal by additional ornaments, and the presence of man, whom he knows, to clean, take care of, and delight in him. It is not improbable that this great liking, which creatures have for their own individuals, is the principle on which the love to their species is built. Cows and sheep, too dull and lifeless to make any demonstration of this liking, yet herd and feed together, each with his own species, because no others are so like themselves. By this they seem to know, likewise, that they have the same interest, and the same enemies. Cows have often been seen to join in a common defense against wolves. Birds of a feather flock together, and I dare say, that the screech owl likes her own note, better than that of the nightingale.

Hor: Montaigne seems to have been somewhat of your opinion, when he fancied that if brutes were to paint the Deity, they would all draw Him of their own species. But what you call self-liking is evidently pride.

Cleo: I believe it is, or at least the cause of it. I believe, moreover, that many creatures show this liking, when, for want of understanding them, we don't perceive it. When a cat washes her face, and a dog licks himself clean, they adorn themselves as much as it is in their power. Man himself in a savage state, feeding on nuts and acorns, and destitute of all outward ornaments, would have infinitely less temptation, as well as opportunity, of showing this liking of himself, than he has when civilized. Yet if a hundred males of the first, all equally free, were together, within less than half an hour, this liking in question, though their bellies were full, would appear in the desire of superiority, that would be shown among them. And the most vigorous, either in strength or understanding, or both, would be the first that would display it. If, as supposed, they were all untaught, this would breed contention, and there would certainly be war before there could be any agreement among them, unless one of them had some one or more visible excellencies above the rest. I said males, and their bellies full, because if they had women among them, or wanted food, their quarrel might begin on another account.

Hor: This is thinking abstractly indeed. But do you think that two or three hundred single savages, men and women, that never had been under any subjection, and were above twenty years of age, could ever establish a society, and be united into one body, if, without being acquainted with one another, they should meet by chance?

Cleo: No more, I believe, than so many horses. But societies never were made that way. It is possible that several families of savages might unite, and the heads of them agree upon some sort of government or other, for their common good. But among them it is certain likewise; that, though superiority was tolerably well settled, and every male had females enough, strength and prowess in this uncivilized state would be infinitely more valued than understanding. I mean in the men; for the women will always prize themselves for what they see the men admire in them. Hence it would follow that the women would value themselves, and envy one another for being handsome; and that the ugly and deformed, and all those that were least favored by nature, would be the first that would fly to art and additional ornaments. Seeing that this made them more agreeable to the men, it would soon be followed by the rest, and in a little time they would strive to outdo one another, as much as their circumstances would allow of; and it is possible, that a woman with a very handsome nose might envy her neighbor with a much worse, for having a ring through it.

Hor: You take great delight in dwelling on the behavior of savages. What relation has this to politeness?

Cleo: The seeds of it are lodged in this self-love and self-liking, which I have spoken of, as will soon appear, if we consider what would be the consequence of them in the affair of self-preservation, and a creature endued with understanding, speech, and risibility. Self-love would first make it scrape together everything it wanted for sustenance, provide against the injuries of the air, and do everything to make itself and young ones secure. Self-liking would make it seek for opportunities, by gestures, looks, and sounds, to display the value it has for itself, superior to what it has for others. An untaught man would desire everybody that came near him to agree with him in the opinion of his superior worth, and be angry, as far as his fear would let him, with all that should refuse it. He would be highly delighted with, and love everybody, whom he thought to have a good opinion of him, especially those, that by words or gestures should own it to his face. Whenever he met with any visible marks in others of inferiority to himself, he would laugh, and do the same at their misfortunes, as far as his own pity would give him leave, and he would insult everybody that would let him.

Hor: This self-liking, you say, was given to creatures for self-preservation. I should think rather that it is hurtful to men, because it must make them odious to one another; and I cannot see what benefit they can receive from it, either in a savage or a civilized state. Is there any instance of its doing any good?

Cleo: I wonder to hear you ask that question. Have you forgotten the many virtues which, I have demonstrated, may be counterfeited to gain applause, and the good qualities a man of sense in great fortune may acquire, by the sole help and instigation of his pride?

Hor: I beg your pardon. Yet what you say only regards man in the society, and after he has been perfectly well educated. What advantage is it to him as a single creature? Self-love I can plainly see induces him to labor for his maintenance and safety, and makes him fond of everything which he imagines to tend to his preservation. But what good does the self-liking to him?

Cleo: If I should tell you that the inward pleasure and satisfaction a man receives from the gratification of that passion is a cordial that contributes to his health, you would laugh at me, and think it farfetched.

Hor: Perhaps not. But I would set against it the many sharp vexations and heart-breaking sorrows that men suffer on the score of this passion, from disgraces, disappointments, and other misfortunes, which, I believe, have sent millions to their graves, much sooner than they would have gone, if their pride had less affected them.

Cleo: I have nothing against what you say. But this is no proof, that the passion itself was not given to man for self-preservation; and it only lays open to us the precariousness of sublunary happiness, and the wretched condition of mortals. There is nothing created that is always a blessing. The rain and sunshine themselves, to which all earthly comforts are owing, have been the causes of innumerable calamities. All animals of prey, and thousand others, hunt after food with the hazard of their lives, and the greater part of them perish in their pursuits after sustenance. Plenty itself is not less fatal to some, than want is to others. And of our own species, every opulent nation has had great numbers, that in full safety from all other dangers, have destroyed themselves by excesses of eating and drinking. Yet nothing is more certain than that hunger and thirst were given to creatures to make them solicitous after, and crave those necessities, without which it would be impossible for them to subsist.

Hor: Still I can see no advantage accruing from this self-liking to man, considered as a single creature, which can induce me to believe that nature should have given it us for self-preservation. What you have alleged is obscure. Can you name a benefit every individual person receives from that principle within him, that is manifest, and clearly to be understood?

Cleo: Since it has been in disgrace, and everybody disowns the passion, it seldom is seen in its proper colors, and disguises itself in a thousand different shapes. We are often affected with it, when we have not the least suspicion of it. But it seems to be that which continually furnishes us with that relish we have for life, even when it is not worth having. Whilst men are pleased, self-liking has every moment a considerable share, though unknown, in procuring the satisfaction they enjoy. It is so necessary to the well-being of those that have been used to indulge it that they can taste no pleasure without it; and such is the deference, and the submissive veneration they pay to it, that they are deaf to the loudest calls of nature, and will rebuke the strongest appetites that should pretend to be gratified at the expense of that passion. It doubles our happiness in prosperity, and buoys us up against the frowns of adverse fortune. It is the mother of hopes, and the end as well as the foundation of our best wishes. It is the strongest armor against despair, and as long as we can like any ways our situation, either in regard to present circumstances, or the prospect before us, we take care of ourselves. And no man can resolve upon suicide, whilst self-liking lasts. But as soon as that is over, all our hopes are extinct, and we can form no wishes but for the dissolution of our frame, untill at last our being becomes so intolerable to us, that self-love prompts us to make an end of it, and seek refuge in death.

Hor: You mean self-hatred; for you have said yourself, that a creature cannot love what it dislikes.

Cleo: If you turn the prospect, you are in the right. But this only proves to us what I have often hinted at, that man is made up of contrarieties. Otherwise, nothing seems to be more certain, than that whoever kills himself by choice, must do it to avoid something, which he dreads more than that death which he chooses. Therefore, how absurd soever a person's reasoning may be, there is in all suicide a palpable intention of kindness to oneself.

(. . .)

Hor: But when shall we come to the origin of politeness?

Cleo: We are at it now, and we need not look for it any further than in the self-liking, which I have demonstrated every individual man to be possessed of. Do but consider these two things; first, that from the nature of that passion it must follow, that all untaught men will ever be hateful to one another in conversation, where neither interest nor superiority are considered. For if of two equals one only values himself more by half, than he does the other, though that other should value the first equally with himself, they would both be dissatisfied, if their thoughts were known to each other. But if both valued themselves more by half than they did each other, the difference between them would still be greater, and a declaration of their sentiments would render them both insufferable to each other—which among uncivilized men would happen every moment, because without a mixture of art and trouble, the outward symptoms of that passion are not to be stifled. The second thing I would have you consider is the effect which in all human probability this inconvenience, arising from self-liking, would have upon creatures, endued with a great share of understanding, that are fond of their ease to the last degree, and as industrious to procure it. These two things, I say, do but duly weigh, and you shall find, that the disturbance and uneasiness, that must be caused by self-liking, whatever strugglings and unsuccessful trials to remedy them might precede, must necessarily produce at long run, what we call good manners and politeness.

Hor: I understand you, I believe. Everybody, in this undisciplined state, being affected with the high value he has for himself, and displaying the most natural symptoms, which you have described, they would all be offended at the barefaced pride of their neighbors. And it is impossible that this should continue long among rational creatures, but the repeated experience of the uneasiness they received from such behavior, would make some of them reflect on the cause of it; which, in tract of time, would make them find out, that their own barefaced pride must be as offensive to others, as that of others is to themselves.

Cleo: What you say is certainly the philosophical reason of the alterations that are made in the behavior of men by their being civilized. But all this is done without reflection, and men by degrees, and great length of time, fall as it were into these things spontaneously.

Hor: How is that possible, when it must cost them trouble, and there is a palpable self-denial to be seen in the restraint they put upon themselves?

Cleo: In the pursuit of self-preservation men discover a restless endeavor to make themselves easy, which insensibly teaches them to avoid mischief on all emergencies. And when human creatures once submit to government, and are used to live under the restraint of laws, it is incredible how many useful cautions, shifts, and stratagems they will learn to practice by experience and imitation from conversing together; without being aware of the natural causes, that oblige them to act as they do, [that is,] the passions within, that, unknown to themselves, govern their will and direct their behavior.

Hor: You'll make men as mere machines as Descartes does brutes.

Cleo: I have no such design. But I am of opinion, that men find out the use of their limbs by instinct, as much as brutes do the use of theirs; and that, without knowing anything of geometry or arithmetic, even children may learn to perform actions that seem to bespeak great skill in mechanics, and a considerable depth of thought and ingenuity in the contrivance besides.

Hor: What actions are they, which you judge this from?

Cleo: The advantageous postures which they'll choose in resisting force, in pulling, pushing, or otherwise removing weight; from their slight and dexterity in throwing stones, and other projectiles, and the stupendous cunning made use of in leaping.

Hor: What stupendous cunning, I pray?

Cleo: When men would leap or jump a great way, you know, they take a run before they throw themselves off the ground. It is certain that by this means they jump further, and with greater force, than they could do otherwise. The reason likewise is very plain. The body partakes of, and is moved by, two motions; and the velocity, impressed upon it by leaping, must be added to so much, as it retained of the velocity it was put into by running. Whereas the body of a person who takes his leap, as he is standing still, has no other motion than what is received from the muscular strength exerted in the act of leaping. See a thousand boys, as well as men, jump, and they'll all make use of this stratagem, but you won't find one of them, that does it knowingly for that reason. What I have said of this stratagem made use of in leaping, I desire you would apply to the doctrine of good manners, which is taught and practiced by millions who never thought on the origin of politeness, or so much as knew the real benefit it is of to society. The most crafty and designing will everywhere be the first, that for interest-sake will learn to conceal this passion of pride, and in a little time nobody will show the least symptom of it, while he is asking favors, or stands in need of help.

Hor: That rational creatures should do all this, without thinking or knowing what they were about, is inconceivable. Bodily motion is one thing, and the exercise of the understanding is another. And therefore agreeable postures, a graceful mien, an easy carriage, and a genteel outward behavior, in general, may be learned and contracted perhaps without much thought. But good manners are to be observed everywhere, in speaking, writing, and ordering actions to be performed by others.

Cleo: To men who never turned their thoughts that way it certainly is almost inconceivable to what prodigious height, from next to nothing, some arts may be and have been raised by human industry and application, by the uninterrupted labor, and joint experience of many ages, though none but men of ordinary capacity should ever be employed in them. What a noble as well as beautiful, what a glorious machine is a first-rate man of war, when she is under sail, well rigged, and well manned! As in bulk and weight it is vastly superior to any other moveable body of human invention, so there is no other that has an equal variety of differently surprising contrivances to boast of. There are many sets of hands in the nation, that, not wanting proper materials, would be able in less than half a year to produce, to fit out, and navigate a first-rate [ship]: yet it is certain that this task would be impracticable if it was not divided and subdivided into a greater variety of different labors; and it is certain that none of these labors require any other, than working men of ordinary capacities.

Hor: What would you infer from this?

Cleo: That we often ascribe to the excellence of man's genius, and the depth of his penetration, what is in reality owing to the length of time, and the experience of many generations, all of them very little differing from one another in natural parts and sagacity. And to know what it must have cost to bring that art of making ships for different purpose to the perfection in which it is now, we are only to consider, in the first place that many considerable improvements have been made in it within these fifty years and less; and in the second, that the inhabitants of this island did build and make use of ships eighteen hundred years ago, and that from that time to this, they have never been without.

Hor: Which all together make a strong proof of the slow progress that art has made, to be what it is.

Cleo: The chevalier [Bernard] Reneau [d'Eliçagary] has wrote a book [*The Theory of Maneuvering Sailing Vessels*], in which he shows the mechanism of sailing, and accounts mathematically for everything that belongs to the working and steering of a ship. I am persuaded that neither the first inventors of ships and sailing, or those who have made improvements since in any part of them, ever dreamed of those reasons, any more than now the rudest and most illiterate of the vulgar do, when they are made sailors, which time and practice will do in spite of their teeth. We have thousands of them, that were first hauled on board and detained against their wills, and yet in less than three years' time knew every rope and every pulley in the ship, and without the least scrap of mathematics had learned the management, as well as use of them, much better than the greatest mathematician could have done in all his lifetime, if he had never been at sea. The book I mentioned, among other curious things, demonstrates what angle the rudder must make with the keel, to render its influence upon the ship the most powerful. This has its merit; but a lad of fifteen, who has served a year of his time on board of a hoy [a small sloop], knows everything that is useful in this demonstration practically. Seeing the poop always answering the motion of the helm, he only minds the latter, without making the least reflection on the rudder, until in a year or two more his knowledge in sailing, and capacity of steering his vessel become so habitual to him, that he guides her as he does his own body, by instinct, though he is half asleep, or thinking on quite another thing.

Hor: If, as you said, and which I now believe to be true, the people, who first invented, and afterwards improved upon ships and sailing, never dreamed of those reasons of Monsieur Reneau, it is impossible that they should have acted from them, as motives that induced them *a priori*, to put their inventions and improvements in practice, with knowledge and design; which, I suppose, is what you intended to prove.

Cleo: It is. And I verily believe, not only that the raw beginners, who made the first essays in either art, good manners as well as sailing, were ignorant of the true cause, the real foundation those arts are built upon in nature; but likewise that, even now both arts are brought to great perfection, the greatest part of those that are most expert, and daily making improvements in them, know as little of the rationale of them, as their predecessors did at first. Though I believe at the same time Monsieur Reneau's reasons to be very just, and yours as good as his; that is, I believe that there is as much truth and solidity in your accounting for the origin of good manners as there is in his for the management of ships. They are very seldom the same sort of people, those that invent arts, and improvements in them, and those that enquire into the reason of things. This latter is most commonly practiced by such as are idle and indolent, that are fond of retirement, hate business, and take delight in speculation. Whereas none succeed oftener in the first, than active, stirring, and laborious men, such as will put their hand to the plough, try experiments, and give all their attention to what they are about.

Hor: It is commonly imagined, that speculative men are best at invention of all sorts.

Cleo: Yet it is a mistake. Soap-boiling, grain-dying, and other trades and mysteries, are from mean beginnings brought to great perfection. But the many improvements that can be remembered to have been made in them have for the generality been owing to persons who either were brought up to, or had long practiced and been conversant in those trades, and not to great proficients in chemistry or other parts of philosophy, whom one would naturally expect those things from. In some of these arts, especially grain or scarlet-dying, there are processes really astonishing; and by the mixture of various ingredients, by fire and fermentation, several operations are performed, which the most sagacious naturalist cannot account for by any system yet known; a certain sign, that they were not invented by reasoning *a priori*. When once the generality begin to conceal the high value they have for themselves, men must become more tolerable to one another. Now new improvements must be made every day, until some of them grow impudent enough, not only to deny the high value they have for themselves, but likewise to pretend that they have greater value for others than they have for themselves. This will bring in complaisance, and now flattery will rush in upon them like a torrent. As soon as they are arrived at this pitch of insincerity, they will find the benefit of it, and teach it their children. The passion of shame is so general, and so early discovered in all human creatures, that no nation can be so stupid as to be long without observing and making use of it accordingly. The same may be said of the credulity of infants, which is very inviting to many good purposes. The knowledge of parents is communicated to their offspring, and everyone's experience in life, being added to what he learned in his youth, every generation after this must be better taught than the preceding; by which means, in two or three centuries, good manners must be brought to great perfection.

Hor: When they are thus far advanced, it is easy to conceive the rest. For improvements, I suppose, are made in good manners, as they are in all other arts and sciences. But to commence from savages, men I believe would make but a small progress in good manners the first three hundred years. The Romans, who had a much better beginning, had been a nation above six centuries, and were almost masters of the world before they could be said to be a polite people. What I am most astonished at, and which I am now convinced of, is, that the basis of all this machinery is pride. Another thing I wonder at is, that you chose to speak of a nation that entered upon good manners before they had any notions of virtue or religion, which I believe there never was in the world.

Cleo: Pardon me, Horatio. I have nowhere insinuated that they had none, but I had no reason to mention them. In the first place, you asked my opinion concerning the use of politeness in this world, abstract from the considerations of a future state. Secondly, the art of good manners has nothing to do with virtue or religion, though it seldom clashes with either. It is a science that is ever built on the same steady principle in our nature, whatever the age or the climate may be, in which it is practiced.

Hor: How can anything be said not to clash with virtue or religion, that has nothing to do with either, and consequently disclaims both?

Cleo: This I confess seems to be a paradox, yet it is true. The doctrine of good manners teaches men to speak well of all virtues, but requires no more of them in any age, or country, than the outward appearance of those in fashion. And as to sacred matters, it is everywhere satisfied with a seeming conformity in outward worship. For all the religions in the universe are equally agreeable to good manners, where they are national. And pray, what opinion must we say a teacher to be of, to whom all opinions are probable alike? All the precepts of good manners throughout the world have the same tendency, and are no more than the various methods of making ourselves acceptable to others, with as little prejudice to ourselves as is possible: by which artifice we assist one another in the enjoyments of life, and refining upon pleasure; and every individual person is rendered more happy by it, in the fruition of all the good things he can purchase, than he could have been without such behavior. I mean happy, in the sense of the voluptuous. Let us look back on old Greece, the Roman Empire, or the great Eastern nations that flourished before them, and we shall find that luxury and politeness ever grew up together, and were never enjoyed asunder; that comfort and delight upon Earth have always employed the wishes of the *beau monde*; and that, as their chief study and greatest solicitude, to outward appearance, have ever been directed to obtain happiness in this world, so what would become of them in the next seems, to the naked eye, always to have been the least of their concern. . . .

The Sixth Dialogue
between Horatio and Cleomenes

(. . .)

Cleomenes: Man, as I have hinted before, naturally loves to imitate what he sees others do, which is the reason that savage people all do the same thing. This hinders them from meliorating their condition, though they are always wishing for it. But if one will wholly apply himself to the making of bows and arrows, whilst another provides food, a third builds huts, a fourth makes garments, and a fifth utensils, they not only become useful to one another, but the callings and employments themselves will in the same number of years receive much greater improvements, than if all had been promiscuously followed by every one of the five.

Horatio: I believe you are perfectly right there. And the truth of what you say is in nothing so conspicuous, as it is in watch-making, which is come to a higher degree of perfection, than it would have been arrived at yet, if the whole had always remained the employment of one person. I am persuaded, that even the plenty we have of clocks and watches, as well as the exactness and beauty they may be made of, are chiefly owing to the division that has been made of that art into many branches.

Cleo: The use of letters must likewise very much improve speech itself, which before that time cannot but be very barren and precarious.

Hor: I am glad to hear you mention speech again. I would not interrupt you, when you named it once before. Pray what language did your wild couple speak, when first they met?

Cleo: From what I have said already it is evident that they could have had none at all; at least, that is my opinion.

Hor: Then wild people must have an instinct to understand one another, which they lose when they are civilized.

Cleo: I am persuaded that nature has made all animals of the same kind, in their mutual commerce, intelligible to one another, as far as is requisite for the preservation of themselves and their species. And as to my wild couple, as you call them, I believe there would be a very good understanding, before many sounds passed between them. It is not without some difficulty that a man born in society can form an idea of such savages and their condition. And unless he has used himself to abstract thinking, he can hardly represent to himself such a state of simplicity in which man can have so few desires, and no appetites roving beyond the immediate call of untaught nature. To me it seems very plain that such a couple would not only be destitute of language, but likewise never find out or imagine that they stood in need of any; or that the want of it was any real inconvenience to them.

Hor: Why do you think so ?

Cleo: Because it is impossible that any creature should know the want of what it can have no idea of. I believe moreover, that if savages, after they are grown men and women, should hear others speak, be made acquainted with the usefulness of speech, and consequently become sensible of the want of it in themselves, their inclination to learn it would be as inconsiderable as their capacity. And if they should attempt it, they would find it an immense labor, a thing not to be surmounted, because the suppleness and flexibility in the organs of speech, that children are endued with, and which I have often hinted at, would be lost in them. And they might learn to play masterly upon the violin, or any other the most difficult musical instrument, before they could make any tolerable proficiency in speaking.

Hor: Brutes make several distinct sounds to express different passions by: as, for example, anguish, and great danger dogs of all sorts express with another noise than they do rage and anger; and the whole species express grief by howling.

Cleo: This is no argument to make us believe that nature has endued man with speech. There are innumerable other privileges and instincts which some brutes enjoy, and men are destitute of: chickens run about as soon as they are hatched; and most quadrupeds can walk without help, as soon as they are brought forth. If ever language came by instinct, the people that spoke it must have known every individual word in it. And a man in the wild state of nature would have no occasion for a thousandth part of the most barren language that ever had a name. When a man's knowledge is confined within a narrow compass, and he has nothing to obey but the simple dictates of nature, the want of speech is easily supplied by dumb signs; and it is more natural to untaught men to express themselves by gestures, than by sounds. But we are all born with a capacity of making ourselves understood, beyond other animals, without speech. To express grief, joy, love, wonder and fear, there are certain tokens that are common to the whole species. Who doubts that the crying of children was given them by nature, to call assistance and raise pity, which latter it does so unaccountably beyond any other sound?

Hor: In mothers and nurses, you mean.

Cleo: I mean in the generality of human creatures. Will you allow me that warlike music generally rouses and supports the spirits, and keeps them from sinking?

Hor: I believe I must.

Cleo: Then I'll engage, that the crying . . . of helpless infants will stir up compassion in the generality of our species that are within the hearing of it, with much greater certainty than drums and trumpets will dissipate and chase away fear, in those they are applied to. Weeping, laughing, smiling, frowning, sighing, exclaiming; we spoke of before how universal, as well as copious, is the language of the eyes, by the help of which the remotest nations understand one another at first sight, taught or untaught, in the weightiest temporal concern that belongs to the species. And in that language our wild couple would at their first meeting intelligibly say more to one another without guile, than any civilized pair would dare to name without blushing.

Hor: A man without doubt may be as impudent with his eyes, as he can be with his tongue.

Cleo: All such looks, therefore, and several motions that are natural, are carefully avoided among polite people, upon no other account than that they are too significant. It is for the same reason that stretching ourselves before others, whilst we are yawning, is an absolute breach of good manners, especially in mixed company of both sexes. As it is indecent to display any of these tokens, so it is unfashionable to take notice of, or seem to understand, them. This disuse and neglect of them is the cause that whenever they happen to be made either through ignorance or willful rudeness, many of them are lost and really not understood by the *beau monde* that would be very plain to savages without language, who could have no other means of conversing than by signs and motions.

Hor: But if the old stock would never either be able or willing to acquire speech, it is impossible they could teach it their children. Then which way could any language ever come into the world from two savages?

Cleo: By slow degrees, as all other arts and sciences have done, and length of time; [for example,] agriculture, physics, astronomy, architecture, painting, etc. From what we see in children that are backward with their tongues, we have reason to think, that a wild pair would make themselves intelligible to each other by signs and gestures, before they would attempt it by sounds. But when they lived together for many years, it is very probable that for the things they were most conversant with they would find out sounds to stir up in each other the ideas of such things, when they were out of sight. These sounds they would communicate to their young ones. And the longer they lived together the greater variety of sounds they would invent, as well for actions as the things themselves. They would find that the volubility of tongue and flexibility of voice were much greater in their young ones than they could remember it ever to have been in themselves. It is impossible, [because contrary to Scripture,] but some of these young ones would, either by accident or design, make use of this superior aptitude of the organs at one time or other, which every generation would still improve upon; and this must have been the origin of all languages, and speech itself, that were not taught by inspiration. I believe, moreover, that after language (I mean such as is of human invention) was come to a great degree of perfection, and even when peo ple had distinct words for every action in life, as well as everything they meddled or conversed with, signs and gestures still continued to be made for a great while to accompany speech, because both are intended for the same purpose.

Hor: The design of speech is to make our thoughts known to others.

Cleo: I don't think so.

Hor: What! Don't men speak to be understood?

Cleo: In one sense they do. But there is a double meaning in those words, which I believe you did not intend. If by man's speaking to be understood, you mean that when men speak, they desire that the purport of the sounds they utter should be known and apprehended by others, I answer in the affirmative. But if you mean by it that men speak in order that their thoughts may be known, and their sentiments laid open and seen through by others, which likewise may be meant by speaking to be understood, I answer in the negative. The first sign or sound that ever man made, born of a woman, was made in behalf, and intended for the use, of him who made it; and I am of opinion, that the first design of speech was to persuade others, either to give credit to what the speaking person would have them believe; or else to act or suffer such things, as he would compel them to act or suffer, if they were entirely in his power.

Hor: Speech is likewise made use of to teach, advise, and inform others for their benefit, as well as to persuade them in our own behalf.

Cleo: And so by the help of it men may accuse themselves and own their crimes. But nobody would have invented speech for those purposes; I speak of the design, the first motive and intention that put man upon speaking. We see in children that the first things they endeavor to express with words are their wants and their will, and their speech is but a confirmation of what they asked, denied, or affirmed, by signs before.

Hor: But why do you imagine that people would continue to make use of signs and gestures after they could sufficiently express themselves in words?

Cleo: Because signs confirm words, as much as words do signs. And we see, even in polite people, that when they are very eager they can hardly forbear making use of both. When an infant, in broken imperfect gibberish, calls for a cake or a plaything, and at the same time points at and reaches after it, this double endeavor makes a stronger impression upon us than if the child had either spoken its wants in plain words, without making any signs, or else looked at and reached after the thing wanted, without attempting to speak. Speech and action assist and corroborate one another, and experience teaches us that they move us much more, and are more persuasive jointly than separately . . . , and when an infant makes use of both, he acts from the same principle, that an orator does, when he joins proper gestures to an elaborate declamation.

Hor: From what you have said, it should seem that action is not only more natural, but likewise more ancient than speech itself, which before I should have thought a paradox.

Cleo: Yet it is true; and you shall always find, that the most forward, volatile, and fiery tempers make more use of gestures, when they speak, than others that are more patient and sedate.

Hor: It is a very diverting scene to see how this is overdone among the French, and still more among the Portuguese. I have often been amazed to see what distortions of face and body, as well as other strange gesticulations with hands and feet, some of them will make in their ordinary discourses. But nothing was more offensive to me, when I was abroad, than the loudness and violence which most foreigners speak with, even among persons of quality, when a dispute arises, or anything is to be debated. Before I was used to it, it put me always upon my guard, for I did not question but they were angry; and I often recollected what had been said, in order to consider whether it was not something I ought to have resented.

Cleo: The natural ambition and strong desire men have to triumph over, as well as persuade others, is the occasion of all this. Heightening and lowering the voice, at proper seasons, is a bewitching engine to captivate mean understandings; and loudness is an assistant to speech, as well as action is. Incorrectness, false grammar, and even want of sense, are often happily drowned in noise and great bustle; and many an argument has been convincing, that had all its force from the vehemence it was made with. The weakness of the language itself may be palliatively cured by strength of elocution.

Hor: I am glad that speaking low is the fashion among well-bred people in England; for bawling and impetuosity I cannot endure.

Cleo: Yet this latter is more natural. And no man ever gave in to the contrary practice, the fashion you like, that was not taught it, either by precept or example. And if men do not accustom themselves to it, whilst they are young, it is very difficult to comply with it afterwards. But it is the most lovely, as well as most rational piece of good manners, that human invention has to boast of in the art of flattery. For when a man addresses himself to me in a calm manner, without making gestures, or other motions with head or body, and continues his discourse in the same submissive strain and composure of voice, without exalting or depressing it, he, in the first place, displays his own modesty and humility in an agreeable manner; and, in the second, makes me a great compliment, in the opinion which he seems to have of me. For by such a behavior he gives me the pleasure to imagine that he thinks me not influenced by my passions, but altogether swayed by my reason. He seems to lay his stress on my judgment, and therefore to desire, that I should weigh and consider what he says, without being ruffled or disturbed. No man would do this unless he trusted entirely to my good sense, and the rectitude of my understanding.

(. . .)

Cleo: The superiority of understanding, in the first place, makes man sooner sensible of grief and joy, and capable of entertaining either, with greater difference as to the degrees, than they are felt in other creatures. Secondly, it renders him more industrious to please himself, that is, it furnishes self-love with a greater variety of shifts to exert itself on all emergencies, than is made use of by animals of less capacity. Superiority of understanding likewise gives us a foresight, and inspires us with hopes, of which other creatures have little, and that only of things immediately before them. All these things are so many tools, arguments, by which self-love reasons us into content, and renders us patient under many afflictions, for the sake of supplying those wants that are most pressing. This is of infinite use to a man, who finds himself born in a body politic, and it must make him fond of society; whereas the same endowment before that time, the same superiority of understanding in the state of nature, can only serve to render man incurably averse to society, and more obstinately tenacious of his savage liberty, than any other creature would be, that is equally necessitous.

Hor: I don't know how to refute you. There is a justness of thought in what you say which I am forced to assent to. And yet it seems strange. How come you by this insight into the heart of man, and which way is that skill of unraveling human nature to be obtained?

Cleo: By diligently observing what excellencies and qualifications are really acquired in a well-accomplished man; and having done this impartially, we may be sure that the remainder of him is nature. It is for want of duly separating and keeping asunder these two things that men have uttered such absurdities on this subject, alleging as the causes of man's fitness for society, such qualifications as no man ever was endued with, that was not educated in a society, a civil establishment, of several hundred years' standing. But the flatterers of our species keep this carefully from our view. Instead of separating what is acquired from what is natural, and distinguishing between them, they take pains to unite and confound them together.

Hor: Why do they? I don't see the compliment, since the acquired as well as natural parts belong to the same person; and the one is not more inseparable from him than the other.

Cleo: Nothing is so near to a man, nor so really and entirely his own, as what he has from nature. And when that dear self, for the sake of which he values or despises, loves or hates everything else, comes to be stripped and abstracted from all foreign acquisitions, human nature makes a poor figure. It shows a nakedness, or at least an undress, which no man cares to be seen in. There is nothing we can be possessed of that is worth having which we do not endeavor closely to annex, and make an ornament of to ourselves. Even wealth and power, and all the gifts of fortune, that are plainly adventitious, and altogether remote from our persons, whilst they are our right and property, we don't love to be considered without them. We see likewise that men, who are come to be great in the world from despicable beginnings, don't love to hear of their origin.

Hor: That is no general rule.

Cleo: I believe it is, though there may be exceptions from it; and these are not without reasons. When a man is proud of his parts, and wants to be esteemed for his diligence, penetration, quickness and assiduity, he'll make perhaps an ingenuous confession, even to the exposing of his parents. And in order to set off the merit that raised him, be speaking himself of his original meanness. But this is commonly done before inferiors, whose envy will be lessened by it, and who will applaud his candor and humility in owning this blemish. But not a word of this before his betters, who value themselves upon their families. And such men could heartily wish that their parentage was unknown, whenever they are with those that are their equals in quality, though superior to them in birth, by whom they know that they are hated for their advancement, and despised for the lowness of their extraction. But I have a shorter way of proving my assertion. Pray, is it good manners to tell a man that he is meanly born, or to hint at his descent, when it is known to be vulgar?

Hor: No: I don't say it is.

Cleo: That decides it, by showing the general opinion about it. Noble ancestors, and everything else that is honorable and esteemed, and can be drawn within our sphere, are an advantage to our persons, and we all desire, they should be looked upon as our own.

Hor: Ovid did not think so, when he said, *nam genus & proavos & quae non fecimus ipsi, vix ea nostra voco* [we cannot take credit for our lineage, our grandfathers, or anything we have not done].

Cleo: A pretty piece of modesty in a speech, where a man takes pains to prove that Jupiter was his great-grandfather. What signifies a theory, which a man destroys by his practice? Did you ever know a person of quality pleased with being called a bastard, though he owed his being, as well as his greatness, chiefly to his mother's impudicity?

Hor: By things acquired, I thought you meant learning and virtue. How come you to talk of birth and descent?

Cleo: By showing you that men are unwilling to have anything that is honorable separated from themselves, though it is remote from, and has nothing to do with their persons. I would convince you of the little probability there is, that we should be pleased with being considered abstract from what really belongs to us; and qualifications, that in the opinion of the best and wisest are the only things for which we ought to be valued. When men are well-accomplished, they are ashamed of the lowest steps from which they rose to that perfection. And the more civilized they are, the more they think it injurious, to have their nature seen without the improvements that have been made upon it. The most correct authors would blush to see everything published, which in the composing of their works they blotted out, and stifled; and which yet it is certain they once conceived. For this reason they are justly compared to architects, that remove the scaffolding before they show their buildings. All ornaments bespeak the value we have for the things adorned. Don't you think, that the first red or white that ever was laid upon a face, and the first false hair that was wore, were put on with great secrecy, and with a design to deceive?

Hor: In France painting is now looked upon as part of a woman's dress. They make no mystery of it.

Cleo: So it is with all the impositions of this nature, when they come to be so gross that they can be hid no longer; as men's perukes [hairdresses] all over Europe. But if these things could be concealed, and were not known, the tawny coquette would heartily wish that the ridiculous daubing she plasters herself with, might pass for complexion; and the bald-pated beau would be as glad to have his full-bottomed wig looked upon as a natural head of hair. Nobody puts in artificial teeth, but to hide the loss of his own.

Hor: But is not a man's knowledge a real part of himself?

Cleo: Yes, and so is his politeness. But neither of them belong to his nature, any more than his gold watch or his diamond ring. And even from these he endeavors to draw a value and respect to his person. The most admired among the fashionable people that delight in outward vanity, and know how to dress well, would be highly displeased if their clothes, and skill in putting them on, should be looked upon otherwise than as part of themselves. Nay, it is this part of them only, which, while they are unknown, can procure them access to the highest companies, the courts of princes. Where it is manifest, that both sexes are either admitted or refused, by no other judgment than what is formed of them from their dress, without the least regard to their goodness or their understanding.

Hor: I believe I apprehend you. It is our fondness of that self, which we hardly know what it consists in, that could first make us think of embellishing our persons. And when we have taken pains in correcting, polishing, and beautifying nature, the same self-love makes us unwilling to have the ornaments seen separately from the thing adorned.

Cleo: The reason is obvious. It is that self we are in love with, before it is adorned as well as after, and everything which is confessed to be acquired, seems to point at our original nakedness, and to upbraid us with our natural wants; I would say, the meanness and deficiency of our nature. That no bravery is so useful in war as that which is artificial is undeniable. Yet the soldier that by art and discipline has manifestly been tricked and wheedled into courage, after he has behaved himself in two or three battles with intrepidity, will never endure to hear that he has not natural valor; though all his acquaintance, as well as himself, remember the time, that he was an arrant coward.

Hor: But since the love, affection, and benevolence we naturally have for our species is not greater than other creatures have for theirs, how comes it, that man gives more ample demonstrations of this love on thousand occasions, than any other animal?

Cleo: Because no other animal has the same capacity or opportunity to do it. But you may ask the same of his hatred. The greater knowledge and the more wealth and power a man has, the more capable he is of rendering others sensible of the passion he is affected with, as well when he hates as when he loves them. The more a man remains uncivilized, and the less he is removed from the state of nature, the less his love is to be depended upon.

Hor: There is more honesty and less deceit among plain, untaught people, than there is among those that are more artful. And therefore I should have looked for true love and unfeigned affection among those that live in a natural simplicity rather than anywhere else.

Cleo: You speak of sincerity, but the love which I said was less to be depended upon in untaught than in civilized people, I supposed to be real and sincere in both. Artful people may dissemble love, and pretend to friendship, where they have none. But they are influenced by their passions, and natural appetites, as well as savages, though they gratify them in another manner. Well-bred people behave themselves in the choice of diet and the taking of their repasts very differently from savages; so they do in their amours, but hunger and lust are the same in both. An artful man, nay, the greatest hypocrite, whatever his behavior is abroad, may love his wife and children at his heart, and the sincerest man can do no more. My business is to demonstrate to you that the good qualities men compliment our nature and the whole species with are the result of art and education. The reason why love is little to be depended upon in those that are uncivilized is because the passions in them are more fleeting and inconstant. They more often jostle out and succeed one another than they are and do in well-bred people. Persons that are well educated have learned to study their ease and the comforts of life; to tie themselves up to rules and decorums for their own advantage, and often to submit to small inconveniences to avoid greater. Among the lowest vulgar, and those of the meanest education of all, you seldom see a lasting harmony. You shall have a man and his wife, that have a real affection for one another, be full of love one hour, and disagree the next, for a trifle; and the lives of many are made miserable from no other faults in themselves, than their want of manners and discretion. Without design they will often talk imprudently, untill they raise one another's anger; which neither of them being able to stifle, she scolds at him. He beats her; she bursts out into tears. This moves him, he is sorry; both repent, and are friends again, and with all the sincerity imaginable resolve never to quarrel for the future, as long as they live. All this will pass between them in less than half a day, and will perhaps be repeated once a month, or oftener, as provocations offer, or either of them is more or less prone to anger. Affection never remained long uninterrupted between two persons, without art. And the best friends, if they are always together, will fall out, unless great discretion be used on both sides.

(. . .)

Hor: But what is it at last, that raises opulent cities and powerful nations from the smallest beginnings?

Cleo: Providence.

Hor: But Providence makes use of means that are visible. I want to know the engines it is performed with.

Cleo: All the ground work that is required to aggrandize nations you have seen in *The Fable of the Bees*. All sound politics, and the whole art of governing, are entirely built upon the knowledge of human nature. The great business in general of a politician is to promote, and, if he can, reward all good and useful actions on the one hand; and on the other, to punish, or at least discourage, everything that is destructive or hurtful to society. To name particulars would be an endless task. Anger, lust, and pride may be the causes of innumerable mischiefs, that are all carefully to be guarded against. But setting them aside, the regulations only that are required to defeat and prevent all the machinations and contrivances, that avarice and envy may put man upon, to the detriment of his neighbor, are almost infinite. Would you be convinced of these truths, do but employ yourself for a month or two, in surveying and minutely examining into every art and science, every trade, handicraft and occupation, that are professed and followed in such a city as London; and all the laws, prohibitions, ordinances and restrictions, that have been found absolutely necessary, to hinder both private men and bodies corporate, in so many different stations, first from interfering with the public peace and welfare; [and] secondly, from openly wronging and secretly overreaching, or any other way injuring, one another. If you will give yourself this trouble, you will find the number of clauses and provisos to govern a large flourishing city well to be prodigious beyond imagination. And yet every one of them tending to the same purpose: the curbing, restraining and disappointing the inordinate passions, and hurtful frailties of man. You will find, moreover, which is still more to be admired, the greater part of the articles in this vast multitude of regulations, when well understood, to be the result of consummate wisdom.

Hor: How could these things exist if there had not been men of very bright parts and uncommon talents?

Cleo: Among the things I hint at, there are very few that are the work of one man, or of one generation. The greatest part of them are the product, the joint labor of several ages. . . . The wisdom I speak of is not the offspring of a fine understanding or intense thinking, but of sound and deliberate judgment, acquired from a long experience in business, and a multiplicity of observations. By this sort of wisdom, and length of time, it may be brought about, that there shall be no greater difficulty in governing a large city, than (pardon the lowness of the simile) there is in weaving of stockings.

Hor: Very low indeed.

Cleo: Yet I know nothing to which the laws and established economy of a well-ordered city may be more justly compared, than the knitting-frame. The machine, at first view, is intricate and unintelligible. Yet the effects of it are exact and beautiful, and in what is produced by it, there is a surprising regularity. But the beauty and exactness in the manufacture are principally, if not altogether, owing to the happiness of the invention, the contrivance of the engine. For the greatest artist at it can furnish us with no better work, than may be made by almost any scoundrel after half a year's practice.

Hor: Though your comparison be low, I must own that it very well illustrates your meaning.

Cleo: Whilst you spoke, I have thought of another, which is better. It is common now to have clocks that are made to play several tunes with great exactness. The study and labor, as well as trouble of disappointments, which, in doing and undoing such a contrivance, must necessarily have cost from the beginning to the end, are not to be thought of without astonishment. There is something analogous to this in the government of a flourishing city, that has lasted uninterrupted for several ages. There is no part of the wholesome regulations, belonging to it, even the most trifling and minute, about which great pains and consideration have not been employed, as well as length of time. And if you will look into the history and antiquity of any such city, you will find that the changes, repeals, additions and amendments, that have been made in and to the laws and ordinances by which it is ruled are in number prodigious. But that when once they are brought to as much perfection, as art and human wisdom can carry them, the whole machine may be made to play of itself, with as little skill as is required to wind up a clock. And the government of a large city, once put into good order, the magistrates only following their noses, will continue to go right for a great while, though there was not a wise man in it, provided that the care of Providence was to watch over it in the same manner as it did before.

Hor: But supposing the government of a large city, when it is once established, to be very easy, it is not so with whole states and kingdoms. Is it not a great blessing to a nation, to have all places of honor and great trust filled with men of parts and application, of probity and virtue?

Cleo: Yes; and of learning, moderation, frugality, candor and affability. Look out for such as fast as you can, but in the meantime the places can't stand open, the offices must be served by such as you can get.

Hor: You seem to insinuate that there is a great scarcity of good men in the nation.

Cleo: I don't speak of our nation in particular, but of all states and kingdoms in general. What I would say is that it is the interest of every nation to have their home government, and every branch of the civil administration, so wisely contrived, that every man of middling capacity and reputation may be fit for any of the highest posts. (. . .)

An Enquiry into the Origin of Honor, and the Usefulness of Christianity in War (1732)

The First Dialogue
between Horatio and Cleomenes

Horatio: I wonder you never attempted to guess at the origin of honor, as you had done at that of politeness, and your friend in his *Fable of the Bees* has done at the origin of virtue.

Cleomenes: I have often thought of it, and am satisfied within myself, that my conjecture about it is just, but there are three substantial reasons why I have hitherto kept it to myself, and never yet mentioned to anyone what my sentiments are concerning the origin of that charming sound. . . . The word honor is used in such different acceptations; [it] is now a verb, then a noun, sometimes taken for the reward of virtue, sometimes for a principle that leads to virtue, and, at others again, signifies virtue itself. It would be a very hard task to take in everything that belongs to it, and at the same time avoid confusion in treating of it. This is my first reason. The second is that to set forth and explain my opinion on this head to others with perspicuity would take up so much time, that few people would have patience to hear it, or think it worth their while to bestow so much attention, as it would require, on what the greatest part of mankind would think very trifling.

Hor: This second whets my curiosity: pray, what is your third reason?

Cleo: That the very thing, to which, in my opinion, honor owes its birth, is a passion in our nature, for which there is no word coined yet, no name that is commonly known and received in any language.

Hor: That is very strange.

Cleo: Yet not less true. Do you remember what I said of self-liking . . . when I spoke of the origin of politeness?

Hor: I do. But you know, I hate affectation and singularity of all sorts. Some men are fond of uncouth words of their own making, when there are other words already known that sound better, and would equally

195

explain their meaning. What you called then self-liking at last proved to be pride, you know.

Cleo: Self-liking I have called that great value, which all individuals set upon their own persons; that high esteem, which I take all men to be born with for themselves. I have proved from what is constantly observed in suicide that there is such a passion in human nature, and that it is plainly distinct from self-love. When this self-liking is excessive, and so openly shown as to give offense to others, I know very well it is counted a vice and called pride. But when it is kept out of sight, or is so well disguised as not to appear in its own colors, it has no name, though men act from that and no other principle.

Hor: When what you call self-liking, that just esteem which men have naturally for themselves, is moderate, and spurs them on to good actions, it is very laudable, and is called the love of praise or a desire of the applause of others. Why can't you take up with either of these names?

Cleo: Because I would not confound the effect with the cause. That men are desirous of praise, and love to be applauded by others, is the result, a palpable consequence, of that self-liking which reigns in human nature, and is felt in everyone's breast before we have time or capacity to reflect and think of anybody else. What moralists have taught us concerning the passions is very superficial and defective. Their great aim was the public peace and the welfare of the civil society; to make men governable, and unite multitudes in one common interest.

Hor: And it is possible that men can have a more noble aim in temporals?

Cleo: I don't deny that. But as all their labors were only tending to those purposes, they neglected all the rest; and if they could but make men useful to each other and easy to themselves, they had no scruple about the means they did it by, nor any regard to truth or the reality of things, as is evident from the gross absurdities they have made men swallow concerning their own nature, in spite of what all felt within. In the culture of gardens, whatever comes up in the paths is weeded out as offensive and flung upon the dunghill. But among the vegetables that are all thus promiscuously thrown away for weeds, there may be many curious plants, on the use and beauty of which a botanist would read long lectures. The moralists have endeavored to rout vice, and clear the heart of all hurtful appetites and inclinations. We are beholden to them for this in the same manner as we are to those who destroy vermin, and clear the countries of all noxious creatures. But may not a naturalist detect moles, try experiments upon them, and enquire into the nature of their handicraft, without offense to the mole-catchers, whose business is only to kill them as fast as they can?

Hor: What fault is it you find with the moralists? I can't see what you drive at.

Cleo: I would show you that the want of accuracy in them, when they have treated of human nature, makes it extremely difficult to speak intelligibly of the different faculties of our intellectual part. Some things are very essential and yet have no name, as I have given an instance in that esteem which men have naturally for themselves, abstract[ed] from self-love, and which I have been forced to coin the word self-liking for. Others are mis-called and said to be what they are not. So most of the passions are counted to be weaknesses, and commonly called frailties; whereas they are the very powers that govern the whole machine, and, whether they are perceived or not, determine or rather create the will that immediately precedes every deliberate action.

Hor: I now understand perfectly well what you mean by self-liking. You are of opinion that we are all born with a passion manifestly distinct from self-love; that, when it is moderate and well-regulated, excites in us the love of praise, and a desire to be applauded and thought well of by others, and stirs us up to good actions. But that the same passion, when it is excessive, or ill-turned, whatever it excites in ourselves, gives offense to others, renders us odious, and is called pride. As there is no word or expression that comprehends all the different effects of this same cause, this passion, you have made one, self-liking, by which you mean the passion in general, the whole extent of it, whether it produces laudable actions, and gains us applause, or such as we are blamed for and draw upon us the ill-will of others.

Cleo: You are extremely right; this was my design in coining the word self-liking.

Hor: But you said that honor owes its birth to this passion; which I don't understand, and wish you would explain to me.

Cleo: To comprehend this well, we ought to consider that as all human creatures are born with this passion, so the operations of it are manifestly observed in infants, as soon as they begin to be conscious and to reflect, often before they can speak or go.

Hor: As how?

Cleo: If they are praised, or commended, though they don't deserve it, and good things are said of them, though they are not true, we see that joy is raised in them, and they are pleased. On the contrary, when they are reproved and blamed, though they know themselves to be in fault, and bad things are said of them, though nothing but truth, we see it excites sorrow in them and often anger. This passion of self-liking, then, manifesting itself so early in all children that are not idiots, it is inconceivable that men should not be sensible, and plainly feel, that they have it long before they are grown up. And all men feeling themselves to be affected with it, though they know no name for the thing itself, it is impossible that they should long converse together in society without finding out not only that others are influenced with it as well as themselves, but likewise which way to please or displease one another on account of this passion.

Hor: But what is all this to honor?

Cleo: I'll show you. When A performs an action which, in the eyes of B, is laudable, B wishes well to A; and, to show him his satisfaction, tells him that such an action is an honor to him, or that he ought to be honored for it: by saying this, B, who knows that all men are affected with self-liking, intends to acquaint A, that he thinks him in the right to gratify and indulge himself in the passion of self-liking. In this sense the word honor, whether it is used as a noun or a verb, is always a compliment to make to those who act, have, or are what we approve of. It is a term of art to express our concurrence with others, our agreement with them in our sentiments concerning the esteem and value they have for themselves. From what I have said, it must follow that the greater the multitudes are that express this concurrence, and the more expensive, the more operose and the more humble the demonstrations of it are, the more openly likewise they are made, the longer they last, and the higher the quality is of those who join and assist in this concurrence, this compliment. The greater, without all dispute, is the honor which is done to the person in whose favor these marks of esteem are displayed. So that the highest honor that men can give to mortals, while alive, is in substance no more than the most likely and the most effectual means that human wit can invent to gratify, stir up, and increase in him, to whom that honor is paid, the passion of self-liking.

Hor: I am afraid it is true.

Cleo: To render what I have advanced more conspicuous, we need only look into the reverse of honor, which is dishonor or shame, and we shall find that this could have had no existence any more than honor, if there had not been such a passion in our nature as self-liking. When we see others commit such actions as are vile and odious in our opinion, we say that such actions are a shame to them, or that they ought to be ashamed of them. By this we show that we differ from them in their sentiments concerning the value which we know that they, as well as all mankind, have for their own persons. And we are endeavoring to make them have an ill opinion of themselves, and raise in them that sincere sorrow, which always attends man's reflecting on his own unworthiness. I desire, you would mind, that the actions which we thus condemn as vile and odious need not to be so but in our own opinion; for what I have said happens among the worst of rogues, as well as among the better sort of people. If one villain should neglect picking a pocket, when he might have done it with ease, another of the same gang, who was near him and saw this, would upbraid him with it in good earnest, and tell him that he ought to be ashamed of having slipped so fair an opportunity. Sometimes shame signifies the visible disorders that are the symptoms of this sorrowful reflection on our own unworthiness; at others, we give that name to the punishments that are inflicted to raise those disorders. But the more you will examine into the nature of either, the more you will see the truth of what I have asserted on this head, and [that] all the marks of ignominy, that can be thought of, have a plain tendency to mortify pride, which, in other words, is to disturb, take away and extirpate every thought of self-liking.

(. . .)

Hor: . . . The symptoms of pride and shame are so vastly different, that to me it is inconceivable they should proceed from the same passion.

Cleo: Pray think again with attention, and you'll be of my opinion. My friend compares the symptoms that are observed in human creatures when they exalt in their pride with those of the mortification they feel when they are overwhelmed with shame. The symptoms, and if you will the sensations, that are felt in the two cases, are, as you say, vastly different from one another. But no man could be affected with either, if he had not such a passion in his nature, as I call self-liking. Therefore, they are different affections of one and the same passion, that are differently observed in us, according as we either enjoy pleasure, or are aggrieved on account of that passion; in the same manner as the most happy and the most miserable lovers are happy and miserable on the score of the same passion. Do but compare the pleasure of a man, who with an extraordinary appetite is feasting on what is delicious to him, to the torment of another, who is extremely hungry, and can get nothing to eat. No two things in the world can be more different, than the pleasure of the one is from the torment of the other. Yet nothing is more evident than that both are derived from and owing to the same craving principle in our nature, the desire of food. For when this is entirely lost, it is more vexatious to eat, than it is to let it alone, though the whole body languishes, and we are ready to expire for want of sustenance. Hitherto I have spoken of honor in its first literal sense, in which it is a technical word in the art of civility, and signifies a means which men by converging together have found out to please and gratify one another on account of a palpable passion in our nature, that has no name, and which therefore I call self-liking. In this sense I believe the word honor, both as a verb and a noun, to be as ancient as the oldest language. But there is another meaning besides, belonging to the same sound; and honor signifies likewise a principle of courage, virtue, and fidelity, which some men are said to act from, and to be awed by, as others are by religion. In the latter sense, it is much more modern, and I don't believe to be met with a thousand years ago in any language.

Hor: How! Is it but within these thousand years that there have been men of bravery and virtue . . . ?

Cleo: . . . All ages and most countries have produced men of virtue and bravery; but this I do not enquire into now. What I assert to be modern is the phrase, the term of art. It is that which the ancients knew nothing of. Nor can you with ten words, in either Greek or Latin, express the entire idea which is annexed to the word honor when it signifies a principle. To be a man of honor it is not sufficient that he, who assumes that title, is brave in war, and dares to fight against the enemies of his country. He must likewise be ready to engage in private quarrels, though the laws of God and his country forbid it. He must bear no affront without resenting it, nor refuse a challenge, if it be sent to him in a proper manner by a man of honor. I make no doubt, but this significance of the word honor is entirely Gothic, and sprang up in some of the most ignorant ages of Christianity. It seems to have been an invention to influence men whom religion had no power over. All human creatures have a restless desire of mending their condition. And in all civil societies and communions of men there seems to be a spirit at work, that, in spite of the continual opposition it receives from vice and misfortunes, is always laboring for and seeking after what can never be obtained whilst the world stands.

Hor: What is that pray?

Cleo: To make men completely happy upon Earth. Thus men make laws to obviate every inconvenience they meet with. And as times discover to them the insufficiency of those laws, they make others with an intent to enforce, mend, explain or repeal the former; until the body of laws grows to such an enormous bulk, that to understand it is a tedious prolix study, and the numbers that follow and belong to the practice of it, come to be a grievance almost as great as could be feared from injustice and oppression. Nothing is more necessary than that property should be secured. And it is impossible but on many occasions men must trust one another in the civil society. Now nothing has ever been thought to be more obligatory or a greater tie upon man than religion. (. . .) No large society of men can be well-governed without religion, and that there never was a nation that had not some worship, and did not believe in some deity or other, is most certain. But what do you think is the reason of that?

Hor: Because multitudes must be awed by something that is terrible, as flames of hell, and fire everlasting. And it is evident, that if it was not for the fear of an after-reckoning, some men would be so wicked that there would be no living with them.

Cleo: Pray, how wicked would they be? What crimes would they commit?

Hor: Robbing, murdering, ravishing.

Cleo: And are not often here, as well as in other nations, people convicted of, and punished for those crimes?

Hor: I am satisfied [that] the vulgar could not be managed without religion of some sort or other; for the fear of futurity keeps thousands in awe, who, without that reflection, would all be guilty of those crimes which are now committed only by a few.

Cleo: This is a surmise without any foundation. It has been said a thousand times by divines of all sects, but nobody has ever shown the least probability of its being true, and daily experience gives us all the reason in the world to think the contrary. For there are thousands, who, throughout the course of their lives, seem not to have the least regard to a future state, though they are believers; and yet these very people are very cautious of committing anything which the law would punish. You'll give me leave to observe, by the by, that to believe what you say, a man must have a worse opinion of his species than ever the author of *The Fable of the Bees* appears to have had yet.

Hor: Don't mistake me: I am far from believing that men of sense and education are to be frightened with those bugbears.

Cleo: And what I say, I don't mean of libertines or deists, but men, that to all outward appearance are believers, that go to church, receive the sacrament, and at the approach of death are observed to be really afraid of Hell. And yet of these, many are drunkards, whoremasters, adulterers, and not a few of them betray their trust, rob their country, defraud widows and orphans, and make wronging their neighbors their daily practice.

Hor: What temporal benefit can religion be of to the civil society, if we don't keep people in awe?

Cleo: That's another question. We both agree that no nation or large society can be well-governed without religion. I asked you the reason of this. You tell me, because the vulgar could not be kept in awe without it. In reply to this, I point at a thousand instances where religion is not of that efficacy, and show you withal, that this end of keeping men in awe is much better obtained by the laws and temporal punishment, and that it is the fear of them which actually restrains great numbers of wicked people. I might say all, without exception, of whom there is any hope or possibility that they can be curbed at all, or restrained by anything whatever. For such reprobates as can make a jest of the gallows, and are not afraid of hanging, will laugh likewise at Hell and defy damnation.

Hor: If the reason I allege is insufficient, pray give me a better.

Cleo: I'll endeavor it. The first business of all governments, I mean the task which all rulers must begin with, is to make men tractable and obedient, which is not to be performed unless we can make them believe that the instructions and commands we give them have a plain tendency to the good of every individual, and that we say nothing to them, but what we know to be true. To do this effectively, human nature ought to be humored as well as studied: whoever therefore takes upon him to govern a multitude, ought to inform himself of those sentiments that are the natural result of the passions and frailties which every human creature is born with.

Hor: I don't understand what sentiments.

Cleo: I'll explain myself. All men are born with fear, and as they are likewise born with a desire for happiness and self-preservation, it is natural for them to avoid pain and everything that makes them uneasy; and which, by a general word, is called evil. Fear being that passion which inspires us with a strong aversion to evil, it is very natural to think that it will put us up on enquiring into the means to shun it. I have told you already . . . how this aversion to evil, and endeavor to shun it, this principle of fear, would always naturally dispose human creatures to suspect the existence of an intelligent cause that is invisible, whenever any evil happened to them, which came they knew not whence, and of which the author was not to be seen. If you remember what I said then, the reasons why no nations can be governed without religion, will be obvious. Every individual, whether he is a savage or is born in a civil society, is persuaded within that there is such an invisible cause; and should any mortal contradict this, no multitude would believe a word of what he said. Whereas, on the other hand, if a ruler humors this fear, and puts it out of all doubt, that there is such an invisible cause, he may say of it what he pleases; and no multitude, that was ever taught anything to the contrary, will ever dispute it with him. He may say that it is a crocodile or a monkey, an ox, or a dog, an onion, or a wafer. And as to the essence and the qualities of the individual cause, he is at liberty to call it very good or very bad. He may say of it that it is an envious, malicious, and the most cruel being that can be imagined; that it loves blood, and delights in human sacrifices. Or he may say that there are two individual causes; one the author of good, the other of evil; or that there are three; or that there is really but one, though seemingly there are three, or else that there are fifty thousand. The many calamities we are liable to, from thunder and lightning, hurricanes and earthquakes, plagues and inundations, will always make ignorant and untaught men more prone to believe that the invisible cause is a bad mischievous being, than that it is a good benign one. . . .

Hor: On this head I own I must give up mankind, and cannot maintain the excellency of human nature. For the absurdities in idolatrous worship, that have been and are still committed by some of our own species, are such as no creatures of any other could out-do them in.

Cleo: The Protestant and the Muhammadan are the only national religions now, that are free from idolatry. And therefore the absurdities in the worship of all the rest are pretty much alike; at least, the difference in the degrees of men's folly, as idolaters, is very inconsiderable. For how unknown soever an invisible cause, power, or being may be, that is incomprehensible, this is certain of it, that no clear intelligible idea can be formed of it; and that no figure can describe it. All attempts then, to represent the deity, being equally vain and frivolous, no one shape or form can be imagined of it, that can justly be said to be more or less absurd than another. As to the temporal benefit which religion can be of to the civil society, or the political view which lawgivers and governors may have in promoting it, the chief use of it is in promises of allegiance and loyalty, and all solemn engagements and assertions, in which the invisible power, that, in every country, is the object of the public worship, is invoked or appealed to. For these purposes all religions are equally serviceable, and the worst is better than none. For without the belief of an invisible cause, no man's word is to be relied upon, no vows or protestations can be depended upon. But as soon as a man believes that there is a power somewhere that will punish him, if he forswears himself; as soon, I say, as a man believes this, we have reason to trust to his oath; at least, it is a better test than any other verbal assurance. But what this same person believes further, concerning the nature and the essence of that power he swears by, the worship it requires, or whether he conceives it in the singular or plural number, may be very material to himself. The society has nothing to do with it because it can make no alteration in the security which his swearing gives us. I don't deny the usefulness which even the worst religion that can be may be of to politicians and the civil society. But what I insist upon is that the temporal benefit of it, or the contrivance of oaths and swearing, could never have entered into the heads of politicians if the fear of an invisible cause had not preexisted and been supposed to be universal, any more than they would have contrived matrimony if the desire of procreation had not been planted in human nature and visible in both sexes. Passions don't affect us but when they are provoked. The fear of death is a reality in our nature, but the greatest cowards may, and often do, live forty years and longer, without being disturbed by it. The fear of an invisible cause is as real in our nature as the fear of death. Either of them may be conquered perhaps, but so may lust; and experience teaches us that how violent soever the desire of propagating our species may be whilst we are young, it goes off, and is often entirely lost in old age. When I hear a man say that he never felt any fear of an invisible cause, that was not owing to education, I believe him as much as I do a young married woman in health and vigor who tells me that she never felt any love to a man, that did not proceed from a sense of her duty.

Hor: Does this fear, this acknowledgment of an invisible cause, dispose or excite men any more to the true religion, than it does to the grossest and most abominable idolatry?

Cleo: I don't say it does. But there is no passion in human nature so beneficial, that, according as it is managed, may not do mischief as well as good. What do you think of love? If this fear had not been common to the whole species, none could have been influenced by it; the consequence of which must have been that men would have rejected the true religion as well as the false. There is nothing that men may differ in, in which they will ever be all of the same opinion, and abstruse truths do often seem to be less probable than well-dressed fables, when they are skillfully accommodated to our own way of thinking. That there is but one God, the Creator of Heaven and Earth, that is an all-wise and perfectly good being, without any mixture of evil, would have been a most rational opinion, though it had not been revealed. But reasoning and metaphysics must have been carried on to a great height of perfection before this truth could be penetrated into by the light of nature. Plutarch, who was a man of great learning, and has in many things displayed good sense and capacity, thought it impossible that one being should have been the cause of the whole world, and was therefore of opinion that there must have been two principles, the one to produce all the good; and the other all the evil that is in the world. And some of the greatest men have been of this opinion, both before and since the promulgation of the Gospel. But whatever philosophers and men of letters may have advanced, there never was an age

or a country where the vulgar would ever come into an opinion that con-
tradicted that fear, which all men are born with, of an invisible cause, that
meddles and interferes in human affairs; and there is a greater possibility,
that the most senseless enthusiast should make a knowing and polite
nation believe the most incredible falsities, or that the most odious tyrant
should persuade them to the grossest idolatry, than that the most artful
politician, or the most popular prince, should make atheism to be univer-
sally received among the vulgar of any considerable state or kingdom,
though there were no temples or priests to be seen. From all of which I
would show, that, on the one hand, you can make no multitudes believe
contrary to what they feel, or what contradicts a passion inherent in their
nature, and that, on the other, if you humor that passion, and allow it to be
just, you may regulate it as you please. How unanimous soever, therefore,
all rulers and magistrates have seemed to be on promoting some religion
or other, the principle of it was not of their invention. They found it in
man. And the fear of an invisible cause being universal, if governors had
said nothing of it, every man in his own breast would have found fault
with them, and had a superstition of his own to himself. It has often been
seen, that the most subtle unbelievers among politicians have been forced,
for their own quiet, to counterfeit their attachment to religion, when they
would thousand times rather have done without it.

Hor: It is not in the power then, you think, of politicians to contradict
the passions, or deny the existence of them, but that, when once they have
allowed them to be just and natural, they may guide men in the indulgence of them, as they please.

Cleo: I do so. And the truth of this is evident likewise in another passion, that of love, which I have hinted at before. Marriage was not
invented to make men procreate; they had that desire before, but it was
instituted to regulate a strong passion, and prevent the innumerable mischiefs that would ensue, if men and women should converge together promiscuously, and love and leave one another as caprice and their unruly
fancy led them. Thus we see that every legislator has regulated matrimony
in that way, which, to the best of his skill, he imagined would be the most
proper to promote the peace and felicity in general of those he governed.
And how great an impostor forever Muhammed was, I can never believe
that he would have allowed . . . three or four wives apiece if he had
thought it better that one should be contented with and confined to one
woman; I mean better upon the whole, more beneficial to the civil society,
as well in consideration of the climate he lived in, as the nature and the
temperament of those Arabians he gave his laws to.

(. . .)

Hor: But the belief of an overruling power, that will certainly punish perjury and injustice, being common to all religions, what preeminence has the Christian over the rest, as to the civil society in temporals?

Cleo: It shows and insists upon the necessity of that belief more amply and more emphatically than any other. Besides, the strictness of its morality, and the exemplary lives of those who preached it, gained vast credit to the mysterious part of it. And there never had been a doctrine or philosophy from which it was so likely to expect, that it would produce honor, mutual love and faithfulness in the discharge of all duties and engagements as the Christian religion. The wisest moralists, before that time, had laid the greatest stress on the reasonableness of their precepts, and appealed to human understanding for the truth of their opinions. But the Gospel, soaring beyond the reach of reason, teaches us many things, which no mortal could ever have known, unless they had been revealed to him, and several that must always remain incomprehensible to finite capacities. This is the reason that the Gospel preaches and enjoins nothing with more earnestness than faith and believing.

Hor: But would men be more swayed by things they believed only, than they would by those they understood?

Cleo: All human creatures are swayed and wholly governed by their passions, whatever fine notions we may flatter ourselves with. Even those who act suitably to their knowledge, and strictly follow the dictates of their reason, are not less compelled so to do by some passion or other that sets them to work than others, who bid defiance and act contrary to both, and whom we call slaves to their passions. To love virtue for the beauty of it, and curb one's appetites because it is most reasonable so to do, are very good things in theory. But whoever understands our nature, and consults the practice of human creatures, would sooner expect from them, that they should abstain from vice, for fear of punishment, and do good, in hopes of being rewarded for it.

Hor: Would you prefer that goodness, built upon selfishness and mercenary principles, to that which proceeds from a rectitude of thinking, and a real love of virtue and the reasonableness of men's actions?

Cleo: We can give no better proof of our reasonableness than by judging rightly. When a man wavers in his choice between present enjoyments of ease and pleasure and the discharge of duties that are troublesome, he weighs what damage or benefit will accrue to him upon the whole, as well from the neglect as the observance of the duties that are prescribed to him. And the greater the punishment is he fears from the neglect, and the more transcendent the reward is which he hopes for from the observance, the more reasonably he acts when he sides with his duty. To bear with inconveniences, pain, and sorrow, in hopes of being eternally happy, and refuse the enjoyment of pleasure, for fear of being miserable forever, are more justifiable to reason, and more consonant to good sense, than it is to do it for nothing.

Hor: But our divines will tell you that this slavish fear is unacceptable, and that the love of God ought to be the motive of good actions.

Cleo: I have nothing against the refined notions of the love of God, but this is not what I would now speak of. My design was only to prove that the more firmly men believe rewards and punishments from an invisible cause, and the more this belief always influences them in all their actions, the closer they'll keep to justice and all promises and engagements. It is this that was always most wanted in the civil society. And, before the coming of Christ, nothing had appeared upon Earth from which this grand *desideratum*, this blessing, might so reasonably be expected as it might from his doctrine. In the beginning of Christianity, and whilst the Gospel was explained without any regard to worldly views, to be a soldier was thought inconsistent with the profession of a Christian. But this strictness of the Gospel principles began to be disapproved of in the second century. The divines of those days were most of them become errant priests, and saw plainly that a religion which would not allow its votaries to assist at courts or armies, and comply with the vain world, could never be made national. Consequently, the clergy of it could never acquire any considerable power upon Earth. In spirituals they were the successors of the Apostles, but in temporals they wanted to succeed the pagan priests, whose profession they looked upon with wishful eyes. And worldly strength and authority being absolutely necessary to establish dominion, it was agreed that Christians might be soldiers, and in a just war fight with the enemies of their country. But experience soon taught them that those Christians whose consciences would suffer them to be soldiers, and to act contrary to the doctrine of peace, were not more strict observers of other duties; that pride, avarice and revenge ranged among them as they did among the heathens, and that many of them were guilty of drunkenness and incontinence, fraud and injustice, at the same time that they pretended to great zeal, and were great sticklers for their religion. This made it evident that there could be no religion so strict, no system of morality so refined, nor theory so well-meaning, but some people might pretend to profess and follow it, and yet be loose livers, and wicked in their practice.

Hor: Those who profess to be of a theory, which they contradict by their practice, are, without doubt, hypocrites.

Cleo: I have more charity than to think so. There are real believers that lead wicked lives. And many stick not at crimes which they never would have dared to commit if the terrors of the divine justice, and the flames of Hell, had struck their imagination, and been before them in the same manner as they really believe they shall be; or if at that time their fears had made the same impression upon them, which they do at others, when the evil dreaded seems to be near. Things at a distance, though we are sure that they are to come, make little impression upon us in comparison with those that are present and immediately before us. This is evident in the affair of death. There is nobody who does not believe that he must die. . . . Yet it hardly ever employs people's thoughts, even of those who are most terribly afraid of it whilst they are in perfect health, and have everything they like. Man is never better pleased than when he is employed in procuring ease and pleasure, in thinking on his own worth, and mending his condition upon Earth. Whether this is laid on the Devil or our attachment to the world, it is plain to me that it flows from man's nature, always to mind to flatter, love, and take delight in himself; and that he cares as little as possible ever to be interrupted in this grand employment. As every organ, and every part of man, seems to be made and wisely contrived for the functions of this life only, so his nature prompts him not to have any solicitude for things beyond this world. The care of self-preservation we are born with does not extend itself beyond this life. Therefore every creature dreads death as the dissolution of its being, the term not be exceeded, the end of all. How various and unreasonable soever our wishes may be, and how enormous the multiplicity of our desires, they terminate in life, and all the objects of them are on this side the grave.
(. . .)

Hor: But the ambitious that are in pursuit of glory, and sacrifice their lives to fame and a lasting reputation, sure they have wishes beyond the grave.

Cleo: Though a man should stretch and carry his ambition to the end of the world, and desire not to be forgotten as long as that flood, yet the pleasure that arises from the reflection on what shall be said of him thousands and thousands of years after, can only be enjoyed in this life. If a vain coxcomb, whose memory shall die with him, can be but firmly persuaded that he shall leave an eternal name, the reflection may give him as much pleasure as the greatest hero can receive from reflecting on what shall really render him immortal. A man, who is not regenerated, can have no notion of another world, or future happiness. Therefore, his longing after it cannot be strong. Nothing can affect us forcibly but what strikes the senses, or such things as we are conscious of within. By the light of nature only we are capable of demonstrating to ourselves the necessity of a first cause, a Supreme Being. But the existence of a Deity cannot be rendered more manifest to our reason, than his essence is unknown and incomprehensible to our understanding.

Hor: I don't see what you drive at.

Cleo: I am endeavoring to account for the small effect and little force, which religion, and the belief of future punishments, may be of to mere man, unassisted with the divine grace. The practice of nominal Christians is perpetually clashing with the theory they profess. Innumerable sins are committed in private, which the presence of a child, or the most insignificant person, might have hindered by men who believe God to be omniscient, and never questioned his ubiquity.

Hor: But pray, come to the point, the origin of honor.

Cleo: If we consider that men are always endeavoring to mend their condition and render society more happy as to this world we may easily conceive, when it was evident that nothing could be a check upon man that was absent, or at least appeared not to be present, how moralists and politicians came to look for something in man himself, to keep him in awe. The more they examined into human nature, the more they must have been convinced that man is so selfish a creature, that, while he is at liberty, the greatest part of his time will always be bestowed upon himself; and that whatever fear or reverence he might have for an invisible cause, that thought was often jostled out by others, more nearly relating to himself. It is obvious, likewise, that he neither loves nor esteems anything so well as he does his own individual, and that there is nothing, which he has so constantly before his eyes, as his own dear self. It is highly probable that skillful rulers, having made these observations for some time, would be tempted to try if man could not be made an object of reverence to himself.

Hor: You have only named love and esteem. They alone cannot produce reverence by your own maxim; how could they make a man afraid of himself?

Cleo: By improving upon his dread of shame. And this, I am persuaded, was the case. For as soon as it was found out that many vicious, quarrelsome, and undaunted men, that feared neither God nor the Devil, were yet often curbed and visibly withheld by the fear of shame; and likewise that this fear of shame might be greatly increased by an artful education, and be made superior even to that of death, they had made a discovery of a real tie, that would serve many noble purposes in the society. This I take to have been the origin of honor, the principle of which has its foundation in self-liking. And no art could ever have fixed or raised it in any breast, if that passion had not preexisted and been predominant there.

Hor: But, how are you sure, that this was the work of moralists and politicians, as you seem to insinuate?

Cleo: I give those names promiscuously to all that, having studied human nature, have endeavored to civilize men, and render them more and more tractable, either for the ease of governors and magistrates, or else for the temporal happiness of society in general. I think of all inventions of this sort, the same which told you of politeness, that they are the joint labor of many. Human wisdom is the child of time. It was not the contrivance of one man, nor could it have been the business of a few years, to establish a notion, by which a rational creature is kept in awe for fear of itself, and an idol is set up, that shall be its own worshipper.

Hor: But I deny that in the fear of shame we are afraid of ourselves. What we fear is the judgment of others, and the ill opinion they will justly have of us.

Cleo: Examine this thoroughly, and you'll find that when we covet glory, or dread infamy, it is not the good or bad opinion of others that affects us with joy or sorrow, pleasure or pain, but it is the notion we form of that opinion of theirs, and must proceed from the regard and value we have for it. If it was otherwise, the most shameless fellow would suffer as much in his mind from public disgrace and infamy as a man that values his reputation. Therefore it is the notion we have of things, our own thought and something within ourselves, that creates the fear of shame. For if I have a reason why I forbear to do a thing today, which it is impossible should be known before tomorrow, I must be withheld by something that exists already. For nothing can act upon me the day before it has its being.

Hor: The upshot is, I find, that honor is of the same origin with virtue.

Cleo: But the invention of honor, as a principle, is of a much later date, and I look upon it as the greater achievement by far. It was an improvement in the art of flattery, by which the excellency of our species is raised to such a height, that it becomes the object of our own adoration, and man is taught in good earnest to worship himself.

Hor: But granting you, that both virtue and honor are of human contrivance, why do you look upon the invention of the one to be a greater achievement than that of the other?

Cleo: Because the one is more skillfully adapted to our inward make. Men are better paid for their adherence to honor than they are for their adherence to virtue. The first requires less self-denial and the rewards they receive for that little are not imaginary but real and palpable. But experience confirms what I say. The invention of honor has been far more beneficial to the civil society than that of virtue, and much better answered the end for which they were invented. For ever since the notion of honor has been received among Christians, there have always been, in the same number of people, twenty men of real honor, to one of real virtue. The reason is obvious. The persuasions to virtue make no allowances, nor have any allurements that are clashing with the principle of it. Whereas the men of pleasure, the passionate and the malicious, may all in their turns meet with opportunities of indulging their darling appetites without trespassing against the principle of honor. A virtuous man thinks himself obliged to obey the laws of his country; but a man of honor acts from a principle which he is bound to believe superior to all laws. Do but consider the instinct of sovereignty that all men are born with, and you'll find that in the closest attachment to the principle of honor there are enjoyments that are ravishing to human nature. A virtuous man expects no acknowledgment from others, and if they won't believe him to be virtuous, his business is not to force them to it. But a man of honor has the liberty openly to proclaim himself to be such, and call to an account everybody who dares to doubt of it. Nay, such is the inestimable value he sets upon himself that he often endeavors to punish with death the most insignificant trespass that's committed against him, the least word, look, or motion, if he can find but any farfetched reason to suspect a design in it to undervalue him; and of this nobody is allowed to be a judge but himself. The enjoyments that arise from being virtuous are of that nicety, that every ordinary capacity cannot relish them: as, without doubt, there is a noble pleasure in forgiving of injuries, to speculative men that have refined notions of virtue; but it is more natural to resent them; and in revenging oneself, there is a pleasure which the meanest understanding is capable of tasting. It is manifest then, that there are allurements in the principle of honor, to draw in men of the lowest capacity, and even the vicious, which virtue has not.

(. . .)

Hor: I believe that among the men of honor many were tainted with pride and superstition at the same time, but [that] there were others in whom superlative bravery was united with the strictest virtue.

Cleo: All ages have had men of courage, and all ages have had men of virtue. But the examples of those you speak of, in whom superlative bravery was united with the strictest virtue, were always extremely scarce, and are rarely to be met with, but in legends and romances, the writers of both which I take to have been the greatest enemies to truth and sober sense the world ever produced. I don't deny that by perusing them some might have fallen in love with courage and heroism, others with chastity and temperance. But the design of both was to serve the Church of Rome, and with wonderful stories to gain the attention of the readers, while they taught bigotry, and inured them to believe impossibilities. What I intended was to point at the people that had the greatest hand in reconciling, to outward appearance, the principle of honor with that of the Christian religion, the ages this was done in, and the reasons for which it was attempted. For it is certain that by the maxims I named the Church made herself sure of those who were most to be feared. Do but cast your eyes on the childish farces some popes have made great men the chief actors in, and the apish tricks they made them play, when they found them intoxicated with pride, and that at the same time they were believers without reserve. What impertinence of tedious ceremonies have they made the greatest princes submit to, even such as were noted for being choleric and impatient! What absurdities in dress have they made them swallow for ornaments and marks of dignity! If in all these the passion of self-liking had not been highly gratified as well as played upon, men of sense could never have been fond of them, nor could they have been of that duration. For many of them are still remaining even in Protestant countries, where all the frauds of Popery have been detected long ago, and such veneration is paid to some of them, that it would hardly be safe to ridicule them. It is amazing to think, what immense multitudes of badges of honor have been invented by Popery, that are all distinct from the rest, and yet have something or other to show, that they have a relation to Christianity. What a vast variety of shapes, not resembling the original, has the poor cross been tortured into! How differently has it been placed and represented on the garments of men and women, from head to foot! How inconsiderable are all other frauds that lay-rogues now and then have been guilty of, if you compare them to the barefaced cheats and impudent forgeries, with which the Church of Rome has constantly imposed upon mankind in a triumphant manner! What contemptible baubles has that holy toy shop put off in the face of the sun for the richest merchandise! She has bribed the selfish and penetrating statesmen, with empty sound, and titles without meaning. The most resolute warriors she has forced to desist from their purposes, and to do her dirty work against their own interest. I shall [say] nothing of the Holy War, how often the Church has kindled and renewed it, or what a handle she made of it to raise and establish her own power, and to weaken and undermine that of the temporal princes in Christendom. The authority of the Church has made the greatest princes and most haughty sovereigns fall prostrate before [it], and pay adoration to the vilest trumpery, and accept of, as presents of inestimable worth, despicable trifles, that had no value at all but what was set upon them by the gigantic impudence of the donors, and the childish credulity of the receivers. The Church misled the vulgar, and then made money of their errors. There is not an attribute of God, and hardly a word in the Bible, to which she gave not some turn or other, to serve her worldly interest. The belief of witchcraft was the forerunner of exorcisms, and the priests forged apparitions to show the power they pretended to, of laying spirits, and casting out devils. To make accused persons, sometimes by ordeal, at others by single combat, try the justice of their cause, were both arrows out of her quiver; and it is from the latter, that the fashion of dueling took its rise. But those single combats at first were only fought by persons of great quality, and on some considerable quarrel, when they asked leave of the sovereign to decide the difference between them by feats of arms; which being obtained, judges of the combat were appointed, and the champions entered the list with great pomp, and in a very solemn manner. But as the principle of honor came to be very useful, the notions of it, by degrees, were industriously spread among the multitude, till at last all swordsmen took it in their heads that they had a right to decide their own quarrels, without asking anybody's leave. . . .

APPENDIX

Presentment of the Grand Jury of the County of Middlesex to the Court of King's Bench, July 11, 1723

We the Grand Jury for the County of Middlesex have with the greatest sorrow and concern observed the many books and pamphlets that are almost every week published against the sacred articles of our Holy Religion, and all discipline and order in the Church, and the manner in which this is carried on, seems to us to have a direct tendency to propagate infidelity, and consequently corruption of all morals.

We are justly sensible of the goodness of the Almighty that has preserved us from the plague which has visited our neighboring nation, and for which great mercy, his Majesty was graciously pleased to command by his proclamation that thanks should be returned to Heaven; but how provoking must it be to the Almighty, that his mercies and deliverances extended to this nation, and our thanksgiving that was publicly commanded for it, should be attended with such flagrant impieties.

We know of nothing that can be of greater service to His Majesty and the Protestant succession (which is happily established among us for the defense of the Christian religion) than the suppression of blasphemy and profanity, which has a direct tendency to subvert the very foundation on which His Majesty's government is fixed.

So restless have these zealots for infidelity been in their diabolical attempts against religion, that they have,

First, openly blasphemed and denied the doctrine of the ever Blessed Trinity, endeavoring by specious pretenses to revive the Arian heresy, which was never introduced into any nation, but the vengeance of Heaven pursued it.

Secondly, they affirm an absolute fate, and deny the Providence and government of the Almighty in the world.

Thirdly, they have endeavored to subvert all order and discipline in the Church, and by vile and unjust reflections on the clergy, they strive to bring contempt on all religion; that by the libertinism of their opinions they may encourage and draw others into the immoralities of their practice.

Fourthly, that a general libertinism may the more effectually be established, the universities are decried, and all instructions of youth in the principles of the Christian religion are exploded with the greatest malice and falsity.

Fifthly, the more effectually to carry on these works of darkness, studied artifices and invented colors have been made use of to run down religion and virtue as prejudicial to society, and detrimental to the state; and to recommend luxury, avarice, pride, and all kind of vices, as being necessary to public welfare, and not tending to the destruction of the constitution: nay, the very stews themselves have had strained apologies and forced encomiums made in their favor and produced in print, with design, we conceive, to debauch the nation.

These principles having a direct tendency to the subversion of all religion and civil government, our duty to the Almighty, our love to our country, and regard to our oaths, oblige us to present

as the publisher of a book, entitled, *The Fable of the Bees; or Private Vices, Public Benefits.*

And also [publisher's name left blank] as the publisher of a weekly paper, called the *British Journal*, number 26, 35, 36, and 39.

Glossary of Prominent Persons

Pierre **Bayle** (1647–1706), French philosopher and critic who migrated to Rotterdam in 1681 because of rising intolerance of Protestants in France. Bayle was one of the most important skeptical writers of his generation and, although a staunch Calvinist, one of the foremost proponents of religious toleration, contending that morality is independent of religion. His *Historical and Critical Dictionary* (1697) had a profound influence on the Enlightenment.

George **Berkeley** (1685–1763), Anglo-Irish philosopher, social critic and clergyman, who was made Bishop of Cloyne in 1734. In his most important philosophical works, the *Essay Towards a New Theory of Vision* (1709) and *The Principles of Human Knowledge* (1710), Berkeley argued, against the empiricism of Locke, that there is no existence of matter outside of perception, and that only the observing mind of God makes possible the continued existence of material objects.

François **Bernier** (1620–1688), French physician and travel writer whose accounts of Hindu religion, customs and commerce were among the first European observations of their kind, and a secretary to the philosopher Pierre Gassendi. Bernier's *Abridgment* (1684) of Gassendi's doctrines helped to disseminate the philosoper's ideas.

Lucius Sergius Catilina, or **Catiline** (108?–62 B.C.), Roman politician and soldier who served with Pompey under Pompeius Strabo in the so-called "social war" for dominance of the Roman Republic. In 67 B.C. he began a two-year term as governor in Africa and in 63 B.C. organized a conspiracy against the Republic which was uncovered and extinguished by Cicero.

Marcus Porcius **Cato** the Younger (95–46 B.C.), Roman statesman devoted to the principles of the early Republic, who had one of the greatest reputations for honesty and incorruptibility in ancient times, and whose Stoicism put him above the graft and bribery of his day. He was from the first a violent opponent of Julius Caesar, whom he tried to implicate in Catiline's conspiracy of 63 B.C. He supported Pompey after his break with Caesar and, with Scipio, continued to struggle against Caesar from Africa. After Caesar's defeat of Scipio in 46 B.C., Cato famously committed suicide rather than live under Caesar's dominion, thereby establishing his reputation as a Republican martyr.

Marcus Tullius **Cicero** (106–43 B.C.), the greatest Roman orator and prominent Stoic philosopher. A Republican politician who helped defeat Catiline and was strongly opposed to Caesar, he was put to death when Augustus became Emperor. Among the most important of his voluminous writings are *De Officiis [On Duty]*, *De Finibus [On Human Ends]* and *De Oratore*, one of the most influential classical discussions of rhetoric.

Lucius Quintius **Cincinnatus** (ca. 500 B.C.), legendary Roman patriot who, according to tradition, came from his farm to lead Rome against its rivals, the Aegui and Volscians, who threatened the city, and then, upon returning from battle, resigned as dictator and retired to his farm.

Titus Flavius Clemens, or **Clement of Alexandria** (150?–215), Greek theologian who converted to Christianity. He was one of the first to attempt a synthesis of Platonic and Christian thought, a project carried on by his students and successors in Alexandria. Among his most important works is the *Address to the Greeks*, which argues, against Greek tradition, for the superiority of Christianity.

Cleomenes III (ca. 260–219 B.C.), king of Sparta (235–221 B.C.), regarded as the most energetic of the Spartan kings. He sought to restore the prestige of the city by waging war against the Achaean League (227 B.C.), in which he gained a reputation as a warrior. At home he instituted a radical reform of the Spartan state, including the solidification of the power of the king and the extension of Spartal citizenship. His downfal came in 222 B.C. when a reconstituted Achaean League routed the Spartan army in battle, after which Cleomenes fled to Egypt.

René **Descartes** (1596–1650), French philosopher and mathematician, considered to be one of the founders of modern philosophy. His *Meditations on First Philosophy* (1641), which argued the case for the dualism of mind and body and which included several sets of "Objections" by Thomas Hobbes, Antoine Arnauld and Pierre Gassendi, is a foundational text for epistemology in the West. In 1649 Descartes joined a distinguished circle assembled around Queen Christina of Sweden, whom he instructed in philosophy.

Diogenes (412?–323 B.C.), Greek Cynic philosopher who discarded conventional comforts and lived in a tub, and went about Athens with a lantern "searching for an honest man." He taught that the virtuous life is the simple life. When Alexander the Great asked Diogenes what he might do for him, the philosopher was said to have replied, "Only step out of my sunlight."

Epicurus (341?–270 B.C.), Athenian philosopher who taught in several towns in Asia Minor before settling in Athens, where he purchased the famous garden that became linked with other great schools of Greek philosophy such as Plato's Academy. He defined philosophy as the art of making life happy, a state of serenity rather than needless indulgence, whose greatest pleasures were intellectual. Epicurus was an atomist and materialist who criticized the traditional power of religion. Most of Epicurus's writings have not survived. His doctrines are best known through the Latin poem *De Rerum Natura* by the Roman poet and philosopher Lucretius.

Desiderius **Erasmus** (1466?–1536), Dutch humanist philosopher, priest and scholar born in Rotterdam. His translations, commentaries and personal contacts with some of the most eminent intellectuals of the day established him as perhaps the most prominent humanist in the first half of the sixteenth century. His Latin and Greek edition of the *New Testament* (1516), along with the *Adages* (1500), *The Education of a Christian Prince* (1515) and the satirical *In Praise of Folly* (1509) are among his most influential works.

Euripides (480–406 B.C.), Greek tragic dramatist ranking with Aeschylus and Sophocles who wrote some ninety-two plays and won four first prizes during the annual dramatic competitions at Athens. *Medea* (431), *The Trojan Women* (415), *Orestes* (408) and *Iphigenia in Tauris* (407) are among the best known of his nineteen surviving plays.

Pierre **Gassendi** (1592–1655), French priest, philosopher and scientist who became a professor of rhetoric at twenty-one and taught at the Royal

College in Paris. A critic of Aristotle who ranked with the leading mathematicians of his day, he most influentially revived and interpreted the ancient atomism of Democritus in terms of modern science, along with the philosophy of Epicurus within a Christian context.

Thomas **Gordon** (1693?–1750?), British Republican writer on politics who started the influential newspaper *The Independent Whig* in 1720, of which editions were collected in several volumes and served as a focus for criticism of Anglican High Church politics and politicians.

Lorenzo Baltasar **Gracian** (ca. 1584–1658), the Spanish author of *The Oracle*.

Claude-Adrien **Helvétius** (1715–1771), French philosopher and critic who held the lucrative post of Farmer General (tax collector) and whose father was the first physician to the Queen of France. His *De l'esprit [On the Mind]* (1758) was regarded as an atheist and empiricist attack on conventional politics and was condemned by both the pope and the parlement of Paris. He was a hedonist and utilitarian who judged the good in terms of self-satisfactions and regarded self-interest as the sole motive for human action, views he put forward again in *De l'homme [On Man]*, posthumously published in 1772.

Thomas **Hobbes** (1588–1679), English philosopher with an intense interest in the new science, and who was for a time a member of an intellectual circle which included Descartes and Gassendi. He was born in Malmesbury, Wiltshire, and after attending Magdalen College, Oxford, spent most of his working life as a tutor and secretary to the Cavendish family. A social-contract theorist, in his most profound and inflential works, *De Cive [On the Citizen]* (1642) and *Leviathan* (1651), Hobbes sought to establish the nature of political right, the grounds of political obligation and the nature and purpose of sovereignty.

David **Hume** (1711–1776), British philosopher, essayist and historian, one of the most respected Enlightenment intellectuals, who was born in Scotland and studied at the University of Edinburgh. He subsequently developed a skeptical and empiricist philosophical system of morals and social life, first published in *A Treatise of Human Nature* (1739). Hume's *Natural History of Religion* (1755) was one of the most powerful freethinking works of its day, while his *Political Discourses* (1752) and his multivolume *History of England* (1754–1762) established him as a social thinker of the first order, and a significant influence on his younger friend Adam Smith.

Cornelius **Jansen** (1585–1638), Dutch Catholic theologian who became professor at Louvain University in 1630 and bishop of Ypres in 1636. His most significant accomplishment was the *Augustinus*, a massive treatise on dogma and practice published posthumously in 1642. Jansen's work became a central source for a school of French Augustinians, called Jansenists, composed of priests like Pierre Nicole, and philosophers like Blaise Pascal, who sought to reform Catholic devotional principles and practices, particularly the understanding of grace as an unearned gift, along strict Augustinian lines.

Saint **Jerome** (ca. 347–420?), Christian scholar and Father of the Church, who studied at Rome before journeying to the East where, at Antioch, he experienced a vision in which Christ reproved him for his pagan studies, which he then renounced. After living in the desert as an ascetic for three years, Jerome was ordained and traveled to Rome, where he became papal secretary. He was known for his exposition of Scripture, his pastoral work among aristocratic Roman women, and his critical views of the secular clergy. The last part of his life, when he lived as a monk in Bethlehem, was largely devoted to highly influential Latin translations of the Bible, biographies of Christian writers, and a number of theological disputes, including those with the Pelagians, who denied the doctrine of original sin.

Samuel **Johnson** (1709–1764), British poet, essayist and lexicographer, considered to be the foremost arbiter of literary taste in eighteenth-century Britain. Johnson established his literary reputation through the journal *The Rambler*, which he edited between 1750 and 1752, the novel *Rasselas* (1759), an edition of Shakespeare's works in 1765, *The Lives of the Poets* (1779–1781), and, most important, the *Dictionary of the English Language* (1755). He was immortalized by James Boswell in *The Life of Samuel Johnson, LL.D.* (1791).

Decimus Junius Juvenalis, or **Juvenal** (flourished ca. A.D. 100), Roman satiric poet whose diatribes about Roman manners and morals in sixteen hexameter satires denounced luxury, corruption, tyranny, female immorality and the hypocrisy of the Stoics. Little is known about his life, but his poetry, with its biting criticism of contemporary morals from the point of view of Republican virtue, tells us a great deal about Roman life under the early empire.

Immanuel **Kant** (1724–1804), German philosopher born in Königsberg, a city in East Prussia, where he later taught as professor of logic and metaphysics at the university, and never left. Kant was deeply influenced by the rationalism of Leibniz and Wolff, the most prominent German philosophers of the previous generation, and by the empiricism and skepticism of his near contemporary David Hume. Kant's attempt to resolve the tension between these doctrines formed the foundations of both modern epistemology and metaphysics. His most influential books are the *Critique of Pure Reason* (1781), *Prolegomena to Any Future Metaphysics* (1783), and the *Critique of Practical Reason* (1788).

Jean de **La Fontaine** (1621–1695), French poet and fabulist connected with the skeptical and Epicurean philosophers of his day, and part of the entourage of Madame de la Sablière, a patron of these intellectuals. La Fontaine wrote a number of stories and tales, often drawn from Boccaccio, as well as librettos for opera, but his masterpiece is his *Selected Fables, Put Into Verse* (1668–1694), comprising twelve books of some 250 fables, largely drawn from Aesop. Each fable is a short tale of beasts behaving like men, and each serves to comment satirically upon human behavior.

Titus **Lucretius** Carus (ca. 99–ca. 55 B.C.), probably a Roman, about whose life little is known, save for his being the author of *De rerum natura* [*On the Nature of Things*], a long, six-book poem in hexameter verse espousing and attempting to popularize the atomistic doctrines of Democritus and the hedonism of Epicurus. This didactic poem remains the most complete and coherent surviving exposition of philosophical materialism produced in antiquity.

Niccoló **Machiavelli** (1469–1527), Florentine diplomat, politician and philosopher whose discourse on how princes can acquire and maintain their power, *The Prince* (1514), and general theory of politics and Republican governance, *Discourses on the First Ten Books of Livy's History of Rome* (1516), have become classics of political thought in the West.

Michel Eyquem de **Montaigne** (1533–1592), French magistrate, essayist and skeptical philosopher. He was for some time a member of the parlement of Guyenne and for four years the mayor of Bordeaux. While in retirement between 1571 and 1580, and ostensibly aloof from the religious and political conflicts then engulfing France, he wrote the first two volumes of his *Essays* (1580), to which a third volume was added in 1588. Montaigne is still regarded as a master of the essay form and one of the most powerful skeptical moralists.

Pierre **Nicole** (1625–1695), French priest, theologian and moral philosopher closely associated with the Jansenist abbey at Port-Royal, near Paris, where he studied and taught. He was well known in his own lifetime for working with Pascal on *The Provincial Letters* (1656) and for his coauthorship with Antoine Arnauld of the *Port-Royal Logic* (1676). His *Moral Essays* (1674) were powerful and scrupulous exercises in Augustinian moral psychology, some of which were first translated into English by John Locke for his own use, and then appeared in a complete English edition in 1691.

Publius Ovidius Naso, or **Ovid** (43 B.C.–A.D. 17), Roman poet who enjoyed early and widespread fame under the emperor Augustus, after which he was exiled to Tomi, an outpost on the Black Sea, where he died. He wrote both erotic and mythological poems and, during later life, poems of exile. In the mythological category stands the *Metamorphoses*, a collection of myths concerned with miraculous tranformations, generally agreed to be his masterpiece, and the poem for which he was best known in the eighteenth century.

Blaise **Pascal** (1623–1662), French mathematician, inventor, theologian and philosopher, who was a child prodigy, credited with founding the modern theory of probability, and educated solely by his father, himself a gifted mathematician. Pascal came under the influence of Jansenism as a young man, and in 1654 experienced a conversion, after which he devoted himself entirely to religious and moral questions. Among his most notable works are the anti-Jesuit *Provincial Letters* (1656) and the posthumously published *Pensées*, a masterpiece of French prose and moral philosophy.

Plutarch (A.D. 46?–ca. 120), Greek philosopher and biographer who taught at Rome and was a priest at Delphi for the last thirty years of his life. His great work is *The Parallel Lives*, comprising forty-six surviving biographies arranged in Greek and Roman pairs, whose main purpose is the portrayal of character and its moral implications. Translated into English by

Sir Thomas North in the sixteenth century, the *Lives* supplied source material for a number of Shakespeare's plays.

Pyrrho of Elis (ca. 360–270 B.C.), Greek philosopher, regarded as the father of Skepticism, whose doctrines were carried on by his disciple, Timon of Philus. He accompanied the expedition of Alexander the Great to the Orient, after which he enjoyed a considerable reputation, both in his birthplace Elis, and in Athens. Pyrrho taught that nothing in the social and moral realms can be known with certainty, because the contradictory of every statement can be maintained with equal plausibility. Hence the proper philosophic attitude is one of suspended judgment and imperturbability.

Jean-Jacques **Rousseau** (1712–1778), French philosopher, essayist and novelist, born in Geneva. After wandering in Savoy and Italy as a young man, he settled for a time in Paris, first winning recognition with his *Discourse on the Arts and Sciences* (1749), an antimodernist tract which argues that the progress of knowledge and technical mastery has been accompanied by moral decline, a view he amplified in the *Discourse on the Origins of Inequality* (1755). Rousseau's Republican political theory, *The Social Contract* (1762), his educational views in *Émile* (1762), which were both condemned in Paris and his native Geneva, and his best-selling novel *La nouvelle Héloïse* 1761), made him one of the most well-known European intellectuals. His posthumously published *Confessions* (1781) remains a classic of autobiography.

Friedrich von **Schiller** (1759–1805), German poet, dramatist, historian and sometime cultural critic. A key figure, along with Johann Wolfgang von Goethe (1749–1832), in the "Storm and Stress" literary movement, a precursor of Romanticism, and critical of the German cultural inheritance. Recognized as one of the key figures in the history of German literature, his major works include *The Robbers* (1781), which first won him public acclaim, the *Wallenstein* trilogy (1798–1799), *Wilhelm Tell* (1804), a celebration of political liberty, and the *Ode to Joy* (1795), which was used by Beethoven for the finale for his Ninth Sympohony. His *Letters on the Aesthetic Education of Mankind* (1795) was one of the most influential contemporary pieces of aesthetic and social criticism.

Lucius Annaeus **Seneca** (ca. 3 B.C.–A.D. 65), Roman philosopher, dramatist and politician, who earned a reputation as an orator in his youth and became a tutor to the emperor Nero before beginning his own political career. Involved in a number of power struggles and intrigues at court, Seneca committed suicide by slashing his veins in a death scene considered remarkably noble by the Romans. His writings include *De clementia*, a treatise on the duty of rulers to be merciful, and the highly influential *Dialogi*, essays on Stoic philosophy whose admiration of an unselfishly noble life contrasted with Seneca's own, in which cabals, conspiracies and even connivance at murder figured prominently.

Sextus Empiricus (flourished A.D. 150), a follower of the ancient Skeptical philosopher Pyrrho, and the author of the *Outlines of Pyrrhonism*, *Against the Professors* and *Against the Dogmatists*, whose philosophical style, called *zetesis*, had as its object the Skeptical investigation of both sides of every point in an argument. Sextus's work had as its purpose the demonstration that there is no certain knowledge, and that habit and convention are the basis of everything that men do. The translation of Sextus's work in the third quarter of the sixteenth century played an important part in the early modern revival of Skepticism.

Anthony Ashley Cooper, third Earl of **Shaftesbury** (1671–1713), English philosopher and moralist, who was tutored by John Locke, and Member of Parliament, 1695–1698. Shaftesbury's *Characteristicks of Men, Manners, Opinions, Times* (1711) was one of the most acclaimed works of aesthetics and moral philosophy during the first half of the eighteenth century. He argued that we possess a "moral sense," much like our innate capacity to appreciate beauty, and that these two senses could and should be polished and perfected, producing a balance between altruism and egoism in public life, resulting in a harmony in society and the promotion of the general welfare.

Adam **Smith** (1723–1790), Scottish philosopher and political economist generally regarded as the father of economics. His membership in advanced intellectual circles in Glasgow and Edinburgh, and his professorship of moral philosophy at the University of Glasgow, were among the high points of a regular and ordered bachelor life devoted to philosophy and scholarship. The *Theory of Moral Sentiments* (1759) established his international reputation as a moral philosopher, while his *Inquiry into the Nature and Causes of the Wealth of Nations* (1776), conceived by Smith as a treatise designed for "the science of legislation," became within a generation the foundation for laissez-faire economic arguments and the basis of the work of, for example, David Ricardo and Thomas Malthus.

Sir Richard **Steele** (1672–1729), politician, dramatist and essayist, born in Dublin, educated at Oxford and who worked in London for most of his professional career. Steele was best known for his dramatic and journalistic work. *The Christian Hero* (1701), his first play, established his reputation, while his sentimental comedies, *The Lying Lover* (1703) and *The Conscious Lovers* (1706), gained him a large audience. Steele's absorbing interest was the promotion of moral conduct and polite manners among the middle classes, a goal he sought to accomplish in his famous periodical, *The Tatler* (1709–1711), and in his celebrated partnership with Joseph Addison in *The Spectator* (1711–1712) and *The Guardian* (1713).

John **Trenchard** (1662–1723), political writer, educated in Ireland, who sought to promote radical Whig and Republican doctrines, most notably in his collaboration with Thomas Gordon in the journal *The Independent Whig* (1721–1722) and in a series of essays, *Cato's Letters* (1723), which was one of the most influential Republican tracts in Britain and her North American colonies. The publisher of the latter work was prosecuted for promoting irreligion and political turmoil at the same time as was Mandeville's.

Lucilio Julius Caesar **Vanini** (1585–1619), Italian anti-scholastic and anti-Aristotelian philosopher and member of the Carmelite order, who was nevertheless a freethinker. He was driven from one country after another because of his radical views, and was finally condemned and burned at the stake in Toulouse for atheism and witchcraft, making him a martyr for the cause of toleration and freedom of thought.

Publius Vergilius Maro, or **Virgil** (70–19 B.C.), Roman poet patronized by Augustus and one of the dominant figures in Latin literature. His boyhood experience of life on the farm was an essential part of his education, as can be seen in his *Eclogues*, or *Bucolics* (37 B.C.), and *Georgics* (30 B.C.), interpretations of agricultural life and work. Virgil is best known for the *Aeneid*, one of the greatest epic poems, which he worked on during the last seventeen years of his life, and left incomplete. This national epic, honoring Rome and foretelling of its prosperity to come, follows the life of Aeneas, held up to the reader as the paragon of the most revered Roman virtues: piety, devotion to family and loyalty to the state.

Zeno of Citium (334?–262 B.C.), Greek philosopher, who studied under the Cynics in Athens. Although his works have not survived, it is known that he divided philosophy into logic, physics and ethics, and taught that the first two must serve the last. He argued that the only real good is virtue and the only real evil moral weakness; all else (pain, death, poverty) is indifferent. A wise man who accepts his fate cannot be deprived of his virtue, hence he is happy. Famous for a number of logical paradoxes, Zeno taught in Athens at the Stoa Poecile ("painted porch"), and his followers came to be known as Stoics.

Suggestions for Further Reading

All modern inquiry into Mandeville's thought must begin with the work of F. B. Kaye, whose edition of *The Fable of the Bees* (Oxford: The Clarendon Press, 1924, 2 volumes; reissued by Liberty Classics, 1988) contains valuable essays, notes and bibliographic material. All the works of Mandeville's eighteenth-century commentators mentioned in the Introduction exist in reliable modern editions, while the main British responses to *The Fable* have been collected in J. Martin Stafford (ed.), *Private Vices, Publick Benefits? The Contemporary Reception of Bernard Mandeville* (Solihull, England: Ismeron, 1997). The most useful modern commentary is listed below.

Books:

Goldsmith, M. M. *Private Vices, Public Benefits. Bernard Mandeville's Social and Political Thought.* Cambridge: Cambridge University Press, 1985.

Horne, Thomas. *The Social Thought of Bernard Mandeville. Virtue and Commerce in Early Eighteenth-Century England.* New York: Columbia University Press, 1978.

Hundert, E. J. *The Enlightenment's 'Fable': Bernard Mandeville and the Discovery of Society.* Cambridge: Cambridge University Press, 1994.

Monro, Hector. *The Ambivalence of Bernard Mandeville.* Oxford: The Clarendon Press, 1975.

Primer, Irwin (ed.). *Mandeville Studies.* The Hague: Nijhoff, 1975.

Articles:

Castiglione, Dario. "Excess, Frugality and the Spirit of Capitalism: Readings of Mandeville on Commercial Society." In Joseph Melling and Jonathan Barry (eds.), *Culture in History. Production, Consumption and*

Values in Historical Perspective, pp. 155–79. Exeter: University of Exeter Press, 1992.

————. "Mandeville Moralized." In *Annali della Fondazione Luigi Einaudi* 17 (1983), pp. 239–90.

Colletti, Lucio. "Mandeville, Rousseau and Smith." In *From Rousseau to Lenin. Studies in Ideology and Society*, pp. 195–218. Translated by John Merrington and Judith White. London: New Left Books, 1972.

Dickey, Laurence. "Pride, Hypocricy and Civility in Mandeville's Social and Historical Theory." *Critical Review*, 4, 3 (1990), pp. 387–431.

Gunn, J.A.W. "Mandeville: Poverty, Luxury and the Whig Theory of Government." In *Beyond Liberty and Property: The Process of Self-Recognition in Eighteenth-Century Political Thought*, pp. 96–109. Kingston, Ontario: McGill-Queens University Press, 1983.

Hayek, F. A. "Dr. Bernard Mandeville." *Proceedings of the British Academy*, 52 (1966), pp. 125–41.

Hundert, E. J. "Bernard Mandeville and the Enlightenment's Maxims of Modernity." *Journal of the History of Ideas*, 56 (1995), pp. 577–93.

Jack, Malcolm. "One State of Nature: Mandeville and Rousseau." *Journal of the History of Ideas*, 39 (1978), pp. 119–24.

McTaggart, M. J. "Mandeville: cynic or fool?" *Philosophical Quarterly*, 16 (1966), pp. 221–33.

Rosenberg, Nathan. "Mandeville and Laissez-Faire." *Journal of the History of Ideas*, 24 (1963), pp. 183–96.

Ross, Ellen. "Mandeville, Melon and Voltaire: The Origins of the Luxury Controversy in France." *Studies on Voltaire and the Eighteenth Century*, 155 (1976), pp. 1897–1912.